The Abolitionists
Means, Ends, and Motivations
Third Edition

Edited and with an introduction by

Lawrence B. Goodheart
University of Connecticut

Hugh Hawkins
Amherst College

D. C. HEATH AND COMPANY
Lexington, Massachusetts   Toronto

Address editorial correspondence to:
D. C. Heath and Company
125 Spring Street
Lexington, MA 02173

Acquisitions Editor: James Miller
Developmental Editor: Patricia Wakeley
Production Editor: Celena Sun
Designer: Kenneth Hollman
Photo Researcher: Mary Stuart Lang
Production Coordinator: Charles Dutton
Permissions Editor: Margaret Roll

Cover: Frederick Douglass speaking while a mob and the Boston police break up an abolitionist meeting at the Tremont Temple on 3 December 1860 commemorating the first anniversary of the execution of John Brown: contemporary colored engraving. (*The Granger Collection, New York*)

International Standard Book Number: 0–669–35079–6

Library of Congress Catalog Number: 93–80574

10 9 8 7 6 5 4 3 2 1

The Abolitionists
Means, Ends, and Motivations

The frontispiece shows the central image of the abolitionist crusade in the United States and Britain. A kneeling slave man and woman raise their enchained hands heavenward as they invoke white people to honor the Biblical injunction: "Remember them that are in bonds, as bound with them." Yet, in actuality, African Americans, slave and free, were active anti-slavery agents, challenging white supremacy in manifold ways on a variety of fronts. (*Courtesy of the Boston Athenaeum*)

For Anna and Jacob

—L. B. G.

The Editors

Lawrence B. Goodheart

Born in Washington, D. C., Lawrence B. Goodheart was educated at the University of Rochester, State University of New York at Albany, and the University of Connecticut, where he earned a Ph.D. He taught social studies in the Rochester, New York, public schools and later taught history at Vanderbilt University and Nichols College. Goodheart is now associate professor of history at the University of Connecticut, Hartford. He has written *Abolitionist, Actuary, Atheist: Elizur Wright and the Reform Impulse* (1990) and has coedited with Richard O. Curry, *American Chameleon: Essays on Individualism in Trans-National Context* (1991) and with Richard D. Brown and Stephen G. Rabe, *Slavery in American Society* (1993). The latter work is in this series on *Problems in American Civilization*. His essays have appeared in the *Journal of the Early Republic, Civil War History, Canadian Review of American Studies,* and the *Historian.* He has served on the editorial board of the *Journal of the Early Republic* and as director of the Connecticut Academy for English, Geography and History, a teaching institute.

Hugh Hawkins

Born in Topeka, Kansas, Hugh Hawkins earned his B.A. at DePauw University and his Ph.D. at Johns Hopkins. After military service he taught briefly at the University of North Carolina, Chapel Hill, then moved to Amherst College, where he is presently Anson D. Morse Professor of History and American Studies. His books include *Pioneer: A History of the Johns Hopkins University, 1874–1889* (1960), *Between Harvard and America: The Educational Leadership of Charles W. Eliot* (1972), and *Banding Together: The Rise of National Associations in American Higher Education, 1887–1950* (1992); and he was coauther of *Education at Amherst Reconsidered: The Liberal Studies Program* (1978). In the *Problems in American Civilization* series, he has edited, besides the current volume, *Booker T. Washington and His Critics* and *The Emerging University and Industrial America.* His articles have appeared in *Change, History of Education Quarterly, Journal of American History, New England Quarterly,* and *School and Society.* Among his honors and awards are the Moses Coit Tyler Prize of the American Historical Association, a Guggenheim Fellowship, two National Endowment for the Humanities fellowships, and Fulbright visiting professorships at the Universities of Goettingen and Hamburg.

Preface

Since the last edition of this book, scholarship on abolitionism has been extensive and creative. Historians no longer debate whether abolitionists were irresponsible fanatics or flawless reformers. Nor do scholars feel compelled to rehabilitate William Lloyd Garrison and his colleagues in order to rebut earlier critics. During the last two decades, the interpretative framework has been more analytical than polemical, more evenhanded than emotional. The rhetoric may have cooled, but not the interest in the crucial issues of racial relations and social change.

The civil rights and Black Power movements of the 1950s and 1960s renewed appreciation for the abolitionists' courage and commitment. Yet, to paraphrase the prophetic words of the Kerner Commission in 1968, America's persistent polarization into two separate societies—one black, one white, separate and unequal—has continued, just as it did after the incomplete revolution of the first Reconstruction. Just as changing present-day concerns influence the questions historians ask of the past, so too has the historiography of abolitionism shifted focus. This third edition makes the exciting current literature on this crucial subject readily available for classroom use.

Much is new in this anthology. A substantial introduction surveys abolitionism from the colonial period through Reconstruction, and a chronology lists the dates of critical events. A new section of antislavery illustrations complements the written text. All the secondary sources are new, as are many of the contemporary documents. Part I, "The Origins of Abolitionism," provides an overview of the changing conditions in the Western world that encouraged the emergence of an antislavery ideology. Part II, "The Antebellum Period," and Part III, "Civil War and Reconstruction," place abolitionism in the context of the general reform movement, in addition to focusing on specific subjects—race, gender, and class as well as religion, economics, and politics. Headnotes introduce each selection, and an updated bibliography provides ready reference for research.

We thank the authors and publishers for permission to reprint their work in this volume. *The Abolitionists* has also benefited from a number of readers who offered constructive criticism. They include Robert H. Abzug, The University of Texas at Austin; Ellen Embardo, University of Connecticut; Louis S. Gerteis, University of Missouri—St. Louis; Lewis Perry, Vanderbilt University; Ronald G. Walters, The Johns Hopkins University; and Bertram Wyatt-Brown, University of Florida.

L. B. G.
H. H.

Contents

III. Civil War and Reconstruction 145

Introduction

The first substantial indictment of slavery in British North America occurred at the time of the American Revolution. The justification of colonial independence on grounds of humanity's inalienable natural right to liberty conflicted with the enslavement of 500,000 blacks, one-sixth of the total population of the thirteen colonies.

The egalitarian ideology of the Revolution challenged a racial caste system that had evolved throughout Anglo-American society during the seventeenth century. Although regional differences in racial relations developed, white supremacy prevailed everywhere. Unless holding written proof of their free status, Africans and their descendants (unlike indentured servants) were legally defined as perpetually owned chattel, movable property comparable to horses or wagons. Free blacks were routinely denied full legal rights and economic opportunity, let alone social acceptance.

Nonetheless, blacks were never passive victims of a brutal system. During the colonial period, they responded in a variety of ways to lessen their degradation. Some fled bondage, as did Crispus Attucks, the patriot killed in the 1770 Boston Massacre; others revolted, as in the 1739 Stono Rebellion in South Carolina, the only North American colony where blacks constituted a majority of the population. For most African Americans, such options were not possible in light of their minority status and the power of the institutions arrayed against them. By the mid-eighteenth century, a distinctive African-American culture had taken hold. Music, family life, religion, and rich folkways set blacks, both slave and free, apart from whites. At the same time, significant fusion of African and European traditions took place on the common ground of America. Important variations in black culture developed from the North, where blacks were concentrated in port cities and constituted a small fraction of the total population, to the tobacco fields of the Chesapeake region and the rice and indigo plantations of the Lower South, where a large and growing number of slaves worked. Nevertheless, African Americans created the cultural basis for a resistance to white domination, a response that the American Revolution would further transform.

The Society of Friends, particularly Quakers in the Philadelphia area, initiated the first consistent questioning of slavery in the British colonies among whites. Emphasizing the intuitive theology of the Protestant Reformation, Quakers testified to the oneness of humankind, the universality of divine love, and the evil of physical coercion. These beliefs made them conscientious objectors to war and predisposed some to identify slavery as sin. The Germantown Friends in 1688 and the Quaker dissident George Keith in 1693 indicted the cruelty of slavery and affirmed the humanity of blacks. This early abolitionism went largely unheeded, however, because racial hierarchy at the time was considered part of the natural order. By the mid-eighteenth century, however, the revivalist emphasis on personal accountability for sin, preached during the Great Awakening, and the commercial connections of American Quakers that brought them into contact with emerging antislavery sentiment in Britain provided the catalyst for change. The humanitarian arguments of Benjamin Lay, John Woolman, and Anthony Benezet triumphed at the 1758 Yearly Meeting in Philadelphia. There the Quakers disowned members who engaged in the slave trade or slave ownership. In 1775 Philadelphia Quakers created the first antislavery society in the world, a model for a host of similar organizations in America, Britain, and France.

Above all, republican ideology of the American Revolution undermined the legitimacy of racial slavery. Enlightenment intellectuals argued that reason, natural law and order, progress, happiness, and liberty governed the good society, values antithetical to the whip, branding iron, and shackle. If Britain could be regarded as reducing the colonies to political slavery through "a long train of abuses and usurpations," then a number of patriots concluded with Thomas Paine that the actual slaves the colonists held ought to be free also. For the virtuous republic, slavery posed a blatant moral contradiction.

Revolutionary fervor led to extensive antislavery measures. On the national level, the Continental Congress urged in 1774 the abolition of the international slave trade, and a half dozen states, including Virginia (which had a surplus of slaves), quickly complied. Some 5,000 slaves who enlisted in the patriot cause gained their freedom through military service, though Maryland was the only southern state to offer such "freedom by the flintlock." Other slaves petitioned northern state legislatures for their freedom. Benjamin Banneker, a talented free black, wrote a notable letter to

Thomas Jefferson countering the Virginian's negative racial views. The Confederation Congress during the 1780s banned slavery in the Northwest Territory to facilitate settlement by an independent yeomanry. And in 1787 the new federal Constitution permitted the ending of slave importation after twenty years, a step that was taken on January 1, 1808, a year after Parliament had passed a comparable law for the British Empire.

In the North, where slavery was neither extensive nor an economic necessity, laws for gradual emancipation were enacted. By 1804 all the original states north of Maryland and Delaware had taken legal action to end slavery within their borders. As early as 1790 no slaves were held in Massachusetts; in 1840 New Jersey was the only northern state where any bondage still existed. Southern states, where blacks were numerous and slavery was firmly entrenched, did not adopt a policy of abolition. But, in the Upper South as in the North, small antislavery groups, often led by Quakers, organized until they were silenced by overwhelming opposition. The Upper South, unlike the Carolinas and Georgia, did ease restrictions on manumission; this change coincided with a shift from tobacco to grain production in the Chesapeake that undercut the need for slave labor. The free black population in Maryland thus constituted 25 percent of that state's African Americans in 1810, up from a mere 4 percent in 1755.

Despite the enactment of important antislavery measures, the paradox of slavery and freedom remained. Indeed, historian Edmund Morgan argues that precisely because white Virginians in the most populous slave state were racially united across class lines in their common suppression of blacks, they could agitate for revolution against Britain without fear of provoking social upheaval. Nor did northerners press for national emancipation. Instead the Constitution of 1787 included a series of concessions over sectional issues that left slavery firmly in place. It also allowed the passage of the first fugitive slave law in 1793. In the same year, the invention of the cotton gin and the rise of textile manufacturing in Britain and the North encouraged a vast demographic shift of masters and slaves that, in a few decades, extended a profitable system of bondage westward to Texas and Missouri.

In 1800 the free black population had expanded to 11 percent (108,000 people) of the total African-American population, but the number of slaves approached one million. Slavery, confined to the South, became its "peculiar institution." Along with the denial of liberty to slaves, the restrictions on free blacks that persisted everywhere fostered a popular belief in white supremacy. The argument that blacks were intrinsically inferior, lazy, and sexually wanton (ideas that Thomas Jefferson espoused in his *Notes on the State of Virginia,* published in 1787) gained currency in justifying a national caste system based on color. The successful slave insurrection on the West Indian island of Santo Domingo (which began in 1791 and culminated in the bloody defeat of French colonialism in 1803) as well as the discovery in 1800 of Gabriel Prosser's planned uprising in Richmond escalated white fears about oppressed blacks dwelling among whites. Frustrated by pervasive white hostility and racial segregation, free blacks, especially in the Upper South and North, turned inward after 1790, nurturing their own distinctive institutions. These community organizations—churches, schools, mutual aid societies, and small businesses—provided the leadership and mass support for subsequent black agitation for abolition and racial justice.

The first national organization dedicated to emancipation, the American Colonization Society (founded in December 1816), exemplified the country's racial contradictions. The white northern evangelicals and Upper South slaveholders who dominated the society looked with alarm at the rapid increase of a population of African descent. Indeed, from 1800 to 1830 the number of free blacks tripled to 320,000, while the slave population more than doubled to two million. In response, the society promoted the voluntary expatriation of free blacks to a colony in Liberia, which it hoped would encourage gradual manumission. Slaveholders were particularly interested in removing free blacks, whom they feared would destabilize southern society. However much northern evangelicals deplored slavery, they accepted white supremacy as inevitable and regarded colonization as a benevolent reform. Despite support by leading politicians, however, including President James Monroe, the society by 1830 had transported only 1,420 blacks to Liberia.

The limitations of African recolonization were soon apparent. Meeting in Bishop Richard Allen's African Methodist Episcopal Church in January 1817, prominent Philadelphia blacks organized the first of many large rallies to denounce the policy. They demanded their rights as U.S. citizens and expressed solidarity with the slaves. These views found support in *Freedom's Journal* (the first black newspaper, started in 1827 in New York) and in the annual conventions of northern blacks that began in 1830 in Philadelphia. From Boston, David Walker issued a revolutionary *Appeal* in 1829, excoriating white hypocrisy on race and alarming officials who charged that black sailors distributed the pamphlet in southern ports. Indeed, Denmark Vesey's 1822 insurrection of blacks in Charleston was foiled only at the last minute, while in Virginia Nat Turner in 1831 led the bloodiest slave rebellion in U.S. history. Later that same year a massive slave revolt took place in Jamaica. Mounting antislavery opinion swept Parliament in the early 1830s, leading to the 1834 emancipation in the British West Indies of some 780,000 slaves; they were placed in an apprenticeship plan to prepare them for freedom, with £20 million in economic compensation provided to slaveholders.

In addition, regional antagonism in the United States, simmering from the War of 1812, erupted into sectional discord over the next two decades. The divisive issue of slavery underlay political confrontations over Missouri statehood, the Tariff of Abomination, and the Nullification Crisis, and artful compromise quieted them only temporarily. Growing national attention to the volatile racial situation developed alongside the burgeoning religious revivals of the Second Great Awakening, which promised the immediate blessing of grace from a benevolent deity whenever a sinner repented. Tens of thousands responded.

During this time of ferment, William Lloyd Garrison, an impecunious Boston printer, extended the religious message of redemption to what he identified as the national sin of slavery. On January 1, 1831, he founded *The Liberator,* vowing, "I will not retreat a single inch—AND I WILL BE HEARD." The evil of slavery, he declared, was not only the brutalization of fellow human beings but the prevention of blacks from being free moral agents ultimately accountable to God, not an interposed human master. Instead of the immoral expedient of gradual abolition espoused by colonizationists, Garrison called for a revolution in race relations, an immediate cessation of the sin of slavery and the full acceptance of African Americans as fellow citizens. Though his term "immediate abolition" was more of a rallying cry than a specific plan, the idealistic Garrison attracted a devoted following of blacks and whites, women and men, who embraced his radical doctrine.

Above all, the early immediate abolitionists recognized that slavery and its resulting pattern of race relations contravened fundamental republican principles and Christian ethics. During the antebellum period the North moved toward an urban, manufacturing economy, while the cotton boom made the South an assertive, expansive slave society. Though the economies of the two regions were interdependent, important values diverged. In the North free labor, with its ideology of individual opportunity and middle-class virtues, was associated with free institutions and national identity. In the South the influential planter class no longer excused racial slavery as a necessary evil. Rather, it proclaimed that slavery was a positive good in contrast to northern wage slavery—unmitigated, they charged, by the paternalism of a benevolent master. The abolitionists were instrumental in legitimating an antislavery perspective in the North, especially when, after the Mexican War, both sections clashed over the extension of slavery into the western territories. But because of pervasive white supremacy, antislavery sentiment grew without a corresponding popular commitment to black equality, a tragic irony that the abolitionists were not able to overcome.

Abolitionists pointed to paradoxes in American society, yet their own crusade was not exempt from contradiction and confusion. Initially Garrison's anticolonization arguments rallied a new breed of youthful abolitionists from New England to Ohio. Spurred by British abolition, they formed the American Anti-Slavery Society in 1833, a national organization whose principal leaders were Garrison and Arthur and Lewis Tappan, wealthy New York evangelicals who subsidized the effort. The prospect of immediate abolition, however, divided the religious. Procolonization trustees at Ohio's Western Reserve College and at Lane Theological Institute in Cincinnati attempted to silence abolitionist faculty and students. As a result, many of the latter left to work for the American Anti-Slavery Society or went to Oberlin College and Oneida Institute, pioneers in biracial education. Theodore Weld, charismatic leader of those at Lane who favored immediate abolition, became the leading lecturer of the national society during the 1830s.

Widespread hostility, however, accompanied Weld wherever he spoke, earning him the title of the most mobbed man in America. Though their racial message was radical, immediatists (those who supported immediate abolition) romantically believed that they would win the pious to the cause, creating a tide of righteousness that would wash away the stain of slavery. They saw abolition as an extension of similar reforms, such as temperance, Bible distribution, and African colonization, that evangelicals had launched in their so-called Benevolent Empire to reorder the republic in a time of social change. Masters of moral suasion, immediatists turned out millions of pieces of literature, women gathered thousands of signatures on antislavery petitions, and agents canvassed the North, organizing affiliates of the national society.

The antiabolition violence of the 1830s was often directed by "gentlemen of property and standing," leading pillars of the community who had a vested interest in the racial status quo. White mobs were easily enraged by charges that abolitionists encouraged "amalgamation" (racial intermarriage) or were otherwise challenging the color caste code. In 1834 a New York mob gutted Lewis Tappan's house; in 1835 Garrison was nearly lynched in Boston; and in 1837 Elijah Lovejoy was killed defending his antislavery press in Alton, Illinois. Afraid to upset the delicate party alliance between the sections, President Andrew Jackson endorsed a ban on sending abolitionist literature to the South. And Congress from 1836 to 1843 enforced a "gag rule" that automatically tabled the numerous antislavery petitions presented to it, despite John Quincy Adams' eloquent protestations. It seemed only when white lives and rights were abused did the immediatists gain credibility.

The unanticipated backlash that immediatists encountered during the mid-1830s forced them to reconsider their means and ends. Garrison concluded that human institutions in general, not just slavery, were inherently flawed because they ultimately rested on the use of coercion. In reaction, he advocated nonresistance, an extreme pietism that embraced pacifism, urged spiritual perfection, and pledged allegiance to the moral government of God. In 1838 Garrison and his Boston circle formed the New England Non-Resistant Society, which reviled the corruption of established religion and the political process. Five years later Garrison burned the

U.S. Constitution—a proslavery document, he charged, that was "a covenant with death, and an agreement with Hell."

Garrisonian nonresistance provoked contention among immediatists whose original solidarity against colonization had waned with the decline of that common foe. The precipitating event was Garrison's sponsorship of an 1837 speaking tour of Angelina and Sarah Grimké. These sisters, ardently opposed to slavery, had renounced their slaveholding origins in South Carolina and converted to Quakerism in Philadelphia. Women often spoke in Quaker meetings, but conservative reformers, especially clerics, were outraged that the Grimkés defied convention to lecture to "promiscuous" assemblies, mixed groups of men and women, instead of to single-sex audiences. Nonresistance, with its indictment of physical force, lent itself also to a feminist indictment of "domestic slavery," the tyranny of patriarchy, a position the Grimkés developed in 1838 in response to their critics. When abolitionists Lucretia Mott and Elizabeth Cady Stanton were banished to the women's balcony at the 1840 World's Anti-Slavery Convention in London, Garrison joined them rather than fraternize on the floor with the male delegates. Abolitionism gave women an egalitarian ideology and common ground from which to protest their plight. Mott and Stanton, for example, organized the Women's Rights Convention of 1848 at Seneca Falls, New York, where exslave Frederick Douglass spoke on behalf of women's suffrage. Yet abolitionists subordinated women's rights to the greater priority of emancipation of slaves, a tension that led to bitter disputes across gender and racial lines.

The election of Abby Kelly, a nonresistant feminist, to the executive committee of the American Anti-Slavery Society in 1840 crystallized a three-way schism among abolitionists. Garrisonians now dominated the national society, but church-oriented and political abolitionists repudiated nonresistance, including feminism. They also were divided among themselves. Church-oriented abolitionists who were centered around Lewis Tappan organized the rival American and Foreign Anti-Slavery Society in 1840. This evangelical faction endorsed the antislavery ballot but not a third party, adamantly opposed women's rights, and hoped to further abolition through the conversion of the ministry. The political wing backed a "human rights" party, saw the "woman question" as a diversion from abolition, and was alienated from the churches, which remained largely opposed to abolition.

After 1840, as national contention over slavery escalated, most abolitionists turned to political action. Even Garrison, who refused to vote, urged those whose consciences permitted them to do so to cast an antislavery ballot. Concern with the nation's republican ideals had always been a central motivation for abolitionists. During the mid-1830s they entered the political realm by petitioning Congress to adopt antislavery measures and by questioning candidates of the major parties about slavery. Outrage in some northern constituencies over the "gag rule" and other violations of constitutional rights encouraged dissident Whigs and Democrats to agitate for abolition in Congress, though party leaders resisted for the sake of intersectional harmony.

Seeking to increase the leverage of the antislavery vote in closely contested elections, New York abolitionists Myron Holley and Alvah Stewart directed the organization of an abolitionist party in 1839. This Liberty party nominated former slaveholder James G. Birney for president in 1840 and 1844. His platform called for the end of the domestic slave trade, the restriction of slavery in the western territories, and abolition in the District of Columbia, all areas where it was thought that the federal government had jurisdiction. In 1844, though Birney gained a mere 16,000 votes in New York, he attracted enough antislavery Whig support from Henry Clay to give the Empire State and the presidency to the proslavery Democrat James Polk.

Polk's proslavery policies encouraged the annexation of Texas and the resulting Mexican War. These events, in turn, popularized the Liberty party's warning that a Slave Power conspiracy of planters and northern "doughfaces" had enveloped the government. In addition to charging that Slave Power threatened the fundamental freedoms of all citizens, political abolitionists blamed the long-lasting depression that began in 1837 on profligate planters. They extolled the virtues of free labor, which meant self-ownership for blacks as well as whites, with the opportunity to work for fair wages, and they proclaimed the promise of free soil in the West for America's laboring classes. Significantly the Liberty party's moral indictment of slavery coincided with the nineteenth-century liberal credo that individual autonomy and personal freedom defined the good society.

Yet abolitionism moved into the political mainstream only by moderating its demand for black rights. The more inclusive Free Soil party named former Democratic president Martin Van Buren as its standard bearer in 1848, even though he had been an early opponent of immediatism. The platforms of the antislavery Free-Soil and Republican parties opposed the extension of slavery into the western territories but said nothing about racial equality. After all, pervasive white supremacy in the North sanctioned racial bias. Massachusetts was unusual when in 1855 it desegregated public schools, integrated its railroad cars, and added African-American men to the jury rolls. Indeed, most northern states barred or restricted black suffrage, limited job opportunities, and practiced other forms of legal discrimination.

Besides racial insults and mob violence, black abolitionists encountered condescending colleagues. Though blacks and whites joined together in the abolitionist crusade, whites expected to lead. Garrison, for example, vilified Frederick Douglass in 1847 when he broke with Garrison, who had been his patron, and founded his own abolitionist newspaper, *The North Star,* in Rochester. African Americans, having experienced relentless discrimination, knew that racism, however expressed, was the fundamental problem. They asserted independent leadership through numerous lectures and published slave narratives that authenticated the brutality of slavery, as Douglass did in the 1845 account of his bondage in Maryland. Harriet Tubman became a legendary conductor on the Underground Railroad, while local vigilance committees aided fugitive slaves. In 1851 Boston blacks freed Shadrack (Fred Wilkins) from federal officers and spirited him to sanctuary in Canada. Defying the pacifist doctrine of Garrisonian nonresistance, Henry Highland Garnet at the Buffalo Convention of the Free People of Color in 1843 justified slave revolution. Disillusioned with the Free Soil party's accommodation to racism, Martin Delaney in 1855 chastised white abolitionists and called for the creation of a black nation, the *sine qua non* of freedom.

Nonetheless, the escalation of sectional tension during the 1850s compelled most black and white abolitionists to support the Republican party. The Compromise of 1850, with its strengthened fugitive slave law, provoked open defiance; blacks in Christiana, Pennsylvania killed two "kidnappers" hunting for fugitives in 1851, and northern legislatures passed personal liberty laws that refused compliance with the federal statute. Northern outrage over the proslavery "betrayal" of the Missouri Compromise of 1820 by the Kansas-Nebraska Act of 1854 and the resulting strife in "bleeding Kansas" led most abolitionists, including nonresistants, to endorse the use of force. Abolitionists eulogized the executed John Brown as a martyr for his 1859 raid on the federal arsenal at Harpers Ferry, Virginia.

With the election of Abraham Lincoln to the presidency in 1860, southern states seceded from the Union, fearing that the South ultimately would be destroyed by Republican policies restricting the westward expansion of slavery. Abolitionists, with their nationalistic commitment to a Union based on free soil, free labor, and free men, endorsed Lincoln's refusal to allow the South to secede, even though that policy meant war.

As they had done for the past thirty years, abolitionists acted as critics after the outbreak of hostilities at Fort Sumter on April 15, 1861. They prodded the president and Congress, especially the radical Republicans, to transform the Civil War into a struggle against slavery, to recruit black soldiers, and to ensure equal justice for the freed people. Although the war was first fought to preserve the Union, slavery became the critical issue by September 1862, when military strategy compelled Lincoln to issue his Preliminary Emancipation Proclamation. Thereafter, it was clear that Union victory would mean an end to slavery. Lincoln had reacted less to the influence of abolitionists than to the need to weaken the Confederates, placate the loyal slave states, and keep Britain neutral. However, African Americans pressed the issue; thousands of slaves fled to Union lines, and starting in 1862, the enrollment of almost 180,000 black troops significantly strengthened Union forces.

When the Thirteenth Amendment ending slavery was adopted in 1865, Garrison closed *The Liberator* and urged the dissolution of the American Anti-Slavery Society, its work done. Garrison felt vindicated by the course of the Civil War and by the unaccustomed public acclaim he was receiving as America's leading abolitionist. Wendell Phillips, however, disagreed with his old comrade. In a contentious election, Phillips became president of the national society and directed its mission toward the four million ex-slaves. Unlike Garrison, Phillips had sharply criticized Lincoln's restricted racial policies and had endorsed the more progressive

John C. Frémont for the 1864 Republican nomination. Despite Phillips' eloquence, however, those dedicated to black rights, including Radical Republicans in Congress, remained few in number. Committed blacks and whites, women and men, did minister to the former slaves, some as early as 1862 in the Union-occupied islands off South Carolina. Nonetheless, abolitionists never had the power to dictate the terms of Reconstruction to the vanquished South.

Instead, postbellum racial policies were constrained by compromise, factionalism, and the prevailing conceptions of social change. Abolitionists in Congress such as Thaddeus Stevens and Charles Sumner had to contend not only with minority status within the Republican party but also with unsympathetic Democrats, former Confederates, and northern racists. The dominant belief in *laissez faire* capitalism allowed only a few to advocate redistribution of rebel plantations or any economic compensation for two centuries of slave labor. Furthermore, the legislation creating the Freedmen's Bureau, as well as the Fourteenth and Fifteenth Amendments, compelled accommodation to moderate and conservative forces. The latter amendment was ironically intended to enfranchise black men in the North, where most states prohibited their voting. (Congressional Reconstruction had already mandated black male suffrage in the South.)

The expedient exclusion of women's suffrage from the Fifteenth Amendment alienated white, middle-class feminists such as Elizabeth Cady Stanton and Susan B. Anthony from the cause of black rights. In 1869 they formed the National Woman Suffrage Association, thus institutionalizing the schism between feminists and abolitionists. In the cause of the female franchise, Stanton even reverted to racial recrimination.

The ratification of the Fifteenth Amendment in 1870 led Phillips and his supporters to dissolve the American Anti-Slavery Society. The franchise, it was naively thought, would ensure equality under the law. Phillips, like most abolitionists, turned to other issues then agitating northern society—temperance, labor unrest, women's rights, and civil service reform. The election of 1872 further divided abolitionists between "stalwarts," who remained loyal to President Grant as the best way to protect the freed people, and "liberals," who opposed the incumbent because of endemic corruption in his administration. Abolitionists rallied, however, on behalf of the much-compromised Civil Rights Act of 1875, which sought to ban discrimination in public accommodations, the last significant effort at Reconstruction legislation. But in 1883 the Supreme Court rendered the law a dead letter by limiting federal supervision of individual behavior, a ruling similar to others that severely curtailed black rights. The Compromise of 1877, which reflected the desire for sectional reconciliation, sounded the full national retreat from Reconstruction. In brief, the effort to achieve equality in the postbellum South failed just as it had faltered in the post-revolutionary North.

Unlike earlier generations, today's historians no longer damn or canonize the abolitionists. The conservative reaction to the civil rights and Black Power movements of the 1950s and 1960s makes clearer the moral fortitude of the abolitionists as well as the constraints on social change. The abolitionists recognized the paradox of slavery and freedom, but they did not fully appreciate the pervasiveness of white racism, even within their own ranks. The expansion of northern antislavery sentiment after 1850 did not produce a popular commitment to black equality. Instead, it was military force that brought about emancipation, while leaving virtually intact the national dilemma of a color caste system. Nineteenth-century restraints on federal power, the tradition of states' rights, the emphasis on self-help, and the lack of financial redress for servitude set the stage for segregation and sharecropping sustained by lynch law. Fatefully, the abolition of slavery left a legacy that still shapes race relations today.

Chronology

1772   Somerset decision by Chief Justice Mansfield ends slavery in Britain but not in its colonies.

1775   Philadelphia Quakers form the world's first antislavery society. In November Lord Dunmore, royal governor of Virginia, offers land to free slaves who left patriot masters for the British.

1776   In April the Continental Congress votes that "no slaves be imported into any of the thirteen colonies."

1777   Vermont's constitution abolishes slavery.

1780   Pennsylvania passes a gradual abolition law.

1782   Virginia eases the laws that allow manumission, a move that influences other states in the Upper South.

1783   A judicial decision outlaws slavery in Massachusetts.

1784   Rhode Island and Connecticut enact gradual emancipation laws.

1787   The United States bans slavery from the Northwest Territory. Britain establishes Sierra Leone as a colony for exslaves. The London Society for Effecting the Abolition of the Slave Trade is founded.

1788   The *Société des Amis des Noirs* organizes in France.

1791   Slave revolution begins in the French colony of Santo Domingo and in 1803 achieves the final defeat of colonialism.

1793   Upper Canada enacts a gradual abolition law.

1794   The National Convention abolishes slavery in the French colonies, but Napoleon revokes the law in 1802.

1799   New York passes a gradual emancipation law.

1800   Gabriel Prosser's attempted slave insurrection in Richmond, Virginia is suppressed.

1804   New Jersey adopts a gradual manumission law.

1807   Parliament abolishes international slave trade in the British Empire.

1808   After January 1, the United States ends the international importation of slaves.

1813   Argentina enacts gradual abolition.

1815   Napoleon ends the French slave trade.

1816   In December the American Colonization Society is founded.

1820   In Jonesboro, Tennessee, Elihu Embree publishes *The Emancipator,* the first newspaper in the United States devoted exclusively to abolition. The United States declares that involvement in the international slave trade constitutes piracy, a crime punishable by death. The Missouri Compromise bars slavery north of 36°30′ in the Louisiana Purchase territory.

1822   Denmark Vesey plots a black uprising in Charleston, South Carolina.

1824   Slavery is abolished in Central America and flourishes only in Brazil, Cuba, and the United States in the New World.

1827 In New York City Samuel Cornish and John Russwurm found *Freedom's Journal,* the first black newspaper.

1829 David Walker publishes his *Appeal.* Mexico abolishes slavery.

1830 There are more than two million slaves in the United States, constituting one-sixth of its total population and more than one-third of all slaves in the New World. The U.S. population of free blacks is about 320,000.

1831 In January William Lloyd Garrison begins publication of *The Liberator.* In August Nat Turner leads a bloody slave rebellion in Southampton County, Virginia. A far larger slave uprising occurs in British Jamaica that December.

1832–1833 Nullification crisis.

1832 Garrison founds the New England Anti-Slavery Society in Boston.

1833 The British Emancipation Acts end slave-holding throughout the British Empire as of August 1, 1834.

1833 In December immediatists organize the American Anti-Slavery Society in Philadelphia.

1834 In January Theodore Weld at Lane Institute in Cincinnati leads the conversion of students to immediatism. In July mobs attack abolitionists and blacks in New York City.

1835 A mob nearly lynches Garrison in Boston.

1836–1844 "Gag rules" automatically table abolitionist petitions presented to Congress.

1837   Abolitionists Angelina and Sarah Grimké begin their controversial lecture campaign. On November 7 a mob kills abolitionist Elijah P. Lovejoy in Alton, Illinois.

1837–1840   Abolitionist schism.

1838   In September Frederick Douglass flees slavery in Maryland. Later that month Garrison and his supporters found the New England Non-Resistance Society.

1840   Garrisonians dominate the American Anti-Slavery Society; Lewis Tappan forms the rival American and Foreign Anti-Slavery Society. The Liberty party runs James G. Birney for president.

1843   Garrison damns the Constitution as a proslavery document. Henry Highland Garnet openly calls for slave insurrection.

1844   Birney receives 62,000 votes as the Liberty party's candidate for president.

1845   Frederick Douglass publishes his fugitive slave autobiography. Texas is admitted to the Union as a slave state.

1846   The United States declares war with Mexico. The Wilmot Proviso is introduced.

1848   The Woman's Rights Convention is held at Seneca Falls, New York. The Free-Soil party runs Martin Van Buren for president. France and Denmark abolish slavery in their colonies.

1850   A strengthened Fugitive Slave Law provokes widespread resistance in the North.

I

The Origins of

Abolitionism

David Brion Davis

JOHN WOOLMAN'S PROPHECY

Slavery is an ancient institution that originated in the dawn of civilization. For most of its long history, the practice of human bondage was accepted as a natural form of social and economic organization. Europeans after 1500 used this to explain the enslavement of large numbers of Africans, a people of different race and culture, in their New World colonies. The emergence of antislavery sentiment during the mid-eighteenth century, such as that of Quaker John Woolman, then represented, in David Brion Davis's words, "a turning point in Western culture." During this era, Enlightenment thinkers assumed that human will and reason could improve society, a transformation that would include the abolition of slavery. In this selection, Davis, Sterling Professor of History at Yale University, explains the religious and social context of Woolman's prophetic indictment of slavery.

In 1746 a young West Jersey tailor named John Woolman felt a "concern" in his mind to visit fellow Quakers in Virginia and North Carolina. Woolman's urge to travel may have been influenced by the fact that his employer's retirement had left him without a job at a time when living costs were being elevated by the prosperity of neighboring Quaker merchants, who were making fortunes in the West India trade. And yet ascetic travel had long been accepted by Quakers as a means of self-discipline and social purification. John Pemberton, whose family was deeply involved in West Indian rum and sugar, would soon be traveling as a missionary in Great Britain, denouncing worldliness and corruption, and warning sinners of the impending Day of Judgment. Samuel Fothergill, brother of the cosmopolitan London physician, would soon be telling Maryland Quakers that slavery was corroding their religious purity.

Woolman had long felt a poignant fear of the vanities, luxuries, and selfish interests of the world. Having steeped himself in the writings of English and French mystics, he had come to see the sufferings and rewards of this life as a succession of tests through which man must seek eternity. But although his religious exercises had

From David Brion Davis, *The Problem of Slavery in Western Culture* (Ithaca, N.Y.: Cornell University Press, 1966), 483–493. Reprinted by permission of the author.

helped him overcome youthful frivolity and wantonness, he was troubled by the memory of one crucial failure. When his master had asked him to write a bill of sale for a Negro woman, he had complied against the promptings of his conscience. In the South he was similarly uneasy over accepting food and lodging from Quaker slaveowners, especially as he saw how the white youth, relieved from the healthful discipline of work, were led to idleness and worldly vice. The depraving effects of slavery became deeply impressed on Woolman's mind as he traveled through Virginia, where the institution appeared "as a dark gloominess hanging over the land." Soon after returning to Burlington County, he gave expression to his anxieties by writing *Some Considerations on the Keeping of Negroes.* But though encouraged by his dying father to consult leading Friends on the advisability of publishing the tract, Woolman kept his opinions to himself until 1754.

The mid-eighteenth century was not an auspicious time to launch an antislavery crusade. When Woolman made his first southern trip, officials in Georgia had virtually abandoned efforts to impede the importation of slaves, and in four years an act of Parliament would officially end the single experiment to exclude Negroes from an American colony. Nearly a decade before Woolman's journey, Benjamin Lay had published his blistering indictment of slaveholders, but in 1746 Lay was a forgotten eccentric who lived in isolation, disowned and ostracized by the Society of Friends. The most admired and envied of Woolman's Quaker acquaintances—the Pembertons, the Logans, the Smiths—owned slaves. The most advanced position that could win acceptance from the Quaker elite was probably epitomized by a printed epistle of 1741 from John Bell, an English Friend. The essence of Bell's message was the necessity of spreading the Gospel light after a long night of apostasy. True Christians must "be as Lights to those who yet remain in Darkness." They should treat their slaves with compassion, and convert servitude into an agency of conversion. But Bell's interpretation of the Golden Rule assumed that slavery was not incompatible with Christian duty. His exhortation was no more than the conventional attempt to apply the dualisms of Saint Paul to an exploitive and speculative economic institution.

And yet the eight years that intervened between Woolman's southern trip and the publication of his first antislavery tract represented a turning point in the history of Western culture. To both religious and secular writers the period brought an almost explosive consciousness of man's freedom to shape the world in accordance with his own will and reason. And as the dogmas and restraints of the past lost their compelling force, there was a heightened concern for discovering laws and principles that would enable human society to be something more than an endless contest of greed and power. This quest for moral assurance led inevitably to examinations of inequality, sovereignty, and servitude. Two years after Woolman's trip, Montesquieu's *L'Esprit des lois* demolished the traditional justifications for slavery, and placed the subject on the agenda of the French Enlightenment. In 1752 James Foster's *Discourses* judged the institution by the ethics of latitudinarian theology, and David Hume focused attention on the relation of slavery to population growth. The year 1755 saw the appearance of Hutcheson's *System of Moral Philosophy*, Rousseau's *Discours sur l'inégalité*, de Jaucourt's first antislavery article in the *Encyclopédie*, and Franklin's calculations on the economic wastefulness of slave labor.

One may also note that the publication of Woolman's *Considerations* coincided with the outbreak of hostilities on the Pennsylvania frontier, and hence with the beginning of a war which soon involved English, Spanish, and French colonies from Grenada to Gorée, and from Cuba to Bengal. The loss by France of most of her colonial empire, and the acquisition of Canada by Britain, quite naturally stimulated a searching reassessment of all aspects of imperial economics and administration. And the postwar inquiries of economists and statesmen came at a time when the British sugar islands were suffering from the effects of exhausted soil and antiquated methods of production, and were increasingly dependent on an artificially protected market; when French and Spanish sugar was glutting the European market and depressing prices; when the cost of African slaves was rising; when debts and depleted soil in the North American tobacco colonies were forcing planters to turn to crop diversification and westward expansion. Such conditions provided a favorable context for questioning slavery on economic and political grounds. And if this was not enough, the Seven Years' War gave added force to the feelings of physical insecurity which had long plagued colonists who lived among vast populations of slaves. Since the war proved that whole empires were vulnerable to military conquest, colonists had new reason to fear the unlimited importation of men who might someday look to an invader for liberation.

Given this convergence of cultural, intellectual, economic, and strategic developments, it is not surprising that the climate of opinion on slavery should have changed by 1769, when John Woolman felt obliged to make a missionary trip to the West Indies. In this study we have not been concerned with events which led directly to the international antislavery movements of the late eighteenth century. We should not conclude our inquiry, however, without taking note of certain patterns of communication and influence that were developing on the eve of the American Revolution.

Benjamin Rush was one of the focal points of converging intellectual currents. A member of an old Pennsylvania family which had originally been Quaker and which had connections with the Keithian antislavery schismatics, Rush was educated and deeply influenced by the "New Light" Presbyterian, Samuel Finley. A friend of the revivalists George Whitefield and Samuel Davies, he was also close to Benjamin Franklin and, as a student at Edinburgh, to David Hume and William Robertson. With Arthur Lee he visited John Wilkes in prison. In Paris, thanks to Franklin's introductions, he became acquainted with the Physiocrats, the elder Mirabeau, and Diderot, the latter entrusting him with correspondence to deliver to Hume. As we have seen, it was in 1769 that Rush's letter to Barbeu Dubourg prompted Du Pont de Nemours to link the Quakers' manumission of their slaves with the hope of universal emancipation, the rise of an American empire, and the economic reformation of Europe. In 1773 Rush was encouraged by his friend Anthony Benezet to initiate a long and fruitful correspondence with Granville Sharp and to write an antislavery pamphlet which drew on the recently published theories of John Millar.

In 1769 *The Weekly Magazine or Edinburgh Amusement* printed one of the strongest indictments of slavery yet to appear in a British journal. The author's arguments were chiefly derived from Montesquieu. In the same year Granville Sharp, who had become involved in a legal battle to free a Negro in London, published *A Representation of the Injustice and Dangerous Tendency of Tolerating Slavery in England*. This work, which was also indebted to Montesquieu, was thought by later abolitionists to have signaled the beginning of the British antislavery crusade. By 1769 Sharp had become so convinced that slavery was an innovation which violated fundamental rights that he was addressing appeals to everyone from William Blackstone to the Archbishop of Canterbury, and was warning his erring land of the certainty of God's judgments. In 1767 he had been browsing in a bookstall and had stumbled upon Anthony Benezet's *A Short Account of That Part of Africa, Inhabited by the Negroes.* Sharp was so impressed by the pamphlet that he had it reprinted right away. Originally published in Philadelphia in 1762, the work presented favorable descriptions of Africa . . . and quoted antislavery passages from Hutcheson, Foster, Richard Savage, J. Philmore, and George Wallace, none of whom were American. Even before Sharp had reprinted Benezet's tract in England, it had been translated into French.

In 1772, just as John Woolman was beginning the travels in England which resulted in his death, Sharp learned of his own victory in the celebrated Somerset case, in which Chief Justice Mansfield ruled that the power claimed by a slaveholder had never been acknowledged in English law. At almost the same moment, Sharp received his first letter from Anthony Benezet, who had already reprinted an abridgement of *A Representation of the Injustice and Dangerous Tendency of Tolerating Slavery in England,* along with William Warburton's sermon of 1766 to the SPG. Though Sharp regarded Benezet as "unhappily involved in the errors of Quakerism," this letter initiated a highly significant correspondence which was to touch leaders of the Church of England as well as Benjamin Franklin.

While the Quakers provided a striking model of humanitarianism and were praised by John Wesley as well as by Turgot and Voltaire, the Society of Friends was hardly in advance of enlightened opinion on both sides of the Atlantic. In 1767, when one of Benezet's pamphlets was being reprinted and distributed by the London Meeting for Sufferings, the author himself was sending out copies of an antislavery address which has just appeared in *The Virginia Gazette.* Only a few years later there was a flurry of antislavery agitation in New England, where Arminians, revivalists, Quakers, and revolutionaries seemed to have found a common cause. It was in 1771 that the Massachusetts legislature passed a bill to outlaw the importation of slaves, and that Du Pont de Nemours, after trying to synthesize an antislavery philosophy of utility and sensibility, vowed to employ all his powers to break the Negro's chains. Two years later Thomas Day of Birmingham, an intimate of Erasmus Darwin, Matthew Boulton, Josiah Wedgwood, and Joseph Priestly, wrote his immensely popular *The Dying Negro*, a poem which cited Montesquieu, Hutcheson, and Adam Smith, and the second edition of which was dedicated to Rousseau.

Illustrations could easily be multiplied, but the central point should now be clear. By the early 1770's a large number of moralists, poets, intellectuals, and reformers had come to regard American slavery as an unmitigated evil. In Britain, France, and the North American colonies there were forces in motion that would lead to organized movements to abolish the African trade and the entire institutional framework which permitted human beings to be treated as things. Although slavery was nearly as old as human history, this was something new to the world. . . . On one side were the classical and Christian theories of servitude which tended to rationalize the brute fact that forced labor had been an integral part of the American experience. On the other side were increasing strains in the traditional system of values, the emergence of new modes of thought and feeling, and a growing faith in the possibility of moral progress which was to some extent associated with the symbolic meaning of the New World. But in the last analysis, such trends and contexts and backgrounds are only abstractions. No matter how "ripe" the time, there would be no coalescing of antislavery opinion until specific decisions and commitments were taken by individual men.

This is not to say that a John Woolman or Anthony Benezet singlehandedly awakened the world. One can easily exaggerate the importance of the fact that Granville Sharp, John Wesley, and Thomas Clarkson were all inspired by Benezet's words. The ideas, as we have seen, were in the air. Yet when all allowances are made for cultural trends and climates of opinion, one must ultimately come down to the men who precipitated change. If the Western world became more receptive to antislavery thought between the time when Woolman left for North Carolina in 1746 and when he arrived in England in 1772, the self-effacing Quaker was a major instrument of the transformation.

At first sight it is difficult to understand why Woolman should have been so revered by later antislavery historians. He was not a fearless castigator of sin like Benjamin Lay. He was not a compiler and publicist like Anthony Benezet. He was not an antislavery theorist like George Keith, Francis Hutcheson, and Montesquieu. His enduring contribution to antislavery literature was not an inflammatory tract or an eloquent manifesto, but rather the journal of his own life. For the secret of Woolman's influence was his sense of personal involvement, his ability to see Negro slavery as something more than an abstract institution, his conviction that he shared the profound guilt of all America.

His *Journal* has too often been read as the expression of a man at peace with himself and the world, of a man who has found perfect serenity of soul. It is actually the inner record of a soul tormented by a ceaseless conflict between yearnings for peace and purity. John Woolman was acutely sensitive to the opinions of others and valued consensus and accord. He was familiar with all the self-righteous disguises of his own ego. And yet few men have been so aware of the subtle ways in which society accommodates the individual conscience to self-interest. So far as slavery was concerned, he was too devout to be contemptuous of Biblical sanctions, or of the traditional ideal of the paternalistic master and humble servant. He knew pious men whose consciences were apparently not troubled by the ownership of Negroes. But as a shopkeeper and scrivener, Woolman had to make decisions which either supported or questioned the rightness of slaveholding. In 1753 he began refusing to write wills that bequeathed slave property. The following year, in executing the will of a deceased Quaker, he sold a small Negro boy for a term of service that would end at the age of thirty, and applied the money to the estate. The transaction haunted Woolman's conscience, and in later years he sought to make restitution for the sin. His sense of guilt was augmented by the fact that he had long sold West Indian sugar and molasses. These were the pressures behind Woolman's plan of 1769 to make a pilgrimage to the Caribbean. He would apply the profits he had made from slave-grown produce to a holy cause.

He was troubled, however, by the thought of traveling on a ship engaged in the deadly trade which nourished the slave system. Recalling how David could not bring himself to drink water for which his men had risked their lives, merely to satisfy his "delicacy of taste," Woolman had for some years declined to eat sugar. He was willing to face the charge of eccentricity by wearing clothes and even a hat untainted by dyes. But how could one go to minister to the unrighteous without partaking of their unrighteousness? On his second journey through the South, in 1757, Woolman had left money for the slaves who served him in each house where he stayed, so that he might be free from all association with unrequited labor. He felt he should pay more than the usual passage money to the West Indies, on the assumption that the low fare was the result of an unnatural trade. He thought of hiring a ship to sail in ballast. He acknowledged, however, that if trade with the West Indies were to be suddenly stopped, "many there would suffer for want of bread." In the end, the burden of decision proved too great, and after vacillating in his plans, Woolman became seriously ill. He was thus spared the sight of field gangs on a West India plantation.

By 1769 Woolman was showing signs of mental strain and personal oddity which were only partly related to his continuing testimony against slavery. By that time he no longer stood virtually alone, as he had at mid-century. In 1761 London Yearly Meeting had ruled that dealing in slaves merited disownment. For eleven years Philadelphia Yearly Meeting had been excluding Friends who bought or sold slaves from participation in the business affairs of the society. The rule of 1758 was being used as a weapon by local visiting committees who made it clear to slaveholders that total disownment would be the penalty for a continuing refusal to prepare their Negroes for eventual emancipation. The evolution of these policies owed much to the stimulus of the Seven Years' War, to the general reform movement within the Society of Friends, and to the activities of such men as the Fothergills, John Churchman, and Anthony Benezet. And yet Woolman had written the influential epistle sent out by Philadelphia Yearly Meeting in 1754, which expressed concern over the Quakers' growing involvement in slavery, and which announced the new ideal of educating Negroes for ultimate freedom. He had been instrumental in securing official approval for the rule of 1758; and in the face of stiffening resistance, he had led the way in visiting and exhorting slaveholders to cleanse themselves of corruption. On a tour of New England he had urged prominent Quakers to petition their assemblies to prohibit further importation of slaves. Traveling through Delaware, he had given encouragement to the followers of Joseph Nichols, who in 1768 decided to free their slaves.

While John Woolman's chief influence lay in his face-to-face confrontation with slaveholders, we may assume that the substance of his thought can be found in *Some Considerations on the Keeping of Negroes*, the second part of which appeared in 1762. These essays are infused with a calm and charitable spirit that reinforces the simplicity and moral earnestness of the author's message. Woolman is always careful to refrain from judging slaveowners as a group. He does not demand immediate and universal emancipation. But he writes in the language of an Old Testament prophet, and his judgments have the authority of man's universal conscience.

There are two great themes in Woolman's work. To those who held to the ancient dualisms of body and soul, who maintained that external condition had no effect on internal freedom and purity, Woolman replied with devastating candor. Theoretically, a master might retain his slave for only the highest motives. But could any slaveholder affirm that his perception had not been distorted by custom, self-love, and racial prejudice? Could he honestly imagine himself in his bondsman's place, and think that he would still approve a system which led to wars and kidnapping in Africa, to the Middle Passage, and to the subjugation of one race for the benefit of another? In Woolman's view human beings were not saintly enough to make Negro slavery conform to the Christian ideal. The degradation of Negroes was so complete that even the most humane masters were misled by a false association of ideas. The notion of racial inferiority blocked the flow of natural affections and opened the floodgates to self-love and aggression. Bit by bit the evils fed upon themselves and the darkness thickened and became fastened upon the land.

The full meaning of self-delusion and personal guilt could be understood only when one remembered that the God of our fathers "furnished a table for us in the wilderness, and made the deserts and solitary places to rejoice." The Lord had operated a New World to mankind, and as with Israel of old, had blessed His chosen people with freedom and material plenty. And instead of being humbled by such success, and being content with the satisfaction of simple wants, the people had succumbed to greed. They had become absorbed in the pursuit of luxury, which they sought to pass on to their children, instead of "an inheritance incorruptible." God's displeasure was already manifest in a succession of wars and calamities. And it was the prophecy of John Woolman that if Americans continued to be unfaithful to their high destiny, their descendants would face the awful retribution of God's justice.

Howard Temperley

THE IDEOLOGY OF ANTISLAVERY

Abolition is a radical disjunction from the norm of slavery in much of the civilized past. Remarkably, little more than a century elapsed from the formation of the first antislavery society by Philadelphia Quakers in 1775 to the end of slavery in the New World with Brazilian emancipation in 1888. The essential historical questions are: why at this time and why in Western culture? Rejecting a purely moral cause or an entirely economic explanation, Howard Temperley of the University of East Anglia in the United Kingdom argues that a broad constellation of values rooted in changing material conditions had shaped an antislavery ideology in Britain and the northern United States by the late eighteenth century. The emergence of dynamic free labor economies in both nations linked progress with human freedom, making slavery appear a moral abomination and an economic anachronism. Temperley's thesis also helps to explain the affinity between British and American abolitionists and the escalation of sectional tension in the United States over slavery.

The problem is easily stated: What was it, in the late eighteenth and early nineteenth centuries, that made men turn against an institution which, in one form or another, had existed since time immemorial? Why was slavery attacked *then?* Why not in the seventeenth century, or the sixteenth? Why, indeed, was it attacked at all?

From Howard Temperley, "The Ideology of Antislavery," in David Elitis and James Walwin, eds., *The Abolition of the Atlantic Slave Trade: Origins and Effects in Europe, Africa, and the Americas* (Madison, Wis.: University of Wisconsin Press, 1981), 21–34. Reprinted by permission of the publisher.

Traditionally, the answers given to this question have taken two forms.

One is to describe how ideas, initially expressed by a handful of thinkers, were taken up, elaborated, added to, and ultimately incorporated into the beliefs of the population at large. This was essentially the approach of Thomas Clarkson, whose *History of Abolition* (1808) is notable both as the first attempt to provide a comprehensive account of the origins of the antislavery movement and as a model for later writers. In a foldout map which appears at the end of the introductory section of his work he shows how, beginning far back in the sixteenth century as tiny springs and rivulets, each marked with the name of some prominent thinker or statesman, the waters converge to become rivers, eventually "swelling the torrent which swept away the slave-trade." As Clarkson saw it, the victory of the abolitionists represented the triumph of right thinking over error, of the forces of light over the forces of darkness. It had been a long struggle, extending over centuries, but in the end truth had prevailed.

Until a generation ago few historians felt disposed to dissent from this view. Although less overtly Manichean in their approach, they were prepared to accept Clarkson's analysis, at least to the extent that they saw the ideas which eventually came together and energized the antislavery crusade as having originated in the distant past, in most cases with identifiable individuals or groups. . . . This, for example, is the approach . . . of most early twentieth century writers and many later writers, a notable recent example being David Brion Davis's *The Problem of Slavery in Western Culture* (1966).

The principal challenge to this view has come from those historians who have seen the abolition of the slave trade and slavery as having been the result, not of moral, but of economic pressures. The classic statement of this case was Eric Williams's *Capitalism and Slavery* (1944). Williams, it is true, did not entirely discount the influence of moral teaching, to the extent that he saw the abolitionists as a "spearhead." They spoke "a language the masses could understand" and thereby "were successful in raising anti-slavery sentiments almost to the status of a religion in England." In this sense they helped the process along. But at bottom it was the forces of economic rather than moral change that mattered. It was "mercantilism" that created the slave system and "mature capitalism" that destroyed it. He states his case forcefully: "The attack falls into three phases: the attack on the slave trade, the attack on slavery, the attack on the preferential sugar duties. The slave trade was abolished in 1807, slavery in 1833, the sugar preference in 1846. These three events are inseparable."

Leaving aside for the moment the question of whether the evidence will actually support this view, we may simply note that what we have here are two fundamentally contradictory explanations as to why abolition occurred at the time it did. In the one case it is seen as the product of a long process of intellectual inquiry. The antislavery argument that was presented to Parliament and the British public in the 1780s and 1790s was not, and given its complexity could not conceivably have been, the achievement of one group or even of one generation. Inevitably it was the work of many hands extending back over many generations. In the same way, the economic explanation is also dependent on the notion of gradual maturation which initially fostered slavery but ultimately created a conjunction of interests which destroyed it. In each case abolition is seen as the result of an extended chain of events which by the late eighteenth and early nineteenth centuries had created a situation in which the slave trade, and later slavery itself, could no longer be regarded as acceptable.

Comparing these two explanations, it may be noted that in one respect at least the economic view scores over what, for want of a better term, we may call the intellectual diffusionist account in that it is more firmly rooted in what are commonly regarded as the major developments of the period. Much of the plausibility of Williams's account, indeed, derives from the fact that Britain, the first nation to industrialize, also took the lead in the campaign to abolish the slave trade and slavery. This is a development which the intellectual diffusionist account virtually ignores. Moreover, there is something patently unsatisfactory about any explanation of a historical event, particularly a historical event as important as the abolition of the slave trade and slavery, which is based on developments in the realm of ideas and which fails, at least in any detailed way, to relate those ideas to the actual lives of people of the period. Most ideas, as we know, have long pedigrees. Often, too, they are capable of acquiring a momentum of their own and can develop, almost regardless of changes in the material world, according to an inner logic of their own. But equally plainly ideas are shaped by circumstance, and the longer the time span the greater the likelihood of this happening. Thus in accounting for the attack on slavery we need to know not simply when ideas originated and who first formulated them, but what it was at a certain point in time that made man choose, out of all the ideas available, those particular ideas, and furthermore to act on them. To assume, as the abolitionists frequently did, that their ideas were right and that virtue requires no explanation is inadequate, since plainly not everyone agreed with them. We still need to be shown why what seemed right to the abolitionists—and, more to the point, to an increasingly large proportion of their contemporaries—had not seemed right to their predecessors.

Yet, if the intellectual diffusionist account has its pitfalls, so also does the economic explanation, the principal one being that it is exceedingly difficult to show that the overthrow of either the slave trade or slavery would actually have influenced the material interests of those who pressed for it, except, in some cases, adversely. So far as the attack on the British slave trade is concerned, as Seymour Drescher has recently argued in *Econocide: British Slavery in the Era of Abolition* (1977), the whole theory of West Indian decline upon which Williams bases his thesis is without foundation. West Indian decline was the result, rather than the cause, of abolition. Much the same may be said of the abolition of slavery itself, which further accelerated the decline process. As I attempted to show in an appendix to *British Antislavery, 1833–1870* (1972), the attack on West Indian slavery could not have been an attack on monopoly, since before 1833 a large proportion of the West Indian sugar crop was sold on the world market, which determined the price. Rather, it was the abolition of slavery, which reduced production below that necessary to supply British needs, that created a monopoly, thus driving up prices and creating a demand for an end to differential tariffs. Nor is it easy to fall back on the alternative argument, often used in such cases, and say that what mattered were not economic realities but how men perceived them, since in each instance the results that ensued were widely predicted. Plausible though it might appear at first sight, and attractive though it might remain in theory, the truth is that the economic explanation fails to take account of the fact that slavery was itself very much a capitalist institution, that in general it offered a good return on investment, that it provided a plentiful supply of cheap raw materials, and that the usual effect of emancipation was to drive up the price of the products upon which the burgeoning industries of Europe and America depended.

But if neither the economic nor the intellectual diffusionist accounts provide a satisfactory explanation, what alternatives are there? One obvious tactic, of course, is to try to link the two together. The problem here is that simple mixing does nothing to improve the quality of the initial ingredients. If both are defective, the same will inevitably be true of the final mixture. . . .

One possible way of getting out of this impasse, however, is to look again at the conceptual framework which historians have used. And here we may begin by noting that there is something essentially artificial about the way in which altruism and self-interest have been juxtaposed, as if they were the only motives from which the participants acted. Williams is plainly guilty of this, but so also are the traditionalists in their emphasis on those elements of right thinking and self-dedication which led W. E. H. Lecky in his *History of European Morals* (1884) to describe the crusade against slavery as "among the three or four perfectly virtuous pages comprised in the history of nations." Large numbers of people, and certainly groups as large and variegated as those responsible for the overthrow of the slave trade and slavery, which of course included not only the abolitionists but all those who voted against these practices in Parliament and Congress, together with those who supported them in their efforts, are simply not moved, or at least not entirely moved, by abstract benevolence. Nor, for that matter, is economics, Adam Smith notwithstanding, merely the pursuit of individual self-interest. Adam Smith himself, significantly enough, disapproved of slavery for reasons which turn out on examination to have nothing to do with its immediate cost-effectiveness. Thus even in his system, and no less strikingly in those of his successors, economics in this broader sense is seen as being concerned not merely, or even primarily, with how best to pursue short-term individual gains, but with the way in which societies actually do, or in theory should, order their affairs. Viewed in this way economics and benevolence no longer appear as opposing principles. As the Victorians in particular were well aware, the two could not only be reconciled but were often mutually supportive. Thus, whether we look at economic thought or at the possible range of motives which led large numbers of individuals, the great majority of whom were not abolitionists in the narrow sense, to turn against the slave trade and slavery, we find ourselves dealing with large-scale, and in many respects overlapping, systems of belief which are far too complex to be categorized in terms of either self-interest or benevolence.

To call these systems ideologies is, perhaps, to invite misunderstanding, although it is not clear what other word will suffice. Certainly it is not intended here to postulate a rigid set of assumptions which everyone opposed to slavery shared. Perhaps the word could be used in that sense with regard to some antislavery groups which expected a strict orthodoxy of belief on the part of their members, although even then there are distinctions that would need to be recognized. But if we take ideology to mean an assortment of beliefs and values shared by the members of a society and used by them to explain and guide social action, no such rigidity need be assumed. Such an ideology would be expected to change along with the society that produced it, and whose aspirations and beliefs it reflected. Nor should we expect that it would be logically consistent. Much of the impulse for change would come, in fact, from attempts to reconcile internal contradictions. Not surprisingly, many within the society would claim that their beliefs were not simply personal, or for that matter social, but represented universal truths. But whether they did or not is a question which might appropriately be left to philosophers or theologians; for present purposes they should be regarded as social products.

So how might such a concept be used to explain the development of the antislavery movement? One way to begin is to examine the character of the two societies, Britain and the northern United States, which found themselves in the forefront of the struggle. And here we may start by noting that both had experienced remarkable rates of economic growth in the course of the eighteenth century. Probably nowhere else in the world was the relative increase in wealth and population more striking than in the thirteen colonies. This, as we all know, was one of the factors which persuaded the British government to attempt to tighten its hold on the colonists, and so helped to precipitate the break with the mother country. Yet Britain's own rate of growth during these years, although less marked in relative terms, was also impressive, whether we compare it with what had happened in previous centuries or with the experiences of her political rivals. This was, as economic historians continually remind us, a period of crucial importance for the Western world. Instead of the rhythmic expansion and contraction of populations and their products which had taken place over the previous millennium, the gains of the eighteenth century represented the departure point from which began the sustained growth that has characterized the modern world. Britain and her ex-colonies were in the forefront of this development. Materially speaking, they had reason to feel proud of their achievement.

A second characteristic that Britain and the northern states (as opposed to the South) shared was the fact that they had achieved this prosperity without direct recourse to slave labor, at least on any significant scale. To be sure, there was slavery in Britain right up to the end of the eighteenth century (the Somerset decision notwithstanding), and it lingered on in the northern states even longer. As late as 1820 there were still eighteen thousand slaves in the northeastern United States, and at the time of the first census in 1790 the figure was more than double that; but compared with the situation south of the Mason-Dixon line this represented a relatively modest stake in the institution. It must also be remembered that both Britain and the northern states had profited, and were continuing to profit on an ever-increasing scale, from the employment of slaves elsewhere. Nevertheless, the fact remains that, so far as their domestic arrangements were concerned, both were committed to an essentially free-labor system.

These points are too obvious to dwell on. Yet they are worth emphasizing if only because they help to explain why men in these two societies were so ready to accept ideas of progress, and in particular ideas of progress which linked individual freedom to material prosperity. The two, needless to say, are not necessarily connected. More often than not they have been seen as opposing principles, the assumption being that the pursuit of the one must necessarily entail the sacrifice of the other. Implicit in the whole idea of government is the belief that individual freedom must be given up to secure the benefits of an ordered society; among which must be included a measure of material satisfaction. How much freedom needs to be sacrificed is a matter of opinion, but history is not wanting in examples of societies welcoming tyrants because the alternatives of anarchy and lawlessness were regarded as even less acceptable. So the commonly expressed eighteenth century view that freedom and prosperity were not only reconcilable but mutually supportive, and that the more you had of the one the more you could expect of the other, is something that needs explaining. The explanation, I suggest, is to be found not in the ideas of the philosophers, still less in theories about the general progress of the human mind, but in the immediate lives of people of the period.

This, then, is one way of relating material and intellectual developments, and one that throws a good deal of light on the thinking of such figures as Adam Smith and the exponents of the secular antislavery argument generally. For what is striking about the secular case against slavery is the *assumption* that slavery was an economic anachronism. Smith's own attitudes are particularly revealing, because of all eighteenth century commentators he was probably the one best qualified to argue the case against it on strictly economic grounds. Yet, as already noted, the case he actually presents is not based on economics at all, at least not in any cost-accounting sense, but on the general proposition that greater freedom would lead to greater prosperity. Like other eighteenth century thinkers he expresses himself in terms of universal principles, but at bottom it is a historical argument, derived from his own beliefs about the nature of the historical process. Whatever the objective truths of Smith's arguments, the fact remains that they are very much the product of one kind of society, and indeed of one particular class within that society.

An obvious objection to this argument is that, while it may very well be true that Adam Smith rejected slavery for the reasons suggested, it is by no means clear that other people did. Very few, after all, were Smithians. The point that is being made here, however, is not that Smith was important for his teachings (although Clarkson was happy to cite him) so much as for what he reflected about the continuing processes that characterized the age in which he lived. Of course, not even Smith himself realized that the Western world was entering a new economic era. Nevertheless, it is evident that substantial increases in trade and improvements in agriculture had begun to be made long before Smith's time and so were readily observable by his contemporaries. Furthermore, if what is at issue here is the origin of the Western idea of progress, it should be borne in mind that this owed at least as much to developments in the field of knowledge as to material changes. Certainly by the end of the seventeenth century men not only knew more than their predecessors but knew that they knew more.

Yet even if we grant that these developments go some way toward explaining the secular case against slavery, it by no means follows that they motivated the early leaders of the antislavery movement, most of whom, if we may judge by the arguments they used, believed that they were acting out of religious principles. This is a tricky problem because by and large these principles stem directly from the Christian tradition. But if, instead of following the Clarkson method of attempting to trace them back to their origins, we ask simply what it was that brought them to the fore at this particular point in time, we can perhaps make a start by observing that what was fundamental to the whole attack on slavery was the belief that it was removable. Politics, we are continually reminded, is the art of the practical, but so also are ethics practical in the sense that what is irremovable may be deplorable, inconvenient, or embarrassing, but can scarcely be unethical. Ethics, in other words, implies optionality. Moralists may be more stringent in their views than politicians, but in this respect at least the underlying considerations are the same.

In a sense, of course, slavery always was removable to the extent that institutions men establish they can, given an adequate stimulus, usually get around to disestablishing. But until the eighteenth century that stimulus was generally lacking, with the result that slavery was accepted with that fatalism which men commonly reserve for aspects of nature which, whether they are to be celebrated or deplored, have to be borne. To argue against slavery was to argue against the facts of life. Before slavery could become a political issue—or even, in the proper sense, a moral issue—what needed to be shown was that the world could get along without it. And what better demonstration could there be than the development, within the heartland of Western civilization, of societies which not only did without slavery but which did very well without it, and which furthermore appeared to owe their quite remarkable dynamism to the acceptance of principles which represented the direct negation of the assumptions upon which slavery was founded.

This was not, of course, a development particularly likely to impress the inhabitants of those societies which relied directly on slave labor. They knew perfectly well how much they owed to their slaves, not only in a strictly economic sense, but for the maintenance of their whole way of life. They also knew that they were contributing in no small way to the prosperity of the free-labor societies by providing them with cheap raw materials and foodstuffs. And, by virtue of their position, they were well placed to judge the revolutionary nature of the abolitionists' demands—what a rapid shift from slave to free labor would mean in terms of political and social power. Often what they said in this regard was a great deal more realistic than anything said by their opponents. Yet the fact remains that as societies they were overshadowed by cultures whose values, deriving from a quite different set of historical experiences, were in the process of changing in ways that made the justification of slavery, even on hardhearted economic grounds, increasingly difficult.

What I am suggesting, in other words, is that the attack on slavery can be seen as an attempt by a dominant metropolitan ideology to impose its values on the societies of the economic periphery. And what I am also suggesting is that this attack was the product of a widening ideological gap occasioned by the extraordinary success, not least in material terms, of those societies which practiced a free-labor system, among which Britain and the northern United States were outstanding examples. For if we suppose that the manner in which societies gain their existence helps to form the ideas of their members as to how people in general should live, we must also, I think, concede that there were very powerful reasons why men in these two societies (and one could add France as a third) should have come to regard slavery as not only immoral but anachronistic.

This, of course, is a very different thing from saying that the promotion of their own economic interests *required* the abolition of slavery, because in most cases it did not. Nor is it necessary to argue that relative to the slaveholding societies the free-labor societies were becoming more powerful, although sometimes this was so. It was much easier for Britain to attack slavery after the departure of the American colonies. But by the same token it became correspondingly more perilous for the Americans themselves to do anything about it, and in the event little was done to remove the institution until war made action possible. Thus any general account which attributes the rise of the antislavery movement to considerations of economic necessity is open to serious objections.

Such objections can be avoided, however, if we think of the widening gap between the slaveholding and the nonslaveholding societies in ideological terms, always allowing that men tend to generalize from their own experiences, and that in the eighteenth century they took these sufficiently seriously to enunciate universal laws on the basis of them. It also seems to me that this approach has advantages over the intellectual diffusionist argument in that it does, from the outset, take account of the fact that ideas are rooted in the material conditions of life. The intellectual diffusionists do not, of course, ignore this fact, but their recognition of it is too often reluctant and belated, as when they argue that general trends in Protestant religious thought were antagonistic to slavery, and then admit that actually, in the slaveholding societies, precisely the opposite tendencies are evident. Southern clergymen, far from being critics of slavery, were among its principal defenders. Altogether it makes much more sense to admit from the start that the thrust for abolition emanated from the nonslaveholding societies and reflected their increasing buoyancy and self-confidence.

Yet even when this is taken into account it does not fully explain why, having decided that slavery was an anachronism, reformers in the metropolitan societies should have invested so much energy in securing its removal. After all, the perception of ideological differences, even differences affecting fundamental beliefs, does not necessarily or even usually lead to action. If slavery was indeed an anachronism, why not simply let it wither away? Even in the case of the slave trade, disapproval did not necessarily require that anything be *done* about it, still less that Britain, having herself withdrawn from the traffic, should go to such lengths to ensure that other nations did the same. Nor are historical parallels of much help. In the fourteenth and fifteenth centuries, the Italian commercial city-states experienced a tremendous acceleration in wealth and power which pushed them ahead of most of the Mediterranean world economically, with an accompanying cultural gap as well. Commercial labor was free labor, although slave labor continued to be used for agricultural and domestic purposes. Yet there is no evidence that these dominant metropolitan centers tried to impose antislavery values derived from their experience with free labor, even though one might have supposed that domestic slavery would have been easier to remove than plantation slavery. Why, then, did the metropolitan powers of the late eighteenth and early nineteenth centuries feel such a compelling need to reach out and remake the world in their own image?

To explain this phenomenon three further points must be noted. The first is that the achievements of the Italian states, impressive though they were, were confined to one small section of the globe, beyond which lay a vast and unknown world. It was, moreover, a section of the globe which had seen the rise and fall of empires going back over millennia. It is not without relevance that the flowering of these states is known as the Renaissance. By contrast, there was no precedent for the achievements of the dominant powers of the eighteenth and nineteenth centuries. In terms of scientific knowledge and its application in the form of technology they were breaking new ground. Their colonies and trading networks spanned the entire globe. For the first time in history it had become possible—one might almost say necessary—to believe in universal human progress.

The second point to be noted concerns the impact of these developments on religion. The idea that individuals stood in need of improvement lay, of course, at the heart of the whole Christian system of belief. So also did the notion that societies should be ordered in such a way as to bring about such improvement. In theory, at any rate, this was the source from which most European rulers derived their authority. But in practice there had always been room for differences of opinion as to the precise form which improvement should take. In large part this was because of the way in which religious belief and practice reflected social needs and aspirations. Thus in some cases what passed for Christian behavior might have little to do with belief as such, as when the early explorers of Africa, Asia, and America described themselves as Christians and the native peoples they encountered as either heathens or savages.

Few would nowadays regard Europe's rise to dominance as a specifically Christian achievement. Nevertheless, contemporaries could not but be impressed by the fact that it was the Christian nations which had created the new world order. One consequence of Europe's expansion was to open up vast new areas to missionary activity. And, as with other missionary enterprises in the past, it is clear that what was being conveyed was much more than simply Christianity. More to the point, however, is the way in which these developments cast doubt on Christianity as conceived of in a purely spiritual or otherworldly sense. Eric Williams, as already noted, credited the abolitionists with "raising anti-slavery sentiments almost to the status of a religion in England." Some years earlier Gilbert Hobbes Barnes in *The Antislavery Impulse* (1933) noted how, in the United States, changes in Calvinist thinking transformed the Great Revival of the 1820s into the antislavery crusade of the 1830s. More recently, Ronald G. Walters in *The Antislavery Appeal* (1977) has gone a step further by arguing that in its later stages in the United States antislavery actually *was* "a highly generalized, all-encompassing religion of humanity."

Yet if this was the case, and what we know of the history of the American movement in those years suggests that in large part it was, we may wonder whether in some measure the same might not also be true of antislavery generally. What I am suggesting, in other words, is that antislavery can be seen as a secularized or semi-secularized form of Christian evangelism, the secular components of which reflected the ideological set of the dominant metropolitan cultures. Broadly viewed, it was part of that process, observable in relation to other issues too, which led to evangelical beliefs becoming more secular and secular beliefs becoming more evangelical. In this sense, one might say, it represented a halfway house between the religious ideologies of earlier times and the more strictly secular ideologies of the modern era.

The third point that needs to be noted concerns the relationship between these events and the advent of modern nationalism. In his *Caution and Warning* (1767) Anthony Benezet quotes a West Indian visitor's observation that "it is a Matter of Astonishment, how a People who, as a Nation, are looked upon as generous and humane, and so much value themselves for their uncommon Sense of the Benefit of Liberty, can live in the Practice of such extreme Oppression and Inhumanity, without seeing the Inconsistency of such Conduct, and without feeling great Remorse." He himself goes on to comment, "How the *British* Nation [his italics] first came to be concerned in a Practice, by which the Rights and Liberties of Mankind are so violently infringed . . . is indeed surprising." In the same year Nathaniel Appleton, a member of the Boston Committee of Correspondence, in his *Considerations on Slavery* castigated his fellow Bostonians by declaring "Oh! ye sons of liberty, pause a moment, give me your ear. Is your conduct consistent? Can you review our late struggles for liberty, and think of the slave-trade at the same time and not blush?" Thus what concerned even these early critics of the slave trade and slavery—and their message was taken up and repeated endlessly in the debates in Parliament and Congress—was not simply that these practices were wrong, but that it was their own nations that endorsed them. Of course, this was an obvious tactic to adopt, since Parliament and Congress had the power to redress some—in the case of Parliament, all—of their grievances. But it is plain that what the abolitionists were appealing to was also an already widely held belief that their nations were the custodians of certain values which distinguished them from other nations, and which it was the duty of their respective governments to uphold. . . .

What was new, or largely new anyway, was the way in which, particularly in the case of Britain and the United States, this sense of nationhood was now seen as being linked to values associated with growth and progress. This was perhaps most evident in the case of the United States, which saw itself as representing a new departure in human government, one which, as its virtues became apparent, would serve as an inspiration to the rest of mankind. The British, for their part, although less naively optimistic, took a not dissimilar view of themselves, at least to the extent that they saw their nation as leading the world not merely in a political sense but in a technological and economic sense too.

No doubt similar trends, although perhaps less marked, can be identified in the case of other Western powers. Certainly, so far as Britain and the northern United States were concerned, slavery had come to seem not only an anachronism but a challenge to their progressive ideals. For that reason it could not simply be left to disappear of its own accord, which might take a very long time. Indeed, given the political influence and determination of the slaveholding interests, there was no assurance that it would happen at all. Thus the abolition of slavery and, as a first step, the abolition of its most objectionable and vulnerable feature, the slave trade, was something that had to be fought for. Fighting for it, moreover, meant not simply liberating slaves in distant colonies and states, but upholding ideals which would eventually find expression in countless other causes from criminal law reform to women's rights.

That the slave trade and slavery were the principal concerns of early humanitarian reformers is understandable enough. They symbolized in a peculiarly graphic way man's inhumanity to man and the total denial of human liberty. Yet their choice as objects of attack is not without irony. Over the years slavery had contributed significantly to the material prosperity of the metropolitan powers; to a considerable degree it was still doing so. Yet the material prosperity, by opening men's eyes to the potentialities of the new world order, had created an ideology in terms of which neither the slave trade nor slavery could be regarded as either necessary or morally acceptable.

IMAGES OF ABOLITIONISM:
AN ILLUSTRATED ESSAY

This woodcut shows an armed mob on November 7, 1837 assaulting the warehouse in Alton, Illinois where the Reverend Elijah P. Lovejoy and others guarded the press of the antislavery *Observer*. As Lovejoy fled the burning building, he was killed. (*Library of Congress*)

Abolitionists used the recent invention of the steam press to wage a war of words and illustrations against slavery. In 1836 alone they published well over a million pages. This woodcut for the month of September from the almanac issued by the American Anti-Slavery Society depicts the brutality of slavery. (*Courtesy, American Antiquarian Society*)

Angelina Grimké, age about 39. The plain dress, simple bonnet and use of "thee" and "thou" in her speech marked the distance this antislavery Quaker convert had traveled from her aristocratic origins in Charleston, South Carolina, where she was born into a slaveholding family. (*Courtesy of The Boston Atheneaum*)

As the female personification of Liberty watches, this contemporary cartoon sympathetically shows an armed William Lloyd Garrison, Frederick Douglass, and a multiracial band of abolitionists rescuing a black woman from the clutches of the Slave Power. A planter bestrides a servile Daniel Webster, the Massachusetts Whig and proponent of the Fugitive Slave Law of 1850. (*Courtesy of The Chicago Historical Society*)

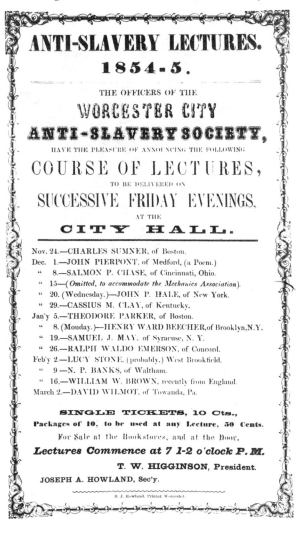

ANTI-SLAVERY LECTURES.

1854-5.

THE OFFICERS OF THE

WORCESTER CITY
ANTI-SLAVERY SOCIETY,

HAVE THE PLEASURE OF ANNOUNCING THE FOLLOWING

COURSE OF LECTURES,

TO BE DELIVERED ON

SUCCESSIVE FRIDAY EVENINGS,

AT THE

CITY HALL.

Nov. 24.—CHARLES SUMNER, of Boston.
Dec. 1.—JOHN PIERPONT, of Medford, (a Poem.)
  " 8.—SALMON P. CHASE, of Cincinnati, Ohio.
  " 15—(*Omitted, to accommodate the Mechanics Association*).
  " 20. (Wednesday.)—JOHN P. HALE, of New York.
  " 29.—CASSIUS M. CLAY, of Kentucky.
Jan'y 5.—THEODORE PARKER, of Boston.
  " 8. (Monday.)—HENRY WARD BEECHER, of Brooklyn, N.Y.
  " 19.—SAMUEL J. MAY, of Syracuse, N. Y.
  " 26.—RALPH WALDO EMERSON, of Concord.
Feb'y 2.—LUCY STONE, (probably.) West Brookfield.
  " 9.—N. P. BANKS, of Waltham.
  " 16.—WILLIAM W. BROWN, recently from England.
March 2.—DAVID WILMOT, of Towanda, Pa.

SINGLE TICKETS, 10 Cts.,
Packages of 10, to be used at any Lecture, 50 Cents.

For Sale at the Bookstores, and at the Door.

Lectures Commence at 7 1-2 o'clock P. M.

T. W. HIGGINSON, President.

JOSEPH A. HOWLAND, Sec'y.

H. J. Howland, Printer, Worcester.

Abolitionist and feminist Thomas Wentworth Higginson, pastor of Worcester's "Free Church," organized weekly antislavery lectures. An audience of blacks and whites, women and men, preachers and politicians heard a variety of abolitionist luminaries, including Henry Ward Beecher and Ralph Waldo Emerson. (*Courtesy, American Antiquarian Society*)

Harper's Weekly intended this realistic drawing as a caricature of the 1859 annual meeting of the American Anti-Slavery Society in New York City. Yet it accurately records the mix of blacks and whites, women and men, as well as the individual intensity and social concerns of the participants. A balding William Lloyd Garrison is seated, arms folded, at center stage. (*Courtesy of The Boston Atheneaum*)

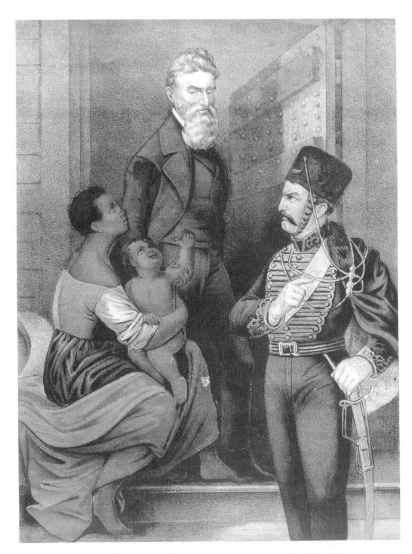

The caption of this 1863 Currier and Ives lithograph reads: "John Brown meeting the slave mother on the steps of Charleston jail on his way to execution. Encouraging them with a look of compassion, Captain Brown stopped and kissed the child then met his fate." The image of Brown's martyrdom with a mother and child contrasts with a guard cloaked in the garb of European aristocracy. (*Courtesy of the Chicago Historical Society*)

The recruiting poster shows dignified and neatly attired black soldiers with a white officer, an effort to overcome white opposition to the enrollment of African Americans in the military. The heroism of black regiments in battles at Fort Wagner, Port Hudson, and Milliken's Bend challenged negative racial stereotypes. Of the some 180,000 blacks who served in the Union forces, about 145,000 came from slave states. (*The Bettmann Archive*)

This photograph, taken shortly after the Civil War, captures the powerful personality of Frederick Douglass, the major black leader of the nineteenth century. In 1838 he fled slavery in Maryland and remained a fugitive until British abolitionists purchased his freedom ten years later for $711. Douglass devoted his considerable oratorical and literary talents to racial equality and women's rights. (*The National Archives*)

The Antebellum Period

Primary Sources

PHILADELPHIA BLACKS PROTEST AGAINST COLONIZATION (1817)

During the Revolutionary era, Thomas Jefferson and others proposed the gradual emancipation of slaves and their emigration from North America. Paul Cuffe, the son of a slave, was a Quaker shipowner and the first American to implement this idea. In 1815 he transported thirty-eight American blacks to Africa at his own expense. Northern white evangelicals and prominent slaveholders in the Upper South joined together to form the American Colonization Society in December 1816 to rid the country of the growing number of manumitted African-Americans, whom they considered a dangerous underclass and a threat to the stability of slavery. Just one month later, on the grounds of republican principle, Christian ethics, and racial solidarity with the slaves, several Philadelphia blacks held a large rally to denounce the racist agenda of this organization. Although James Forten, a prosperous Philadelphia sailmaker and veteran of the Revolutionary War had backed Cuffe, he and numerous blacks opposed the Colonization Society. Not only did the Philadelphia protest spread throughout northern black communities, but its argument would, after 1830, convince William Lloyd Garrison and other white reformers to denounce the Colonization Society. The first rally, convened in 1817 at the African Methodist Episcopal Church founded by Richard Allen, demonstrates that black leadership and institutions were at the heart of abolitionism.

At a numerous meeting of the people of color, convened at Bethel church, to take into consideration the propriety of remonstrating against the contemplated measure, that is to exile us from the land of our nativity; James Forten was called to the chair, and Russell Parrott appointed secretary. The intent of the meeting having been stated by the chairman, the following resolutions were adopted, without one dissenting voice.

Whereas our ancestors (not of choice) were the first successful cultivators of the wilds of America, we their descendants feel

From William Lloyd Garrison, *Thoughts on African Colonization, part II* (Boston: Garrison and Knapp, 1832), 9.

ourselves entitled to participate in the blessings of her luxuriant soil, which their blood and sweat manured; and that any measure or system of measures, having a tendency to banish us from her bosom, would not only be cruel, but in direct violation of those principles, which have been the boast of this republic.

Resolved, That we view with deep abhorrence the unmerited stigma attempted to be cast upon the reputation of the free people of color, by the promoters of this measure, "that they are a dangerous and useless part of the community," when in the state of disfranchisement in which they live, in the hour of danger they ceased to remember their wrongs, and rallied around the standard of their country.

Resolved, That we never will separate ourselves voluntarily from the slave population in this country; they are our brethren by the ties of consanguinity, of suffering, and of wrong; and we feel that there is more virtue in suffering privations with them, than fancied advantages for a season.

Resolved, That without arts, without science, without a proper knowledge of government, to cast into the savage wilds of Africa the free people of color, seems to us the circuitous route through which they must return to perpetual bondage.

Resolved, That having the strongest confidence in the justice of God, and philanthropy of the free states, we cheerfully submit our destinies to the guidance of Him who suffers not a sparrow to fall, without his special providence.

David Walker

THE HYPOCRISY OF WHITES (1829)

David Walker (1785–1830) was a North Carolina free black who relocated in 1825 to Boston, where he ran a secondhand clothing store. An agent for *Freedom's Journal,* the nation's first black newspaper, and an influential member of Massachusetts General Colored Association, Walker was a self-taught intellectual whose wide experiences made him a leader in the African-American community. He financed three editions of his *Appeal,* which first appeared in September 1829.

In this militant essay, Walker lambastes the moral failure of whites, including colonizationists, to extend their religious and political principles to blacks. Near the end of his four-part pamphlet, he concludes in Old Testament terms that divine retribution awaits the nation and its failure to honor the full meaning of the Declaration of Independence. In part, he is assailing Thomas Jefferson, the author of the Declaration, who not only held numerous slaves at Monticello but also strongly suggested in *Notes on Virginia* that blacks were racially inferior. With impassioned rhetoric, Walker extends a Lockean right of revolution to the slaves: "Brethren, arise, arise! Strike for your lives and liberties. Now is the day and the hour." The appearance of the *Appeal* in southern ports led to restrictions on black sailors and the proscription of Walker. In 1830 he died suddenly. Black tradition has it that he was poisoned, though no concrete evidence of murder exists.

A declaration made July 4, 1776

It says,[1] "When in the course of human events, it becomes necessary for one people to dissolve the political bands which have connected them with another, and to assume the Powers of the earth, the separate and equal station to which the laws of nature and of nature's God entitle them. A decent respect for the opinions of mankind requires, that they should declare the causes which impel them to the separation.—We hold these truths to be self

---

[1] See the Declaration of Independence of the United States.

From William Loren Katz, ed., *Walker's Appeal in Four Articles* and Henry Highland Garnet, *An Address to the Slaves of the United States of America* (New York: Arno Press and The New York Times, 1969), 84–86.

evident—that all men are created equal, that they are endowed by their Creator with certain unalienable rights: that among these, are life, liberty, and the pursuit of happiness that, to secure these rights, governments are instituted among men, deriving their just powers from the consent of the governed; that when ever any form of government becomes destructive of these ends, it is the right of the people to alter or to abolish it, and to institute a new government laying its foundation on such principles, and organizing its powers in such form, as to them shall seem most likely to effect their safety and happiness. Prudence, indeed, will dictate, that governments long established should not be changed for light and transient causes; and accordingly all experience hath shewn, that mankind are more disposed to suffer, while evils are sufferable, than to right themselves by abolishing the forms to which they are accustomed. But when a long train of abuses and usurpations, pursuing invariably the same object, evinces a design to reduce them under absolute despotism, it is their right it is their duty to throw off such government, and to provide new guards for their future security." See your Declaration Americans! ! ! Do you understand your own language? Hear your language, proclaimed to the world, July 4th, 1776—☞ "We hold these truths to be self evident—that ALL MEN ARE CREATED EQUAL! ! that they *are endowed by their Creator with certain unalienable rights;* that among these are life, *liberty*, and the pursuit of happiness! !" Compare your own language above, extracted from your Declaration of Independence, with your cruelties and murders inflicted by your cruel and unmerciful fathers and yourselves on our fathers and on us—men who have never given your fathers or you the least provocation! ! ! ! !

Hear your language further! ☞ "But when a long train of abuses and usurpation, pursuing invariably the same object, evinces a design to reduce them under absolute despotism, it is their *right,* it is their *duty,* to throw off such government, and to provide new guards for their future security."

Now, Americans! I ask you candidly, was your sufferings under Great Britain, one hundredth part as cruel and tyranical as you have rendered ours under you? Some of you, no doubt, believe that we will never throw off your murderous government and "provide new guards for our future security." If Satan has made you believe it, will he not deceive you?[2] Do the whites say, I being a black man, ought to be humble, which I readily admit? I ask them, ought they not to be as humble as I? or do they think that they can measure arms with Jehovah? Will not the Lord yet humble them? or will not these very coloured people whom they now treat worse than brutes, yet under God, humble them low down enough?

William Lloyd Garrison

TO THE PUBLIC (1831)

Born in Newburyport, Massachusetts, William Lloyd Garrison (1805–1879) was deserted by an alcoholic father and raised by a poor but pious mother. His early family life may well have inclined a devout Garrison to seek moral perfection as well as social recognition, creating the tension between the spiritual and secular that characterized his reform career. He was a printer in Boston before joining the Quaker Benjamin Lundy in Baltimore as co-editor of the *Genius of Universal Emancipation,* an antislavery newspaper. In 1829 Garrison denounced colonization, breaking with Lundy's gradualism, though he also found the militancy of David Walker's *Appeal* injudicious. Yet Garrison's own rhetoric landed him in jail the next year for libeling a Newburyport merchant as a slave trader. After being bailed out by philanthropist Arthur Tappan, Garrison returned to Boston. There on January 1, 1831, he began publication of *The Liberator,* defiantly declaring, "I will be heard." Sustained by loyal black subscribers and a nucleus of white supporters, Garrison was increasingly heard, launching his journal on a thirty-five-year career dedicated to immediate abolitionism.

The following statement of purpose appeared on page one in the first issue of *The Liberator.*

2 The Lord has not taught the Americans that we will not some day or other throw off their chains and hand-cuffs, from our hands and feet, and their devilish lashes (which some of them shall have enough of yet) from off our backs.

From Wendell Phillips Garrison and Francis Jackson Garrison, *William Lloyd Garrison, 1805–1879: The Story of His Life Told by His Children* (New York: The Century Co., 1885), Vol. I, 224–226.

In the month of August, I issued proposals for publishing *The Liberator* in Washington City; but the enterprise, though hailed in different sections of the country, was praised by public indifference. Since that time, the removal of the *Genius of Universal Emancipation* to the seat of government has rendered less imperious the establishment of a similar periodical in that quarter.

During my recent tour for the purpose of exciting the minds of the people by a series of discourses on the subject of slavery, every place that I visited gave fresh evidence of the fact, that a greater revolution in public sentiment was to be effected in the free states—*and particularly in New England*—than at the South. I found contempt more bitter, opposition more active, detraction more relentless, prejudice more stubborn, and apathy more frozen, than among slaveowners themselves. Of course, there were individual exceptions to the contrary. This state of things afflicted, but did not dishearten me. I determined, at every hazard, to lift up the standard of emancipation in the eyes of the nation, *within sight of Bunker Hill and in the birthplace of liberty.* That standard is now unfurled; and long may it float, unhurt by the spoliations of time or the missiles of a desperate foe—yea, till every chain be broken, and every bondman set free! Let Southern oppressors tremble—let their secret abettors tremble—let their Northern apologists tremble—let all the enemies of the persecuted blacks tremble.

I deem the publication of my original prospectus unnecessary, as it has obtained a wide circulation. The principles therein inculcated will be steadily pursued in this paper, excepting that I shall not array myself as the political partisan of any man. In defending the great cause of human rights, I wish to derive the assistance of all religions and of all parties.

Assenting to the "self-evident truth" maintained in the American Declaration of Independence, "that all men are created equal, and endowed by their Creator with certain inalienable rights—among which are life, liberty and the pursuit of happiness," I shall strenuously contend for the immediate enfranchisement of our slave population. In Park-Street Church, on the Fourth of July, 1829, in an address on slavery, I unreflectingly assented to the popular but pernicious doctrine of *gradual* abolition. I seize this opportunity to make a full and unequivocal recantation, and thus publicly to ask pardon of my God, of my country, and of my brethren the poor slaves, for having uttered a sentiment so full of timidity, injustice, and absurdity. A similar recantation, from my pen, was published in the *Genius of Universal Emancipation* at Baltimore, in September, 1829. My conscience is now satisfied.

I am aware that many object to the severity of my language; but is there not cause for severity? I *will* be as harsh as truth, and as uncompromising as justice. On this subject, I do not wish to think, or speak, or write, with moderation. No! no! Tell a man whose house is on fire to give a moderate alarm; tell him to moderately rescue his wife from the hands of the ravisher; tell the mother to gradually extricate her babe from the fire into which it has fallen;— but urge me not to use moderation in a cause like the present. I am in earnest—I will not equivocate—I will not excuse—I will not retreat a single inch—*and I will be heard*. The apathy of the people is enough to make every statue leap from its pedestal, and to hasten the resurrection of the dead.

It is pretended, that I am retarding the cause of emancipation by the coarseness of my invective and the precipitancy of my measures. *The charge is not true.* On this question my influence,— humble as it is,—is felt at this moment to a considerable extent, and shall be felt in coming years—not perniciously, but beneficially—not as a curse, but as a blessing; and posterity will bear testimony that I was right. I desire to thank God, that he enables me to disregard "the fear of man which bringeth a snare," and to speak his truth in its simplicity and power. And here I close with this fresh dedication:

> Oppression! I have seen thee, face to face,
> And met thy cruel eye and cloudy brow;
> But thy soul-withering glance I fear not now—
> For dread to prouder feelings doth give place
> Of deep abhorrence! Scorning the disgrace
> Of slavish knees that at thy footstool bow,
> I also kneel!—but with far other vow
> Do hail thee and thy herd of hirelings base:—
> I swear, while life-blood warms my throbbing veins,
> Still to oppose and thwart, with heart and hand,
> Thy brutalizing sway—till Afric's chains
> Are burst, and Freedom rules the rescued land,—

Trampling Oppression and his iron rod:
Such is the vow I take—so help me God!

William Lloyd Garrison
Boston, January 1, 1831

American Anti-Slavery Society

DECLARATION OF SENTIMENTS (1833)

Inspired by Parliament's emancipation of slaves in the British Empire and disillusioned with the program of the American Colonization Society, immediate abolitionists met in Philadelphia late in 1833 to establish the American Anti-Slavery Society. Though it was modeled on the Protestant evangelical societies of the Benevolent Empire, its goal was not Bible distribution or the containment of Catholicism but "the immediate and total abolition of slavery" through "moral and political action." Among those forming the new organization were evangelicals organized by New York reformers Arthur and Lewis Tappan as well as Philadelphia Quakers. Among the sixty-two participants were an ecumenical mix of Protestants, twenty-one Quakers (including four women), and three black men. Garrison, just back from a triumphal tour of Great Britain, led a New England contingent. He stayed up all night to write the Declaration of Sentiments, which was adopted December 4, 1833.

The Convention, assembled in the City of Philadelphia to organize a National Anti-Slavery Society, promptly seize the opportunity to promulgate the following *Declaration of Sentiments*, as cherished by them in relation to the enslavement of one-sixth portion of the American people.

More than fifty-seven years have elapsed since a band of patriots convened in this place, to devise measures for the deliverance of this country from a foreign yoke. The corner-stone upon which they founded the *Temple of Freedom* was broadly this—"that all men are created equal; that they are endowed by their Creator with certain inalienable rights; that among these are life,

From *The Liberator*, 3 (December 14, 1833), 198.

LIBERTY, and the pursuit of happiness." At the sound of their trumpet-call, three millions of people rose up as from the sleep of death, and rushed to the strife of blood; deeming it more glorious to die instantly as freemen, than desirable to live one hour as slaves.—They were few in number—poor in resources; but the honest conviction that *Truth, Justice,* and *Right* were on their side, made them invincible.

We have met together for the achievement of an enterprise, without which, that of our fathers is incomplete, and which, for its magnitude, solemnity, and probable results upon the destiny of the world, as far transcends theirs, as moral truth does physical force.

In purity of motive, in earnestness of zeal, in decision of purpose, in intrepidity of action, in steadfastness of faith, in sincerity of spirit, we would not be inferior to them.

Their principles led them to wage war against their oppressors, and to spill human blood like water, in order to be free. *Ours* forbid the doing of evil that good may come, and lead us to reject, and to entreat the oppressed to reject, the use of all carnal weapons for deliverance from bondage—relying solely upon those which are spiritual, and mighty through God to the pulling down of strongholds.

Their measures were physical resistance—the marshalling in arms—the hostile array—the mortal encounter. *Ours* shall be such only as the opposition of moral purity to moral corruption—the destruction of error by the potency of truth—the overthrow of prejudice by the power of love—and the abolition of slavery by the spirit of repentance.

Their grievances, great as they were, were trifling in comparison with the wrongs and sufferings of those for whom we plead. Our fathers were never slaves—never bought and sold like cattle—never shut out from the light of knowledge and religion—never subjected to the lash of brutal taskmasters.

But those for whose emancipation we are striving—constituting at the present time at least one-sixth part of our countrymen,—are recognized by the laws, and treated by their fellow beings, as marketable commodities—as goods and chattels—as brute beasts;—are plundered daily of the fruits of their toil without redress;—really enjoy no constitutional nor legal protection from licentious and murderous outrages upon their persons;—are ruthlessly torn asunder—the tender babe from the arms of its frantic mother—the heart-broken wife from her weeping husband—at the caprice or pleasure of irresponsible tyrants;—and, for the crime of having a dark complexion, suffer the pangs of hunger, the infliction of stripes, and the ignominy of brutal servitude. They are kept in heathenish darkness by laws expressly enacted to make their instruction a criminal offense.

These are the prominent circumstances in the condition of more than TWO MILLIONS of our people, the proof of which may be found in thousands of indisputable facts, and in the laws of the slaveholding States.

Hence we maintain—

That in view of the civil and religious privileges of this nation, the guilt of its oppression is unequalled by any other on the face of the earth;—and, therefore,

That it is bound to repent instantly, to undo the heavy burden, to break every yoke, and to let the oppressed go free.

We further maintain—

That no man has a right to enslave or imbrute his brother—to hold or acknowledge him, for one moment, as a piece of merchandise—to keep back his hire by fraud—or to brutalize his mind by denying him the means of intellectual, social and moral improvement.

The right to enjoy liberty is inalienable. To invade it, is to usurp the prerogative of Jehovah. Every man has a right to his own body—to the products of his own labor—to the protection of law—and to the common advantages of society. It is piracy to buy or steal a native African, and subject him to servitude. Surely the sin is as great to enslave an *American* as an *African*.

Therefore we believe and affirm—

That there is no difference, *in principle*, between the African slave trade and American slavery;

That every American citizen, who retains a human being in involuntary bondage is a man-stealer;

That the slaves ought instantly to be set free, and brought under the protection of law;

That if they had lived from the time of Pharaoh down to the present period, and had been entailed through successive generations, their right to be free could never have been alienated, but their claims would have constantly risen in solemnity;

That all those laws which are now in force, admitting the right of slavery, are therefore before God utterly null and void; being an audacious usurpation of the Divine prerogative, a daring infringement on the law of nature, a base overthrow of the very foundations of the social compact, a complete extinction of all the relations, endearments and obligations of mankind, and a presumptuous transgression of all the holy commandments—and that therefore they ought to be instantly abrogated.

We further believe and affirm—

That all persons of color who possess the qualifications which are demanded of others, ought to be admitted forthwith to the enjoyment of the same privileges, and the exercise of the same prerogatives, as others; and that the paths of preferment, of wealth, and of intelligence, shall be opened as widely to them as to persons of a white complexion.

We maintain that no compensation should be given to the planters emancipating their slaves—

Because it would be a surrender of the great fundamental principle that man cannot hold property in man;

Because *Slavery is a crime, and therefore it is not an article to be sold;*

Because the holders of slaves are not the just proprietors of what they claim;—freeing the slaves is not depriving them of property, but restoring it to the right owner;—it is not wronging the master, but righting the slave—restoring him to himself;

Because immediate and general emancipation would only destroy nominal, not real property: it would not amputate a limb or break a bone of the slaves, but by infusing motives into their breasts, would make them doubly valuable to the masters as free laborers; and

Because if compensation is to be given at all, it should be given to the outraged and guiltless slaves, and not to those who have plundered and abused them.

We regard, as delusive, cruel and dangerous, any scheme of expatriation which pretends to aid, either directly or indirectly, in the emancipation of the slaves, or to be a substitute for the immediate and total abolition of slavery.

We fully and unanimously recognize the sovereignty of each State, to legislate exclusively on the subject of the slavery which is tolerated within its limits. We concede that Congress, *under the present national compact,* has no right to interfere with any of the slave States, in relation to this momentous subject.

But we maintain that Congress has a right, and is solemnly bound, to suppress the domestic slave trade between the several States, and to abolish slavery in those portions of our territory which the Constitution has placed under its exclusive jurisdiction.

We also maintain that there are, at the present time, the highest obligations resting upon the people of the free States, to remove slavery by moral and political action, as prescribed in the Constitution of the United States. They are now living under a pledge of their tremendous physical force to fasten the galling fetters of tyranny upon the limbs of millions in the southern States;—they are liable to be called at any moment to suppress a general insurrection of the slaves;—they authorize the slave owner to vote for three-fifths of his slaves as property, and thus enable him to perpetuate his oppression;—they support a standing army at the south for its protection;—and they seize the slave who has escaped into their territories, and send him back to be tortured by an enraged master or a brutal driver.

This relation to slavery is criminal and full of danger; *it must be broken up.*

These are our views and principles—these, our designs and measures. With entire confidence in the overruling justice of God, we plant ourselves upon the Declaration of our Independence, and upon the truths of Divine Revelation, as upon the *everlasting rock.*

We shall organize Anti-Slavery Societies, if possible, in every city, town and village of our land.

We shall send forth Agents to lift up the voice of remonstrance, of warning, of entreaty and rebuke.

We shall circulate, unsparingly and extensively, antislavery tracts and periodicals.

We shall enlist the *pulpit* and the *press* in the cause of the suffering and the dumb.

We shall aim at a purification of the churches from all participation in the guilt of slavery.

We shall encourage the labor of freemen over that of the

slaves, by giving a preference to their productions;—and

We shall spare no exertions nor means to bring the whole nation to speedy repentance.

Our trust for victory is solely in GOD. We may be personally defeated, but our principles never. *Truth, Justice,* and *Humanity,* must and will gloriously triumph. Already a host is coming up to the help of the Lord against the mighty, and the prospect before us is full of encouragement.

Submitting this DECLARATION to the candid examination of the people of this country, and of the friends of liberty all over the world, we hereby affix our signatures to it;—pledging ourselves that, under the guidance and by the help of Almighty God, we will do all that in us lies, consistently with this Declaration of our principles, to overthrow the most execrable system of slavery that has ever been witnessed upon earth—to deliver our land from its deadliest curse—to wipe out the foulest stain which rests upon our national escutcheon—and to secure to the colored population of the United States all the rights and privileges which belong to them as men and as Americans—come what may to our persons, our interests, or our reputations—whether we live to witness the triumph of justice, liberty and humanity, or perish untimely as martyrs in this great, benevolent and holy cause.

Angelina Grimké

LETTER TO CATHARINE E. BEECHER (1837)

Born into a prominent slaveholding family in Charleston, South Carolina, Angelina Grimké (1805–1879) and her elder sister, Sarah, grew dissatisfied with the practice of slavery and the formalism of the Episcopal church. They moved to Philadelphia, became Quakers, and freed the slaves they later inherited as part of their family legacy. Angelina in 1836 published an antislavery pamphlet, *Appeal to the*

From Angelina E. Grimké, *Letters to Catharine E. Beecher, in Reply to an Essay on Slavery and Abolitionism, Addressed to A. E. Grimké* (Boston: Isaac Knapp, 1838), 6–13.

Christian Women of the South, for which she was promptly denounced in her native city. At Garrison's invitation, the abolitionist sisters toured New England in 1837, speaking to "promiscuous" or mixed audiences of men and women. Offended by this breach of convention, socially conservative immediatists, especially clerics, faulted Garrison and the Grimkés, thus contributing to a serious split among abolitionists over the "woman question." Overall, abolitionism provided feminists with an egalitarian ethic and public forum in which to address long-standing gender inequities.

The following open letter by Angelina Grimké answered criticism about immediatism published by Catharine E. Beecher, who was the daughter of Lyman Beecher, America's most prominent minister and former president of Lane Seminary, and the sister of the not-yet-famous Harriet Beecher Stowe. In 1838 Angelina married Theodore Weld, an immediatist who, as a student, had defied Lyman Beecher, a colonizationist, and abolitionized Lane Seminary in 1834.

Letter II. Immediate Emancipation

Brookline, Mass. 6th month, 17th, 1837

Dear Friend: Where didst thou get thy statement of what Abolitionists mean by immediate emancipation? I assure thee, it is a novelty. I never heard any abolitionist say that slaveholders "were physically unable to emancipate their slaves, and of course are not bound to do it," because in some States there are laws which forbid emancipation. This is truly what our opponents affirm; but we say that all the laws which sustain the system of slavery are unjust and oppressive—contrary to the fundamental principles of morality, and, therefore, null and void.

We hold, that all the slaveholding laws violate the fundamental principles of the Constitution of the United States. In the preamble of that instrument, the great objects for which it was framed are declared to be "to establish justice, to promote the *general* welfare, and to secure the blessings of *liberty* to us and to our posterity." The slave laws are flagrant violations of these fundamental principles. Slavery subverts justice, promotes the welfare of the few to the manifest injury of the many, and robs thousands of the *posterity* of our forefathers of the blessings of liberty. This cannot be denied, for Paxton, a Virginia slaveholder, says, "the *best* blood in Virginia flows in the veins of slaves!" Yes, even the blood of a Jefferson. And every southerner knows that it is a common thing for the *posterity of our forefathers* to be sold on the vendue tables of the South. *The posterity of our fathers* are advertised in American papers as runaway slaves. Such advertisements often contain expressions like these: "has sometimes passed himself off as a *white* man,"—"has been mistaken for a *white* man,"—"*quite white,* has *straight* hair, and would not readily be taken for a slave," and so forth.

Now, thou wilt perceive, that, so far from thinking that a slaveholder is bound by the *immoral* and *unconstitutional* laws of the Southern States, we hold that he is solemnly bound as a man, as an American, to *break* them, and that *immediately* and openly; as much so, as Daniel was to pray, or Peter and John to preach—or every conscientious Quaker to refuse to pay a militia fine, or to train, or to fight. *We* promulgate no such time-serving doctrine as that set forth by thee. When *we* talk of immediate emancipation, we speak that we do mean, and the slaveholders understand us, if thou dost not.

Here, then, is another point in which we are entirely at variance, though the *principles* of abolitionism are "generally adopted by our opposers." What shall I say to these things, but that I am glad thou hast afforded me an opportunity of explaining to thee what *our principles* really are? for I apprehend that *thou* "hast not been sufficiently informed in regard to the feelings and opinions" of abolitionists.

It matters not to me what meaning "Dictionaries or standard writers" may give to immediate emancipation. My Dictionary is the Bible; my standard authors, prophets and apostles. When Jehovah commanded Pharaoh to "let the people go," he meant that they should be *immediately emancipated.* I read his meaning in the judgments which terribly rebuked Pharaoh's repeated and obstinate refusal to "let the people go." I read it in the *universal* emancipation of near 3,000,000 of Israelites in *one awful night.* When the prophet Isaiah commanded the Jews "to loose the bands of wickedness, to undo the heavy burdens, and to let the oppressed go free, and that ye break every yoke," he taught no gradual or partial emancipation, but *immediate, universal emancipation. . . .*

If our fundamental principle is right, that no man can rightfully hold his fellow man as *property,* then it follows, of course, that he is bound *immediately* to cease holding him as such, and that, too, in *violation of the immoral and unconstitutional laws* which have been framed for the express purpose of "turning aside the needy from judgment, and to take away the right from the poor of the people, that widows may be their prey, and that they may rob the fatherless." Every slaveholder is bound to cease to do evil *now*, to emancipate his slaves *now*.

Dost thou ask what I mean by emancipation? I will explain myself in a few words. 1. It is "to reject with indignation, the wild and guilty phantasy, that man can hold *property* in man." 2. To pay the laborer his hire, for he is worthy of it. 3. No longer to deny him the right of marriage, but to "let every man have his own wife, and let every woman have her own husband," as saith the apostle. 4. To let parents have their own children, for they are the gift of the Lord to *them*, and no one else has any right to them. 5. No longer to withhold the advantages of education and the privilege of reading the Bible. 6. To put the slave under the protection of equitable laws.

Now, why should not *all* this be done immediately? Which of these things is to be done next year, and which the year after? and so on. *Our* immediate emancipation means, doing justice and loving mercy *to-day*—and this is what we call upon every slaveholder to do.

I have seen too much of slavery to be a gradualist. I dare not, in view of such a system, tell the slaveholder, that "he is physically unable to emancipate his slaves." I say *he is able* to let the oppressed go free, and that such heaven-daring atrocities ought to *cease now*, henceforth and forever. Oh, my very soul is grieved to find a northern woman thus "sewing pillows under all armholes," framing and fitting soft excuses for the slaveholder's conscience, whilst with the same pen she is *professing* to regard slavery as a sin. "An open enemy is better than such a secret friend."

Hoping that thou mayest soon be emancipated from such inconsistency, I remain until then,

Thine *out* of the bonds of Christian Abolitionism,

A. E. Grimké

Elizur Wright

THE EMERGENCE OF POLITICAL ABOLITIONISM (1837–1839)

Widespread anti-abolitionism, including northern mobs, forced immediatists to reevaluate their means and ends, resulting in a three-way schism in their ranks. By 1840 nonresistant Garrisonians in Boston controlled the American Anti-Slavery Society, whereas church-oriented abolitionists led by Lewis Tappan in New York City formed the rival American and Foreign Anti-Slavery Society. A third group, centered in upstate New York, turned to political action and organized the Liberty party.

The following private correspondence of Elizur Wright (1805–1885), the domestic secretary of the American Anti-Slavery Society from 1833 to 1839 and then editor of the anti-Garrisonian *Massachusetts Abolitionist* from 1839 to 1840, illustrates the factionalism among abolitionists. Wright's 1837 letter to Garrison assails the doctrine of nonresistance. In an 1838 letter to Amos Phelps, an antislavery agent and Congregational minister who bridled at the Grimkés' defiance of decorum, Wright complains that the "woman question" is "tying a tin kettle to the tail of our enterprise." And to Henry B. Stanton, an officer of the national society, Wright in 1839 stresses that the American Anti-Slavery Society must nominate abolitionist candidates for president in order to refocus the cause. This confidential letter inadvertently came into Garrison's possession, adding to the acrimony among abolitionists.

To William Lloyd Garrison
November 6, 1837

. . . My last letter, I hope, has convinced you that I do not wish to *gag* you on any subject. Still do I beg of you, as a brother, to let other subjects alone till slavery is finished, *because* this is the work you have taken in hand, it is the most pressing, and needs your whole energy. What if you do not live to communicate to the world your peculiar views of peace, Human Government, Theology, &c., will wisdom die with you? God is not so poverty stricken in regard to the means of accomplishing any of his designs

From the Elizur Wright Papers, Manuscript Division, Library of Congress.

as to be frustrated for the want of any man. You say 'truth is *one*, and not conflictive and multitudinous.' True; but the people are conflictive, and moreover they cannot receive and unitedly act upon more than one great truth at once. Again, abolitionists do not agree on many points not embraced in their Declaration of Sentiments. Hence it is no more than right that those persons and papers that are 'conspicuously identified' with them as a body, and are understood to speak a language common to all, should confine themselves to subjects on which all agree, or rather on which they do not seriously differ. Here is no restriction of liberty more than is due to truth and righteousness. God, by the very nature of things, has forbidden us to attempt everything at once.

But it does appear to me that *your* 'truth' that human government has no rightful authority, does conflict with *our truths*, as expressed in our Declaration of Sentiments as well as with the most important measures by which we seek to accomplish our object. In the Declaration we maintain that 'the slaves ought instantly to be set free and brought under the *protection of law*,' and that 'Congress has the *right* and is solemnly bound to suppress the domestic slave trade' &c. What miserable falsehood if human government has no *right* to exist! You impeach my Christianity, because I 'cannot cease looking to man for *protection* and redress;' how can it consist with your Christianity to demand for others 'the *protection of law*'? If you follow out your doctrine, surely you must cease having anything to do with Congress and State Legislatures. Our action upon them in the direction of humanity, not only recognizes, but tends to confirm their power, for human governments are never so strong as when the weakest enjoy their protection. Having this view of the bearing of your Peace doctrines upon the dear cause of the slave, could I do less than to beg of you to suppress them till our contest is over? I have no fear of the prevalence of your opinions provided they make their home in their own tub—and that stands distinctly on its own bottom. What I fear is that they will suck *you* into a vortex of spiritual Quixotism, and thus absorb energies which might have shaken down the citadel of oppression.

As to the doctrine of 'perfect holiness,' I have not much to say. My observation of men concurs with the little study I have been able to bestow on the Old and New Testaments, in convincing me that men are not completely freed from sin by the grace of God, in this life. The final victory is over the banks of the Jordan. That a marvellous change does take place by the blessing of God upon Gospel truth, I joyfully believe; but that a man, while in the body, is placed by it beyond the power of temptation, I must be allowed to doubt. The history of Christianity is far from furnishing any proof to this effect, and the passages of scripture you quote, when taken in their connection, and with the allowances, exceptions and reservations to which all general propositions, *not founded on strict definitions,* are subject, do not seem to me to prove that a man cannot be holy in his general character without being altogether sinless. He cannot of course be holy and sinful in the same act, and how many times and how far he may sin and yet repent and be forgiven I shall not undertake to decide. There are a great many things that I don't know. But, I must believe the testimony of my own senses, in preference to anybody's interpretation of scripture, for Scripture itself after all rests on the testimony of sense—and according to that testimony I have never yet met with a man who was free from sin. I am obliged to reject your own claim to sinlessness. Your very letter refutes it. Hence, I am obliged to reject your theory, or to believe that the Gospel has never done its appropriate work within the range of my observation. If your theory could be established from scripture, it would only make me an infidel, for I cannot receive a revelation which asserts that which my senses pronounce to be false, nor one which visibly fails to accomplish its object. On your theory I must either believe that the Gospel has been in the world eighteen hundred years for nothing; or I must believe that pride and vanity, flattery and slander are holy affections and righteous acts! To be sure I may be saved from the dilemma by more evidence, but so far as what I have goes, I am transfixed on one horn or the other. Still therefore am I obliged to mourn over your theological position as 'down right fanaticism' and I pronounce it so with about the same confidence that I pronounce slaveholding a sin, but with far different feelings toward the subject of it.

Your theory of perfection, of course, takes away my hopes of salvation, which are not founded as you intimate on the law, but on *God's free grace to sinners,* who, believing in Christ, *desire to be saved from sin.* But I have said more than I intended—more than I shall every say again. I am sick unto death of the selfish, luxurious, good for nothing sort of religion which is eternally inquiring what will become of ME! If there are any men in the world who deserve to be damned, they are your very religious men whose anxiety is, not *to do right,* but to *escape hell.* They libel their Maker and disgrace his Saviour. Let us do what needs to be done to promote the welfare of all within our reach and leave our *salvation* to God.

To Amos A. Phelps
July 11, 1838

. . . Now for a word on the 'woman question'—for I am in a hurry—first of all on a question so delicate and *ridiculous,* I place no great confidence in my own judgment—of course I don't commend it as matter of popery to anybody else. Secondly, my faith and confidence in the '*everlasting distinction*' which has become the parent of another distinction between the bifurcated male galligaskin and the monopetalons tunic of the female, is so strong of itself that it hardly permits me to engage in any *conservative* measures. Truly I am a *conservative* in a certain sense,—I think the tom turkeys ought to do the gobbling. I am opposed to hens crowing, and surely as a general rule, to female-preaching—but I think practically, there is as little need of my conservatism in the one case as the other. I am, therefore, disposed to give the *women people* all the rope they have a mind to take. Do they want to try the man's part? Let them try it as many of them and as long as they please. I have no sympathy with the terror of certain *male women* who quote Paul at the top of their lungs, as if our friend Theodore's wife or Abby Kelly were about to wrench from them their diploma of manhood forever and aye—but I have just no doubt at all that Paul and propriety are both on their side in the *argument.* Paul, if I understand him, however, did no less than hint that his instructions for the regulation of women might without much danger have been left to *nature herself.* And whatever was the confidence of the Apostle in the correctness of his views of propriety, I think he must have been too much of a gentleman to choke a woman with authority, as well as *too wise a man.* After giving his opinion (do his original words mean more?) I fancy he would have left it to nature and the women themselves whether they should exercise their gift in public. There certainly have been cases in which women have done the work of men nobly and well. If nature were called to account for this I imagine she would cry out *Exceptio probat* &c. That this question should be brought up by some of our friends as though it were a twin sister of Anti-Slavery, is mortifying in the extreme. It belittles us—it is tying a tin kettle to the tail of our enterprise. But I don't see what we can do better than to let it take its course. Let the women take as much as they please of the liberty which the terms of our constitution give them—only the few exceptions of '*the female brethren*' will avail themselves of it and experience will in due time teach *them* the needful lesson. As to the terrors of their counterparts of our own gender, they will calm away in time, like all other terrors.

To Henry B. Stanton
October 12, 1839

Saw only the *streak* of you as you passed here. So I *must* say a word in scrawl which I should have said vocally. It is this—as you are a man and no mouse, urge the Am. Soc. at Cleveland to take a decided step toward *Presidential Candidates.* Our labor will be more than half lost without them. It is a step which we have always contemplated as one which Providence *might* force upon us. Has not the time come? What else can we do except to *back out*? The South can outbid us, and hence she will buy up both political parties as to national politics, *ad infinitum.* We *must* have a free northern nucleus—a standard flung to the breeze—something around which to rally. While we are about it let's have *good stuff.* I am satisfied the best we have will do. Let a candidate take well in his own State (1.) and *he* can be made *popular* anywhere else. . . . There are men enough, if they will only stand, and they must be made to. If the thing is done judiciously and deliberately there will be no difficulty. Provided we get *good stuff,* not much will depend upon the previous fame of our candidates—we can manufacture their notoriety as we go along. Perhaps the Society can be got to pass a resolution asserting the propriety of an anti-slavery nomination in case Clay, Van Buren, &c., pro-slavery men, are nominated by the parties, and authorizing the Ex. Com., or a Committee to call a convention expressly to nominate Presidential candidates, when there is no longer any possibility of a proper candidate being nominated by either party. This will give time for minds to *turn,* and get rid of their *repugnancies.* Just about as soon as we can be sure of *good stuff* to stand the racket, our candidates should be brought before the public. We shall certainly gain more than we lose.

Benefits.
1. Something practical for every man to do.
2. Terror struck to the heart of the south from Clay downwards.
3. Concert of action—iron sharpening iron.
4. Leaving non resistance abolitionism *hors du combat.* (What will our "ninety-nine hundredths" do? vote for Clay, Van Buren,— — —, or Scattering or Nobody?)
5. Politics enobled—glorious object—clean skirts.
6. Interest, discussion and liberality increased a hundred fold—the matter being carried *home* to everybody.
7. Consistency—the jewel—the everything of such a cause as ours.

If we gain these points, what can we lose? Have we not now thoroughly tried everything short of this?

Precedents are not to be quoted against us. Anti-Masonry had not such a *quarry.* Its object shrunk away from it. The enterprise was never half baked. Yet it died, not by nominating separate candidates so much as by amalgamating with existing parties. (2.) After all it died for want of *tangible work* more than anything else. Our cause is entirely different.

But you have thought of this more than I. So no more coals to Newcastle. I throw in my mite.

One thing *I know.* Unless you do take such a step, our New Organization [Massachusetts Abolitionist Society] here is a gone case. (3.) It has been, inter nos, shockingly mismanaged. Everything has been made to turn upon the *woman question.* The political has been left to fall out of sight. (4.) In our State politics the Temperance question is so fairly on the ground that we have not room to stand. (5.) I wont do for *us* to start the national politics. (6.) But if the *parent society* does so, and not by *our* move—then we can take hold with all our might, the non resistants will have to be out upon us under a true flag—the *confounded* woman question will be forgotten—and we shall take a *living* position. You certainly *see* this. Take my solemn assurance that it is life and death with us. Make the move, and we will follow and live. How have I wished since this shattered right fist has failed me for *voice*, and brains to match! (7.) But *you* can do it. For the love of heaven and earth, *do it;* and write me the earliest word.

Henry Highland Garnet

A CALL FOR SLAVE REVOLUTION (1843)

At the National Negro Convention held in Buffalo from August 21 to 24, 1843, Henry Highland Garnet (1815–1882), a twenty-seven-year-old Presbyterian minister from Troy, New York, set the standard for militancy in an open call for slave insurrection. His speech, "An Address to the Slaves of the United States," was rejected by a majority of only one vote (including that of Frederick Douglass) from representing an affirmation of the seventy participants. The delegates feared that the speech, which soon attracted national attention, would lead to further repression of free blacks in the South.

Garnet's oratory shocked many black and white abolitionists in its justification of violent means. Nonetheless the sentiments were in the African-American tradition of resistance as exemplified by Denmark Vesey, Nat Turner, Joseph Cinque, and David Walker's *Appeal,* with which the "Address" was jointly published in 1848. The grandson of a Mandingo leader, Garnet fled slavery in Maryland as a youth, suffered the separation of his family by slave catchers in New York City, and, at school in Canaan, New Hampshire, stood off white vigilantes with a shotgun. His "Address" proved prophetic of impending national violence over slavery, including "Bleeding Kansas," the Harpers Ferry raid, and the Civil War itself.

From Henry Highland Garnet, *An Address to the Slaves of the United States of America* (New York: Printed by J. H. Tubitt, 1848).

Fellow-men! patient sufferers! behold your dearest rights crushed to the earth! See your sons murdered, and your wives, mothers, and sisters, doomed to prostitution! In the name of the merciful God ! and by all that life is worth, let it no longer be a debateable question, whether it is better to choose LIBERTY or DEATH!

In 1822, Denmark Veazie, of South Carolina, formed a plan for the liberation of his fellow men. In the whole history of human efforts to overthrow slavery, a more complicated and tremendous plan was never formed. He was betrayed by the treachery of his own people, and died a martyr to freedom. Many a brave hero fell, but History, faithful to her high trust, will transcribe his name on the same monument with Moses, Hampden, Tell, Bruce, and Wallace, Touissaint L'Overteur, Lafayette and Washington. That tremendous movement shook the whole empire of slavery. The guilty soul thieves were overwhelmed with fear. It is a matter of fact, that at that time, and in consequence of the threatened revolution, the slave states talked strongly of emancipation. But they blew but one blast of the trumpet of freedom, and then laid it aside. As these men became quiet, the slaveholders ceased to talk about emancipation: and now, behold your condition to-day! Angels sigh over it, and humanity has long since exhausted her tears in weeping on your account!

The patriotic Nathaniel Turner followed Denmark Veazie. He was goaded to desperation by wrong and injustice. By Despotism, his name has been recorded on the list of infamy, but future generations will number him among the noble and brave.

Next arose the immortal Joseph Cinque, the hero of the Amistad. He was a native African, and by the help of God he emancipated a whole ship-load of his fellow men on the high seas. And he now sings of liberty on the sunny hills of Africa, and beneath his native palm trees, where he hears the lion roar, and feels himself as free as that king of the forest. Next arose Madison Washington, that bright star of freedom, and took his station in the constellation of freedom. He was a slave on board the brig Creole, of Richmond, bound to New Orleans, that great slave mart, with a hundred and four others. Nineteen struck for liberty or death. But one life was taken, and the whole were emancipated, and the vessel was carried into Nassau, New Providence. Noble men! Those who have fallen in freedom's conflict, their memories will be cherished by the true hearted, and the God-fearing, in all future generations; those who are living, their names are surrounded by a halo of glory.

We do not advise you to attempt a revolution with the sword, because it would be INEXPEDIENT. Your numbers are too small, and moreover the rising spirit of the age, and the spirit of the gospel, are opposed to war and bloodshed. But from this moment cease to labor for tyrants who will not remunerate you. Let every slave throughout the land do this, and the days of slavery are numbered. You cannot be more oppressed than you have been—you cannot suffer greater cruelties than you have already. RATHER DIE FREEMEN, THAN LIVE TO BE SLAVES. Remember that you are THREE MILLIONS.

It is in your power so to torment the God-cursed slaveholders, that they will be glad to let you go free. If the scale was turned, and black men were the masters, and white men the slaves, every destructive agent and element would be employed to lay the oppressor low. Danger and death would hang over their heads day and night. Yes, the tyrants would meet with plagues more terrible than those of Pharaoh. But you are a patient people. You act as though you were made for the special use of these devils. You act as though your daughters were born to pamper the lusts of your masters and overseers. And worse than all, you tamely submit, while your lords tear your wives from your embraces, and defile them before your eyes. In the name of God we ask, are you men? Where is the blood of your fathers? Has it all run out of your veins? Awake, awake; millions of voices are calling you! Your dead fathers speak to you from their graves. Heaven, as with a voice of thunder, calls on you to arise from the dust.

Let your motto be RESISTANCE! RESISTANCE! RESISTANCE!— No oppressed people have ever secured their liberty without resistance. What kind of resistance you had better make, you must decide by the circumstances that surround you, and according to the suggestion of expediency. Brethren, adieu. Trust in the living God. Labor for the peace of the human race, and remember that you are three millions.

Martin R. Delaney

BLACK NATIONALISM (1852)

Martin R. Delaney (1812–1885) founded *The North Star* with Frederick Douglass in 1847 at Rochester, New York, and served as co-editor until 1849. Subsequently he studied at Harvard Medical School and was a practicing physician in Pittsburgh, to which his free black parents had migrated from western Virginia. At the same time, the Mexican War and the Compromise of 1850 with a strengthened Fugitive Slave Law, solidified the power of slavery. Frustrated with ubiquitous racism that circumscribed even black professionals, his thoughts turned to a separate African-American nation, and he articulated his views in *The Condition, Elevation, Emigration, and Destiny of the Colored People of the United States* (1852). In his critical examination of racial relations, he found that even white abolitionists who had followed blacks into the cause had reduced their black colleagues to "a mere secondary, underling position." He argued, as in the following excerpt, that emigration to a black state was the only alternative to further degradation in America. Although he organized a National Emigration Convention in 1854, the advent of the Civil War turned his efforts toward the defeat of the Confederacy and the elevation of the ex-slaves in this country. His advocacy of a separate black state foreshadowed the political aspirations of Marcus Garvey and Elijah Muhammad in the twentieth century.

One part of the American people, though living in or near proximity and together, are quite unacquainted with the other; and one of the great objects of the author, is to make each acquainted. Except the character of an individual is known, there can be no just appreciation of his worth; and as with individuals, so it is with classes.

The colored people are not yet known, even to their most professed friends among the white Americans; for the reason, that politicians, religionists, colonizationists, and Abolitionists, have each and all, at different times, presumed to *think* for, dictate to, and *know* better what suited colored people, than they knew for themselves; and consequently, there has been no other knowledge

From *The Condition, Emigration, and Destiny of the Colored People of the United States.* (Philadelphia: M. Delany, 1852).

of them obtained, than that which has been obtained through these mediums. Their history—past, present, and future, has been written by them, who, for reasons well known, which are named in this volume, are not their representatives, and, therefore, do not properly nor fairly present their wants and claims among their fellows. Of these impressions, we design disabusing the public mind, and correcting the false impressions of all classes upon this great subject. A moral and mental, is as obnoxious as a physical servitude, and not to be tolerated; as the one may, eventually, lead to the other. . . .

A project for an Expedition of Adventure, to the Eastern Coast of Africa. Every people should be the originators of their own designs, the projector of their own schemes, and creators of the events that lead to their destiny—the consummation of their desires.

Situated as we are, in the United States, many, and almost insurmountable obstacles present themselves. We are four-and-a-half millions in numbers, free and bond; six hundred thousand free, and three-and-a-half millions bond.

We have native hearts and virtues, just as other nations; which in their pristine purity are noble, potent, and worthy of example. We are a nation within a nation;—as the Poles in Russia, the Hungarians in Austria; the Welsh, Irish, and Scotch in the British dominions.

But we have been, by our oppressors, despoiled of our purity, and corrupted in our native characteristics, so that we have inherited their vices, and but few of their virtues, leaving us in character, really a *broken people.*

Being distinguished by complexion, we are still singled out— although having merged in the habits and customs of our oppressors—as a distinct nation of people; as the Poles, Hungarians, Irish and others, who still retain their native peculiarities, of language, habits, and various other traits. The claims of no people, according to established policy and usage, are respected by any nation, until they are presented in a national capacity.

To accomplish so great and desirable an end, there should be held, a great representative gathering of the colored people of the United States; not what is termed a National Convention, representing en masse, such as have been, for the last few years, held at various times and places; but a true representation of the intelligence and wisdom of the colored freemen; because it will be futile and an utter failure, to attempt such a project without the highest grade of intelligence.

No great project was ever devised without the consultation of the most mature intelligence, and discreet discernment and precaution.

To effect this, and prevent intrusion and improper representation, there should be a CONFIDENTIAL COUNCIL held; and circulars issued, only to such persons as shall be *known* to the projectors to be equal to the desired object.

The authority from whence the call should originate, to be in this wise:—The originator of the scheme, to impart the contemplated Confidential Council, to a limited number of known, worthy gentlemen, who agreeing with the project, endorse at once the scheme, when becoming joint proprietors in interest, issue a *Confidential Circular,* leaving blanks for date, time, and place of holding the Council, sending them to trusty, worthy and suitable colored freemen, in all parts of the United States, and the Canadas, inviting them to attend; who when met in Council, have the right to project any scheme they may think proper for the general good of the whole people—provided, that the project is laid before them after its maturity.

By this Council to be appointed, a Board of Commissioners, to consist of three, five, or such reasonable number as may be decided upon, one of whom shall be chosen as Principal or Conductor of the Board, whose duty and business shall be, to go on an expedition to the EASTERN COAST OF AFRICA, to make researches for a suitable location on that section of the coast, for the settlement of colored adventurers from the United States, and elsewhere. Their mission should be to all such places as might meet the approbation of the people: as South America, Mexico, the West Indies, &c.

The Commissioners all to be men of decided qualifications; to embody among them, the qualifications of physician, botanist, chemist, geologist, geographer, and surveyor—having a sufficient knowledge of these sciences, for practical purposes.

Their business shall be, to make a topographical, geological, and botanical examination, into such part or parts as they may select, with all other useful information that may be obtained. . . .

The National Council shall appoint one or two Special Commissioners, to England, France, to solicit, in the name of the Representatives of a Broken Nation, of four-and-a-half millions, the necessary outfit and support, for any period not exceeding three years, of such an expedition. Certainly, what England and France would do, for a little nation—mere nominal nation, of five thousand civilized Liberians, they would be willing and ready to do, for five millions; if they be but authentically represented, in a national capacity. What was due to Greece, enveloped by Turkey, should be due to United States, enveloped by the United States; and we believe would be respected, if properly presented. To England and France, we should look for sustenance, and the people of those two nations—as they would have everything to gain from such an adventure and eventual settlement on the EASTERN COAST OF AFRICA—the opening of an immense trade being the consequence. The whole Continent is rich in minerals, and the most precious metals, as but a superficial notice of the topographical and geological reports from that country, plainly show to any mind versed in the least, in the science of the earth . . . The land is ours—there it lies with inexhaustible resources; let us go and possess it. In Eastern Africa must rise up a nation, to whom all the world must pay commercial tribute.

WE must MAKE AN ISSUE, CREATE AN EVENT, and ESTABLISH A NATIONAL POSITION FOR OURSELVES: and never may expect to be respected as men and women, until we have undertaken, some fearless, bold, and adventurous deeds of daring—contending against every odds—regardless of every consequence.

John Brown

SPEECH TO THE COURT (1859)

John Brown's raid of October 16–17, 1859, on the federal arsenal at Harpers Ferry, Virginia, was a military failure. As Abraham Lincoln remarked, "It was not a slave insurrection. It was an attempt by white men to get up a revolt among slaves, in which the slaves refused to participate." Though his "army" of eighteen men (including five blacks) was quickly subdued by federal forces under the command of Robert E. Lee, the dramatic event demonstrated how fragile the bonds of union had become.

Long an opponent of slavery, John Brown (1800–1859) had gained notoriety with the "Pottawatomie Massacre" in Kansas. On May 25, 1856, a group under his direction had killed five proslavery settlers to avenge the previous murder of free soil men. As he stated in this speech of November 2, 1859, to the Virginia court that convicted him of treason, the Harpers Ferry raid was to free slaves "on a larger scale" than he had done in Missouri in December 1858. Though he disingenuously denied fomenting a slave rebellion and invoked a "higher law" of divine justice, he was hanged on December 2, 1859. Brown, who had the clandestine support of some prominent abolitionists (the "Secret Six") for his Virginia foray, was eulogized in antislavery circles as a martyr. His prophetic role was captured in a note he handed to a jailer on the gallows: "I John Brown am now quite certain that the crimes of this guilty land will never be purged away but with Blood."

I have, may it please the Court, a few words to say.

In the first place, I deny everything but what I have all along admitted,—the design on my part to free the slaves. I intended certainly to have made a clean thing of that matter, as I did last winter, when I went into Missouri and there took slaves without the snapping of a gun on either side, moved them through the country, and finally left them in Canada. I designed to have done the same thing again, on a larger scale. That was all I intended. I never did intend murder, or treason, or the destruction of property, or to excite or incite slaves to rebellion, or to make insurrection.

From Franklin B. Sandborn, *The Life and Letters of John Brown* (Boston: Roberts Brothers, 1885), 584–585.

I have another objection: and that is, it is unjust that I should suffer such a penalty. Had I interfered in the manner which I admit, and which I admit has been fairly proved (for I admire the truthfulness and candor of the greater portion of the witnesses who have testified in this case),—had I so interfered in behalf of the rich, the powerful, the intelligent, the so-called great, or in behalf of any of their friends,—either father, mother, brother, sister, wife, or children, or any of that class,—and suffered and sacrificed what I have in this interference, it would have been all right; and every man in this court would have deemed it an act worthy of reward rather than punishment.

This court acknowledges, as I suppose, the validity of the law of God. I see a book kissed here which I suppose to be the Bible, or at least the New Testament. That teaches me that all things whatsoever I would that men should do to me, I should do even so to them. It teaches me, further, to "remember them that are in bonds, as bound with them." I endeavored to act up to that instruction. I say, I am yet too young to understand that God is any respecter of persons. I believe that to have interfered as I have done—as I have always freely admitted I have done—in behalf of His despised poor, was not wrong, but right. Now, if it is deemed necessary that I should forfeit my life for the furtherance of the ends of justice, and mingle my blood further with the blood of my children and with the blood of millions in this slave country whose rights are disregarded by wicked, cruel, and unjust enactments,—I submit; so let it be done!

Let me say one word further.

I feel entirely satisfied with the treatment I have received on my trial. Considering all the circumstances, it has been more generous than I expected. But I feel no consciousness of guilt. I have stated from the first what was my intention, and what was not. I never had any design against the life of any person, nor any disposition to commit treason, or excite slaves to rebel, or make any general insurrection. I never encouraged any man to do so, but always discouraged any idea of that kind.

Let me say, also, a word in regard to the statements made by some of those connected with me. I hear it has been stated by some of them that I have induced them to join me. But the contrary is true. I do not say this to injure them, but as regretting their weakness. There is not one of them but joined me of his own accord, and the greater part of them at their own expense. A number of them I never saw, and never had a word of conversation with, till the day they came to me; and that was for the purpose I have stated.

Now I have done.

Secondary Sources

John L. Thomas

ROMANTIC REFORM IN AMERICA, 1815–1865

The religious revivals known as the Second Great Awakening fueled a ferment of reforms in antebellum America, including abolitionism. The theological notion of perfectibility—the belief that sinners could willingly choose to do good and thus achieve salvation—had radical implications at this time. Ironically, it extended beyond the conservative social vision of the Benevolent Empire established by the major Protestant denominations after 1815. The doctrine of perfectibility was romantic, because, as John L. Thomas points out, it assumed the infinite malleability of the individual as the motive force in the regeneration of society. The advent of the Civil War was, however, in Thomas's words, an "intellectual counterrevolution" in which an organic vision of society came to the fore. The primacy of private conscience among abolitionists, for example, was superseded by nationalist concerns, an appreciation that institutional forces were necessary to secure emancipation. Although an individualistic ethic persisted, the widespread antebellum faith in perfectibility was a casualty of the war. John L. Thomas is professor of history at Brown University.

Confronted by the bewildering variety of projects for regenerating American society, Emerson concluded his survey of humanitarian reform in 1844 with the observation that "the Church, or religious party, is falling away from the Church nominal, and . . . appearing in temperance and nonresistance societies; in movements of abolitionists and of socialists . . . of seekers, of all the soul of the soldiery of dissent." Common to all these planners and prophets, he noted, was the conviction of an "infinite worthiness" in man

From John L. Thomas, "Romantic Reform in America, 1815–1860," *American Quarterly,* 17 (1965), 656–681. Reprinted by permission of the author and The Johns Hopkins University Press.

and the belief that reform simply meant removing "impediments" to natural perfection.

Emerson was defining, both as participant and observer, a romantic revolution which T. E. Hulme once described as "split religion." A romantic faith in perfectibility, originally confined by religious institutions, overflows these barriers and spreads across the surface of society, seeping into politics and culture. Perfectibility—the essentially religious notion of the individual as a "reservoir" of possibilities—fosters a revolutionary assurance "that if you can so rearrange society by the destruction of oppressive order then these possibilities will have a chance and you will get Progress." Hulme had in mind the destructive forces of the French Revolution, but his phrase is also a particularly accurate description of the surge of social reform which swept across Emerson's America in the three decades before the Civil War. Out of a seemingly conservative religious revival there flowed a spate of perfectionist ideas for the improvement and rearrangement of American society. Rising rapidly in the years after 1830, the flood of social reform reached its crest at midcentury only to be checked by political crisis and the counterforces of the Civil War. Reform after the Civil War, though still concerned with individual perfectibility, proceeded from new and different assumptions as to the nature of individualism and its preservation in an urban industrial society. Romantic reform ended with the Civil War and an intellectual counterrevolution which discredited the concept of the irreducible self and eventually redirected reform energies.

Romantic reform in America traced its origins to a religious impulse which was both politically and socially conservative. With the consolidation of independence and the arrival of democratic politics the new nineteenth-century generation of American churchmen faced a seeming crisis. Egalitarianism and rising demands for church disestablishment suddenly appeared to threaten an inherited Christian order and along with it the preferred status of the clergy. Lyman Beecher spoke the fears of more than one of the clerical party when he warned that Americans were fast becoming "another people." When the attempted alliance between sound religion and correct politics failed to prevent disestablishment or improve waning Federalist fortunes at the polls, the evangelicals, assuming a defensive posture, organized voluntary benevolent associations to strengthen the Christian character of Americans and save the country from infidelity and ruin. Between 1815 and 1830 nearly a dozen moral reform societies were established to counter the threats to social equilibrium posed by irreligious democrats. Their intense religious concern could be read in the titles of the benevolent societies which the evangelicals founded: the American Bible Society, the American Sunday School Union, the American Home Missionary Society, the American Tract Society. By the time of the election of Andrew Jackson the benevolent associations formed a vast if loosely coordinated network of conservative reform enterprises staffed with clergy and wealthy laymen who served as self-appointed guardians of American morals.

The clerical diagnosticians had little difficulty in identifying the symptoms of democratic disease. Infidelity flourished on the frontier and licentiousness bred openly in seaboard cities; intemperance sapped the strength of American workingmen and the saving word was denied their children. Soon atheism would destroy the vital organs of the republic unless drastic moral therapy prevented. The evangelicals' prescription followed logically from their diagnosis: large doses of morality injected into the body politic under the supervision of Christian stewards. No more Sunday mails or pleasure excursions, no more grog-shops or profane pleasures, no family without a Bible and no community without a minister of the gospel. Accepting for the moment their political liabilities, the moral reformers relied on the homeopathic strategy of fighting democratic excess with democratic remedies. The Tract Society set up three separate printing presses which cranked out hundreds of thousands of pamphlets for mass distribution. The Home Missionary Society subsidized seminarians in carrying religion into the backcountry. The Temperance Union staged popular conventions; the Peace Society sponsored public debates; the Bible Society hired hundreds of agents to spread its propaganda.

The initial thrust of religious reform, then, was moral rather than social, preventive rather than curative. Nominally rejecting politics and parties, the evangelicals looked to a general reformation of the American character achieved through a revival of piety and morals in the individual. By probing his conscience, by convincing him of his sinful ways and converting him to right conduct they hoped to engineer a Christian revolution which would leave the foundations of the social order undisturbed. The realization of their dream of a nonpolitical "Christian party" in America would ensure a one-party system open to moral talent and the natural superiority of Christian leadership. Until their work was completed, the evangelicals stood ready as servants of the Lord to manage their huge reformational apparatus in behalf of order and sobriety.

But the moral reformers inherited a theological revolution which in undermining their conservative defenses completely reversed their expectations for a Christian America. The transformation of American theology in the first quarter of the nineteenth century released the very forces of romantic perfectionism that conservatives most feared. This religious revolution advanced along three major fronts: first, the concentrated antitheocratic assault of Robert Owen and his secular utopian followers, attacks purportedly atheistic and environmentalist but in reality Christian in spirit and perfectionist in method; second, the revolt of liberal theology beginning with Unitarianism and culminating in transcendentalism; third, the containment operation of the "new divinity" in adapting orthodoxy to the criticism of liberal dissent. The central fact in the romantic reorientation of American theology was the rejection of determinism. Salvation, however variously defined, lay open to everyone. Sin was voluntary: men were not helpless and depraved by nature but free agents and potential powers for good. Sin could be reduced to the selfish preferences of individuals, and social evils, in turn, to collective sins which, once acknowledged, could be rooted out. Perfectionism spread rapidly across the whole spectrum of American Protestantism as different denominations and sects elaborated their own versions of salvation. If man was a truly free agent, then his improvement became a matter of immediate consequence. The progress of the country suddenly seemed to depend upon the regeneration of the individual and the contagion of example.

As it spread, perfectionism swept across denominational barriers and penetrated even secular thought. Perfection was presented as Christian striving for holiness in the "new heart" sermons of Charles Grandison Finney and as an immediately attainable goal in the come-outer prophecies of John Humphrey Noyes. It was described as an escape from outworn dogma by Robert Owen and as the final union of the soul with nature by Emerson. The important fact for most Americans in the first half of the nineteenth century was that it was readily available. A romantic religious faith had changed an Enlightenment doctrine of progress into a dynamic principle of reform.

For the Founding Fathers' belief in perfectibility had been wholly compatible with a pessimistic appraisal of the present state of mankind. Progress, in the view of John Adams or James Madison, resulted from the planned operation of mechanical checks within the framework of government which balanced conflicting selfish interests and neutralized private passions. Thus a properly constructed governmental machine might achieve by artifact what men, left to their own devices, could not—gradual improvement of social institutions and a measure of progress. Perfectionism, on the contrary, as an optative mood demanded total commitment and immediate action. A latent revolutionary force lay in its demand for immediate reform and its promise to release the new American from the restraints of institutions and precedent. In appealing to the liberated individual, perfectionism reinforced the Jacksonian attack on institutions, whether a "Monster Bank" or a secret Masonic order, entrenched monopolies or the Catholic Church. But in emphasizing the unfettered will as the proper vehicle for reform it provided a millenarian alternative to Jacksonian politics. Since social evils were simply individual acts of selfishness compounded, and since Americans could attempt the perfect society any time they were so inclined, it followed that the duty of the true reformer consisted in educating them and making them models of good behavior. As the sum of individual sins social wrong would disappear when enough people had been converted and rededicated to right conduct. Deep and lasting reform, therefore, meant an educational crusade based on the assumption that when a sufficient number of individual Americans had seen the light, they would automatically solve the country's social problems. Thus formulated, perfectionist reform offered a program of mass conversion achieved through educational rather than political means. In the opinion of the romantic reformers the regeneration of American society began, not in legislative enactments or political manipulation, but in a calculated appeal to the American urge for individual self-improvement.

Perfectionism radically altered the moral reform movement by shattering the benevolent societies themselves. Typical of these organizations was the American Peace Society founded in 1828 as a forum for clerical discussions of the gospel of peace. Its founders, hoping to turn American attention from the pursuit of wealth to the prevention of war, debated the question of defensive war, constructed hypothetical leagues of amity, and in a general way sought to direct American foreign policy into pacific channels. Perfectionism, however, soon split the Peace Society into warring factions as radical nonresistants, led by the Christian perfectionist, Henry C. Wright, denounced all use of force and demanded the instant creation of an American society modeled on the precepts of Jesus. Not only war but all governmental coercion fell under the ban of the nonresistants who refused military service and political office along with the right to vote. After a series of skirmishes the nonresistants seceded in 1838 to form their own New England Non-Resistant Society; and by 1840 the institutional strength of the peace movement had been completely broken.

The same power of perfectionism disrupted the temperance movement. The founders of the temperance crusade had considered their reform an integral part of the program of moral stewardship and had directed their campaign against "ardent spirits" which could be banished "by a correct and efficient public sentiment." Until 1833 there was no general agreement on a pledge of total abstinence: some local societies required it, others did not. At the first national convention held in that year, however, the radical advocates of temperance, following their perfectionist proclivities, demanded a pledge of total abstinence and hurried on to denounce the liquor traffic as "morally wrong." Soon both the national society and local and state auxiliaries were split between moderates content to preach to the consumer and radicals bent on extending moral suasion to public pressure on the seller. After 1836 the national movement disintegrated into scattered local societies which attempted with no uniform program and no permanent success to establish a cold-water America.

By far the most profound change wrought by perfectionism was the sudden emergence of abolition. The American

Colonization Society, founded in 1817 as another key agency in the moral reform complex, aimed at strengthening republican institutions by deporting an inferior and therefore undesirable Negro population. The cooperation of Southerners hoping to strengthen the institution of slavery gave Northern colonizationists pause, but they succeeded in repressing their doubts until a perfectionist ethic totally discredited their program. The abolitionist pioneers were former colonizationists who took sin and redemption seriously and insisted that slavery constituted a flat denial of perfectibility to both Negroes and whites. They found in immediate emancipation a perfectionist formula for casting off the guilt of slavery and bringing the Negro to Christian freedom. Destroying slavery, the abolitionists argued, depended first of all on recognizing it as sin; and to this recognition they bent their efforts. Their method was direct and intensely personal. Slaveholding they considered a deliberate flouting of the divine will for which there was no remedy but repentance. Since slavery was sustained by a system of interlocking personal sins, their task was to teach Americans to stop sinning. "We shall send forth agents to lift up the voice of remonstrance, of warning, of entreaty, and of rebuke," the Declaration of Sentiments of the American Anti-Slavery Society announced. Agents, tracts, petitions and conventions—all the techniques of the moral reformers—were brought to bear on the consciences of Americans to convince them of their sin.

From the beginning, then, the abolitionists mounted a moral crusade rather than an engine of limited reform. For seven years, from 1833 to 1840, their society functioned as a loosely coordinated enterprise—a national directory of antislavery opinion. Perfectionist individualism made effective organization difficult and often impossible. Antislavery delegates from state and local societies gathered at annual conventions to frame denunciatory resolutions, listen to endless rounds of speeches and go through the motions of electing officers. Nominal leadership but very little power was vested in a self-perpetuating executive committee. Until its disruption in 1840 the national society was riddled with controversy as moderates, disillusioned by the failure of moral suasion, gradually turned to politics, and ultras, equally disenchanted by public hostility, abandoned American institutions altogether. Faced with the resistance of Northern churches and state legislatures, the perfectionists, led by William Lloyd Garrison, deserted politics for the principle of secession. The come-outer abolitionists, who eventually took for their motto "No Union with Slaveholders," sought an alternative to politics in the command to cast off church and state for a holy fraternity which would convert the nation by the power of example. The American Anti-Slavery Society quickly succumbed to the strain of conflicting philosophies and warring personalities. In 1840 the Garrisonians seized control of the society and drove their moderate opponents out. Thereafter neither ultras nor moderates were able to maintain an effective national organization.

Thus romantic perfectionism altered the course of the reform enterprise by appealing directly to the individual conscience. Its power stemmed from a millennial expectation which proved too powerful a moral explosive for the reform agencies. In one way or another almost all of the benevolent societies felt the force of perfectionism. Moderates, attempting political solutions, scored temporary gains only to receive sharp setbacks. Local option laws passed one year were repealed the next. Despite repeated attempts the Sunday School Union failed to secure permanent adoption of its texts in the public schools. The Liberty Party succeeded only in electing a Democratic president in 1844. Generally, direct political action failed to furnish reformers with the moral leverage they believed necessary to perfect American society. The conviction spread accordingly that politicians and legislators, as Albert Brisbane put it, were engaged in "superficial controversies and quarrels, which lead to no practical results." Political results, a growing number of social reformers were convinced, would be forthcoming only when the reformation of society at large had been accomplished through education and example.

The immediate effects of perfectionism, therefore, were felt outside politics in humanitarian reforms. With its confidence in the liberated individual perfectionism tended to be anti-institutional and exclusivist; but at the same time it posited an ideal society in which this same individual could discover his power for good and exploit it. Such a society would tolerate neither poverty nor suffering; it would contain no condemned classes or deprived citizens, no criminals or forgotten men. Impressed with the necessity for saving these neglected elements of American society, the humanitarian reformers in the years after 1830 undertook a huge rescue operation.

Almost to a man the humanitarians came from moral reform backgrounds. Samuel Gridley Howe was a product of Old Colony religious zeal and a Baptist education at Brown; Thomas Gallaudet a graduate of Andover and an ordained minister; Dorothea Dix a daughter of an itinerant Methodist minister, school mistress and Sunday school teacher-turned-reformer; E. M. P. Wells, founder of the reform school, a pastor of a Congregational church in Boston. Louis Dwight, the prison reformer, had been trained for the ministry at Yale and began his reform career as a traveling agent for the American Tract Society. Robert Hartley, for thirty years the secretary of the New York Association for Improving the Condition of the Poor, started as a tract distributor and temperance lecturer. Charles Loring Brace served as a missionary on Blackwell's Island before founding the Children's Aid Society.

In each of these cases of conversion to humanitarian reform there was a dramatic disclosure of deprivation and suffering which did not tally with preconceived notions of perfectibility—Dorothea Dix's discovery of the conditions in the Charlestown reformatory, Robert Hartley's inspection of contaminated milk in New York slums, Samuel Gridley Howe's chance conversation with Dr. Fisher in Boston. Something very much like a conversion experience seems to have forged the decisions of the humanitarians to take up their causes, a kind of revelation which furnished them with a ready-made role outside politics and opened a new career with which they could become completely identified. With the sudden transference of a vague perfectionist faith in self-improvement to urgent social problems there emerged a new type of professional reformer whose whole life became identified with the reform process. . . .

As romantic perfectionism spread across Jacksonian society it acquired an unofficial and only partly acceptable philosophy in the "systematic subjectivism" of transcendental theory. Transcendentalism, as its official historian noted, claimed for all men what a more restrictive Christian perfectionism extended only to the redeemed. Seen in this light, self-culture—Emerson's "perfect unfolding of our individual nature"—appeared as a secular amplification of the doctrine of personal holiness. In the transcendentalist definition, true reform proceeded from the individual and worked outward through the family, the neighborhood and ultimately into the social and political life of the community. The transcendentalist, Frothingham noted in retrospect, "was less a reformer of human circumstances than a regenerator of the human spirit. . . . With movements that did not start from this primary assumption of individual dignity, and come back to that as their goal, he had nothing to do." Emerson's followers, like the moral reformers and the humanitarians, looked to individuals rather than to institutions, to "high heroic example" rather than to political programs. The Brook-Farmer John Sullivan Dwight summed up their position when he protested that "men are anterior to systems. Great doctrines are not the origins, but the product of great lives."

Accordingly the transcendentalists considered institutions—parties, churches, organizations—so many arbitrarily constructed barriers on the road to self-culture. They were lonely men, Emerson admitted, who repelled influences. "They are not good citizens; not good members of society. . . ." A longing for solitude led them out of society, Emerson to the woods where he found no Jacksonian placards on the trees, Thoreau to his reclusive leadership of a majority of one. Accepting for the most part Emerson's dictum that one man was a counterpoise to a city, the transcendentalists turned inward to examine the divine self and find there the material with which to rebuild society. They wanted to avoid at all costs the mistake of their Jacksonian contemporaries who in order to be useful accommodated themselves to institutions without realizing the resultant loss of power and integrity.

The most immediate effect of perfectionism on the transcendentalists, as on the humanitarians, was the development of a set of concepts which, in stressing reform by example, opened up new roles for the alienated intellectual. In the first place, self-culture accounted for their ambivalence toward reform politics. It was not simply Emerson's reluctance to raise the siege on his hencoop that kept him apart, but a genuine confusion as to the proper role for the reformer. If government was simply a "job" and American society the senseless competition of the marketplace, how could the transcendentalist accept either as working premises? The transcendentalist difficulty in coming to terms with democratic politics could be read in Emerson's confused remark that of the two parties contending for the presidency in 1840 one had the better principles, the other the better men. Driven by their profound distaste for manipulation and chicanery, many of Emerson's followers took on the role of a prophet standing aloof from elections, campaigns and party caucuses and dispensing wisdom (often in oblique Emersonian terminology) out of the vast private resources of the self. In this sense transcendentalism, like Christian perfectionism, represented a distinct break with the prevailing Jacksonian views of democratic leadership and the politics of compromise and adjustment. . . .

A somewhat similar faith in the mystical fraternity informed Theodore Parker's plan for spiritual devotion. Like the other perfectionists, Parker began by reducing society to its basic components—individuals, the "monads" or "primitive atoms" of the social order—and judged it by its tendency to promote or inhibit individualism. "Destroy the individuality of those atoms, . . . all is gone. To mar the atoms is to mar the mass. To preserve itself, therefore, society is to preserve the individuality of the individual." In Parker's theology perfectionist Christianity and transcendental method merged to form a loving brotherhood united by the capacity to apprehend primary truths directly. A shared sense of the divinity of individual man held society together; without it no true community was possible. Looking around him at ante-bellum America, Parker found only the wrong kind of individualism, the kind that said, "I am as good as you, so get out of my way." The right kind, the individualism whose motto was "You are as good as I, and let us help one another," was to be the work of Parker's spiritual revolution. He explained the method of revolution as one of "*intellectual, moral* and *religious* education—everywhere and for all men." Until universal education had done its work Parker had little hope for political stability in the United States. He called instead for a new "party" to be formed in society at large, a party built on the idea that "God still inspires men as much as ever; that he is immanent in spirit as in space." Such a party required no church, tradition or scripture. "It believes God is near the soul as matter to the sense. . . . It calls God father and mother, not king; Jesus, brother, not redeemer, heaven home, religion nature."

Parker believed that this "philosophical party in politics,"as he called it, was already at work in the 1850s on a code of universal laws from which to deduce specific legislation "so that each statute in the code shall represent a fact in the universe, a point of thought in God; so . . . that legislation shall be divine in the same sense that a true system of astronomy be divine." Parker's holy band represented the full fruition of the perfectionist idea of a "Christian party" in America, a party of no strict political or sectarian definition, but a true reform movement, apostolic in its beginnings but growing with the truths it preached until it encompassed all Americans in a huge brotherhood of divine average men. Party members, unlike time-serving Whigs and Democrats, followed ideas and intuitions rather than prejudice and precedent, and these ideas led them to question authority, oppose legal injustice and tear down rotten institutions. The philosophical party was not to be bound by accepted notions of political conduct or traditional attitudes toward law. When unjust laws interpose barriers to progress, reformers must demolish them.

So Parker himself reasoned when he organized the Vigilance Committee in Boston to defeat the Fugitive Slave Law. His reasoning epitomized perfectionist logic: every man may safely trust his conscience, properly informed, because it is the repository for divine truth. When men learn to trust their consciences and act on them, they naturally encourage others to do the same with the certainty that they will reach the same conclusions. Individual conscience thus creates a social conscience and a collective will to right action. Concerted right action means moral revolution. The fact that moral revolution, in its turn, might mean political revolt was a risk Parker and his perfectionist followers were willing to take.

Both transcendentalism and perfectionist moral reform, then, were marked by an individualist fervor that was disruptive of American institutions. Both made heavy moral demands on church and state; and when neither proved equal to the task of supporting their intensely personal demands, the transcendentalists and the moral reformers became increasingly alienated. The perfectionist temperament bred a come-outer spirit. An insistence on individual moral accountability and direct appeal to the irreducible self, the faith in self-reliance and distrust of compromise, and a substitution of universal education for partial reform measures, all meant that normal political and institutional reform channels were closed to the perfectionists. Alternate routes to the millennium had to be found. One of these was discovered by a new leadership which made reform a branch of prophecy. Another was opened by the idea of a universal reawakening of the great god self. But there was a third possibility, also deeply involved with the educational process, an attempt to build the experimental community as a reform model. With an increasing number of reformers after 1840 perfectionist anti-institutionalism led to heavy investments in the communitarian movement.

The attraction that drew the perfectionists to communitarianism came from their conviction that the good society should be simple. Since American society was both complicated and corrupt, it was necessary to come out from it; but at the same time the challenge of the simple life had to be met. Once the true principles of social life had been discovered they had to be applied, some way found to harness individual perfectibility to a social engine. This urge to form the good community, as John Humphrey Noyes experienced it himself and perceived it in other reformers, provided the connection between perfectionism and communitarianism, or, as Noyes put it, between "Revivalism" and "Socialism." Perfectionist energies directed initially against institutions were diverted to the creation of small self-contained communities as educational models. In New England two come-outer abolitionists, Adin Ballou and George Benson, founded cooperative societies at Hopedale and Northampton, while a third Garrisonian lieutenant, John Collins, settled his followers on a farm in Skaneateles, New York. Brook Farm, Fruitlands and the North American Phalanx at Redbank acquired notoriety in their own day; but equally significant, both in terms of origins and personnel, were the experiments at Raritan Bay under the guidance of Marcus Spring, the Marlboro Association in Ohio, the Prairie Home Community of former Hicksite Quakers, and the Swedenborgian Brocton Community. In these and other experimental communities could be seen the various guises of perfectionism.

Communitarianism promised drastic social reform without violence. Artificiality and corruption could not be wiped out by partial improvements and piecemeal measures but demanded a total change which, as Robert Owen once explained, "could make an immediate, and almost instantaneous, revolution in the minds and

manners of society in which it shall be introduced." Communitarians agreed in rejecting class struggle which set interest against
interest instead of uniting them through association. "Whoever will
examine the question of social ameliorations," Albert Brisbane
argued in support of Fourier, "must be convinced that *the gradual
perfecting of Civilization* is useless as a remedy for present social
evils, and that the only effectual means of doing away with
indigence, idleness and the dislike for labor is to do away with
civilization itself, and organize Association . . . in its place." Like
the redemptive moment in conversion or the experience of self-
discovery in transcendentalist thought, the communitarian ideal
pointed to a sharp break with existing society and a commitment to
root-and-branch reform. On the other hand, the community was
seen as a controlled experiment in which profound but peaceful
change might be effected without disturbing the larger social order.
Massive change, according to communitarian theory, could also be
gradual and harmonious if determined by the model. . . .

The communitarian experiments in effect were anti-
institutional institutions. In abandoning political and religious
institutions the communitarians were driven to create perfect
societies of their own which conformed to their perfectionist
definition of the free individual. Their communities veered
erratically between the poles of anarchism and collectivism as they
hunted feverishly for a way of eliminating friction without
employing coercion, sure that once they had found it, they could
apply it in a federation of model societies throughout the country.
In a limited sense, perhaps, their plans constituted an escape from
urban complexity and the loneliness of alienation. But beneath the
nostalgia there lay a vital reform impulse and a driving
determination to make American society over through the power of
education.

The immediate causes of the collapse of the communities
ranged from loss of funds and mismanagement to declining interest
and disillusionment with imperfect human material. Behind these
apparent reasons, however, stood the real cause in the person of the
perfectionist self, Margaret Fuller's "mountainous me," that proved
too powerful a disruptive force for even the anti-institutional
institutions it had created. It was the perfectionist ego which
allowed the communitarian reformers to be almost wholly

nonselective in recruiting their membership and to put their trust in the operation of an atomistic general will. Constitution-making and paper bonds, as it turned out, were not enough to unite divine egoists in a satisfactory system for the free expression of the personality. Perfectionist individualism did not make the consociate family. The result by the 1850s was a profound disillusionment with the principle of association which, significantly, coincided with the political crisis over slavery. Adin Ballou, his experiment at Hopedale in shambles, summarized the perfectionist mood of despair when he added that "few people are near enough right in heart, head and habits to live in close social intimacy." Another way would have to be found to carry divine principles into social arrangements, one that took proper account of the individual.

The collapse of the communitarian movement in the 1850s left a vacuum in social reform which was filled by the slavery crisis. At first their failure to consolidate alternative social and educational institutions threw the reformers back on their old perfectionist individualism for support. It was hardly fortuitous that Garrison, Mann, Thoreau, Howe, Parker, Channing, Ripley and Emerson himself responded to John Brown's raid with a defense of the liberated conscience. But slavery, as a denial of freedom and individual responsibility, had to be destroyed by institutional forces which could be made to sustain these values. The antislavery cause during the secession crisis and throughout the Civil War offered reformers an escape from alienation by providing a new identity with the very political institutions which they had so vigorously assailed.

The effects of the Civil War as an intellectual counterrevolution were felt both in a revival of institutions and a renewal of an organic theory of society. The war brought with it a widespread reaction against the seeming sentimentality and illusions of perfectionism. It saw the establishment of new organizations like the Sanitary and the Christian Commissions run on principles of efficiency and professionalism totally alien to perfectionist methods. Accompanying the wartime revival of institutions was a theological reorientation directed by Horace Bushnell and other conservative churchmen whose longstanding opposition to perfectionism seemed justified by the war. The extreme individualism of the ante-bellum reformers was swallowed up in a Northern war effort that made private conscience less important than saving the Union. Some of the abolitionists actually substituted national unity for freedom for the slave as the primary war aim. Those reformers who contributed to the war effort through the Sanitary Commission or the Christian Commission found a new sense of order and efficiency indispensable. Older perfectionists, like Dorothea Dix, unable to adjust to new demands, found their usefulness drastically confined. Young Emersonians returned from combat convinced that professionalism, discipline and subordination, dubious virtues by perfectionist standards, were essential in a healthy society. A new emphasis on leadership and performance was replacing the benevolent amateurism of the perfectionists.

Popular education and ethical agitation continued to hold the post-war stage, but the setting for them had changed. The three principal theorists of social reform in post-war industrial America— Henry George, Henry Demarest Lloyd and Edward Bellamy— denounced class conflict, minimized the importance of purely political reform, and, like their perfectionist precursors, called for moral revolution. The moral revolution which they demanded, however, was not the work of individuals in whom social responsibility developed as a by-product of self-discovery but the ethical revival of an entire society made possible by the natural development of social forces. Their organic view of society required new theories of personality and new concepts of role-playing, definitions which appeared variously in George's law of integration, Lloyd's religion of love, and Bellamy's economy of happiness. And whereas Nemesis in the perfectionist imagination had assumed the shape of personal guilt and estrangement from a pre-established divine order, for the post-war reformers it took on the social dimensions of a terrifying relapse into barbarism. Finally, the attitudes of the reformers toward individualism itself began to change as Darwinism with the aid of a false analogy twisted the prewar doctrine of self-reliance into a weapon against reform. It was to protest against a Darwinian psychology of individual isolation that Lloyd wrote his final chapter of *Wealth Against Commonwealth,* declaring that the regeneration of the individual was only a half-truth and that "the reorganization of the society which he makes and which makes him is the other half."

We can become individual only by submitting to be bound to others. We extend our freedom only by finding new laws to obey. . . . The isolated man is a mere rudiment of an individual. But he who has become citizen, neighbor, friend, brother, son, husband, father, fellow-member, in one is just so many times individualized.

Lloyd's plea for a new individualism could also be read as an obituary for perfectionist romantic reform.

Lawrence B. Goodheart

ABOLITIONISM IN THE SOUTH

According to some accounts, antislavery agitation flourished in the Upper South until a white backlash against Nat Turner's revolt and immediate abolitionism eliminated dissent. In Tennessee, for example, Elihu Embree published *The Emancipator* in 1820, the first newspaper in the United States devoted completely to antislavery. His effort, though heroic, owed more to his penitent Quaker's desire to atone for the sin of slaveholding than to the organizational strength of the Tennessee Manumission Society. Similarly, in 1832, during the last major southern debate over slavery, antislavery delegates in the Virginia legislature failed to pass a resolution condemning slavery in the wake of the Southampton rebellion. In this selection, Lawrence B. Goodheart argues that abolitionists in Tennessee were fragmented and confined to the eastern hill country and that they were ineffectual against the dominant slave power. Professor Goodheart teaches history at the University of Connecticut, Hartford.

According to the antislavery publisher Benjamin Lundy, Tennessee had twenty-five manumission societies with 1,000 members in 1827, more than any other state. John Rankin, the antislavery Presbyterian minister, declared that in his youth "a majority of the people of East Tennessee were abolitionists," and in 1820 Elihu Embree published *The Emancipator,* the first newspaper in the

From Lawrence B. Goodheart, "Tennessee's Antislavery Movement Reconsidered: The Example of Elihu Embree," *Tennessee Historical Quarterly,* 41:3 (Fall 1982), 224–238. Reprinted by permission of the Tennessee Historical Society.

United States solely devoted to the abolition of slavery. Such evidence led some historians to conclude that Tennessee, and much of the Upper South, had a flourishing antislavery movement until 1830. They attributed the rapid decline and virtual disappearance of the southern antislavery movement after 1830 to the growth of white racial solidarity in reaction to the almost simultaneous outbreak of Nat Turner's Rebellion in Southampton County, Virginia, with the emergence of immediate abolitionism in the North. The suggestion is that, without the fanaticism of a Turner or a William Lloyd Garrison, Tennessee might well have dismantled the institution of slavery on its own.

Tennessee, however, did not have an effective or popular antislavery movement. Lundy's citation is an estimate and is probably inflated, given his crusading zeal. Even if the figures are accurate, they are deceptive. The manumission societies in Tennessee were financially destitute and loosely constructed; they met infrequently and were minimally active except for some petitioning of the state legislature. They had little in common with the better organized and more vigorous state affiliates that immediate abolitionists established throughout the North during the 1830s under the aegis of the American Anti-Slavery Society. Antislavery sentiment did exist in Tennessee, but it was confined to the eastern part of the state and decreased rapidly in the area from the Appalachian Mountains and the Cumberland Plateau to the Mississippi River. Even in East Tennessee, John Rankin was overly generous in stating that a majority of whites were abolitionists, unless he counted people who argued that slavery was an evil but a necessary evil. Whatever the region of the state, the consensus among whites was that emancipation constituted a dangerous experiment in race relations.

Anti-abolitionist sentiment increased as the cotton boom spread, and as the proportion of slaves nearly doubled from 13 percent of the total state population in 1800 to 25 percent [by] 1860. Some Tennesseans, including leading abolitionists such as John Rankin and Charles Osborn specifically moved to Ohio and Indiana because the Northwest Ordinance of 1787 had prohibited slavery there. The dominance of an anti-abolitionist persuasion was manifested in the state legislature which enacted statutes that entrenched slavery and restricted the rights of free blacks. As early as 1801, a full two decades before the rise of Turner and Garrison, Tennessee law made the manumission of slaves more difficult at the very time most northern states had enacted gradual abolition laws. During the first decades of the nineteenth century, Tennessee did not offer an environment conducive to a dynamic antislavery movement or to a program of gradual emancipation. The challenge of immediate abolitionism and the fear of slave insurrections after 1830 did result in new statutes, two in 1831 alone, that increased the difficulty of manumission and more closely supervised the activities of both slaves and free blacks. Proslavery partisans did use the occasion to consolidate their opposition to manumission through racist appeals, but the antislavery movement in Tennessee was quite moribund before receiving the *coup de grace*.

The example of Elihu Embree serves to personalize the arduous struggle of abolitionists in Tennessee. During the period 1815 to 1820, Embree was the most active and articulate abolitionist in the state. He was an outstanding representative of the Other South, that small, outspoken group of southerners who consistently challenged the legitimacy of slavery.

Embree's strong stance against slavery had much to do with characteristics that set him apart from his fellow Tennesseans. Born in Washington County on November 11, 1782, and a long-term resident of Jonesborough, Embree lived in the Piedmont of East Tennessee where climate and topography made the practice of slavery less extensive and well established than in the fertile lowlands to the west where slave labor was profitably exploited in growing cotton. In geographic terms alone, Jonesborough was more hospitable to abolitionist sentiment than were Nashville and Memphis. Moreover, Embree was a successful iron manufacturer, not a gentleman planter; he produced nails and hoops, not cotton and tobacco. In the tradition of Adam Smith, he extolled the superior productivity of free labor over slave labor. Although Tennesseans successfully employed slave labor in iron production, Embree rejected industrial slavery as economically and morally wrong. Above all, this East Tennessean industrialist was a pious Quaker who maintained close ties not only with his local brethren but also with the Society of Friends in Philadelphia. It was specifically Embree's reaffirmation of devotion to Quaker ideals, after having lapsed from faith, that provided the motivation and commitment for his abolitionism.

Long-standing Quaker opposition to slavery in Pennsylvania provided Embree with an organization and an ideology with which he could challenge the racial status quo in Tennessee. Thomas Embree, Elihu's father, was a Quaker minister and abolitionist. He migrated from eastern Pennsylvania to East Tennessee some time before 1782 and initiated his son into the antislavery heritage of the Pennsylvania Friends. In 1797, Thomas addressed an open letter "To the Inhabitants of Tennessee" in which he urged the formation of manumission societies and the implementation of gradual emancipation. Although Thomas moved to Ohio about 1800, Elihu remained in Tennessee and later continued his father's Quaker opposition to slavery. Elihu maintained an active correspondence with Joseph M. Paul, a Quaker merchant and abolitionist in Philadelphia. Embree also visited Philadelphia in 1818, received antislavery tracts from Pennsylvania, and borrowed money from Paul.

In addition to Embree's link with the Pennsylvania Friends, he became involved in Quaker-inspired antislavery activities in East Tennessee. In 1815, under the leadership of Charles Osborn, a Quaker minister, eight men founded the Tennessee Society for the Manumission of Slaves at the Lost Creek Friends' Meeting House in Jefferson County. The Tennessee Manumission Society sought the gradual extinction of slavery and argued that the guarantees of the Declaration of Independence and the Constitution applied to blacks as well as whites. The organization required its members to display prominently in their homes the credo that "freedom is the natural right of all men." These abolitionists emphasized the fact that they were concerned American patriots who wished to secure "the blessings of heaven" for the republic by the eradication of slavery. They employed moral suasion, sent petitions to the state legislature, and withheld their votes from candidates who did not support emancipation. Similar societies were formed throughout East Tennessee, and on November 21, 1815, all branches of the Tennessee Manumission Society were consolidated under one constitution at a convention at the Lick Creek Friends' Meeting

House in Greene County. By November 1817, there were a dozen chapters in East Tennessee.

Slavery had been established in Tennessee, while it was a territory under the jurisdiction of North Carolina. After statehood in 1796 the Tennessee legislature enacted a series of laws that continued the practice of chattel slavery based on race. By 1815 the legislature had legitimated the subordination of Afro-Americans through the registering of all free blacks, outlawing certain slave activities, prescribing the type and extent of punishment for blacks, and instituting slave patrols. In addition, the state mandated that slaveholders who desired to manumit slaves must secure the approval of a county court and must post bond in order to protect the county against the expense of supporting indigent, free blacks. State law thus imposed a judicial procedure and financial burden that acted to deter emancipation.

A heightened sense of spiritual regeneration and moral commitment motivated Embree to challenge Tennessee's black codes. After the death of his first wife in 1806 he remarried in 1808 and gained several slaves as part of his second wife's estate. Although he believed slavery to be wrong, he nevertheless became a slaveholder and soon purchased additional slaves. Embree attributed his fall into slaveholding to an attraction for deism, which, in his words, made him "not very scrupulous in adhering to what I believed to be right, as respected much of my moral conduct." With much of his capital invested in about ten slaves, Embree met a note of some $2,000 in November 1809, by selling a family of slaves, all "sound and healthy," to his creditor. With some difficulty, he managed to keep the family of Richard (a hammer man in his iron works), Nancy (Richard's wife and Embree's servant), and four young children (Frank, William, Abigail, and Sophia) together.

In 1813 or 1814, overcome by "shame," Embree repented of his "misconduct" as an owner and seller of slaves. He reaffirmed his patrimony by joining the Quaker meeting and adopting their abolitionist principles. He freed his remaining slaves and provided in his will that the slave Nancy and all of her children, whom he again owned, be emancipated as soon as legally possible according to Tennessee law which prohibited the manumission of minors. He further sought to expiate his guilt in regard to his "faithful servant and slave, black Nancy" by providing that her daughters, Abigail and Sophia, be given forty dollars each for their education, and he pledged part of his estate to the antislavery cause. Although he met the Quaker strictures against slaveholding and now only employed free labor, Tennessee's leading abolitionist legally remained a slaveholder.

The example of Embree illustrates the difficulty of encouraging manumission. The slaveholder not only lost his initial capital investment and the labor power of the slave, but he also had to establish financial surety against his former slave's potential penuriousness. Embree estimated that he lost $4,000 in freeing his slaves. He was only able to emancipate his slaves because his iron manufacturing business could subsidize the cost. As a successful entrepreneur he could fund his abolitionist activities from his own wealth. In contrast, the Tennessee Manumission Society was never able to solicit enough money to sustain itself. . . .

Ironically, Embree's publication of *The Emancipator* further exemplifies the weakness of Tennessee's antislavery movement. *The Emancipator* was a one-man operation. Embree supplied the capital, wrote the articles, did the editing, and distributed the paper himself. Unlike the American Antislavery Society, which subsidized a number of publications, and Garrison's *Liberator,* which affiliated with the Massachusetts Antislavery Society, *The Emancipator* was entirely independent of the Tennessee Manumission Society. The eleventh article of the Society's constitution required that an inspecting committee approve members' publications. Embree found that the eleventh article and the infrequent meetings of the organization made it impossible for him to publish his writings regularly. Embree himself had written the eleventh article in 1815 in the Quaker tradition of consensus decision making, but in April 1820, he urged its revocation. Until that time, he withdrew from membership in the Tennessee Manumission Society in order to publish *The Emancipator* on a monthly basis without violating the constitution. The Society needed its own newspaper that would have disseminated its views, attracted membership, and solicited funds. Similarly, *The Emancipator* needed the structural support and varied resources an organization could provide. Given the already tenuous nature of Tennessee's antislavery movement, the failure of the Tennessee Manumission Society and Embree to coordinate and consolidate their efforts further weakened the state's abolitionist cause.

The publication of *The Emancipator* in Jonesborough from April to October 1820, nevertheless marked a high point in the promulgation of abolitionism in Tennessee, as well as demonstrating Embree's exceptional personal qualities. His newspaper career began with the *Manumission Intelligencer,* which he issued sporadically during 1819. He discontinued the newspaper by December 1819, because the burden of the iron business left him little time for writing. He remained determined to edit a newspaper entirely devoted to abolition, and *The Emancipator* fulfilled that commitment. He wished *The Emancipator* "to advocate the abolition of slavery and to be a repository of tracts on that interesting and important subject." He regularly carried the proceedings and addresses of the Tennessee Manumission Society, with which he remained organizationally separate but ideologically one. Both advocated gradual emancipation and colonization. For a yearly subscription of one dollar, one could read in *The Emancipator* that slavery violated the natural rights of man, destroyed family ties, made southern farms less prosperous than northern ones, and called God's wrath down on America. Embree pledged not to use his paper for any "innovation" regarding antislavery doctrine; he never advocated immediate abolition or the use of violence in overthrowing the slave system.

Embree believed that a strategy of moral suasion, the calculated appeal to the nation's republican and Christian principles, would lead white Tennesseans to embrace abolition. . . . Petitions, memorials, and conscientious voting, Embree believed, would soon undermine support for slavery. He saw *The Emancipator* as the high-water mark of abolition in Tennessee:

> I have no hesitation in believing that less than twenty years ago a man would have been mobbed, and the printing office torn down for printing and publishing any thing like *The Emancipator;* whereas it now meets the approbation of thousands, and is patronized, perhaps, at least equal to any other paper in the state.

Embree could well take pride in his singular accomplishment: circulation of *The Emancipator* was nearly 2,000 people, and he had subscription agents in Philadelphia, Baltimore, and Wilmington. Enthusiasm overwhelmed common sense, however, when he predicted with "mathematical" certainty that by 1840 slavery would be abolished not only in Tennessee but also the "echo will sound from Maine to New Orleans, ALL MEN ARE FREE."

Although Embree did not suffer a fate similar to that of the martyred abolitionist editor, Elijah Lovejoy, proslavery forces in Tennessee did oppose *The Emancipator* and harass its operations. On several occasions Embree complained that the paper was systematically mutilated, undelivered, or misdirected by unsympathetic postal workers. The governors of Georgia, Alabama, North Carolina, and Mississippi to whom Embree sent complimentary copies of *The Emancipator,* returned them and in two cases folded the newspaper in the form of a letter so that Embree would have to pay a higher return postage fee. Governor George Poindexter of Mississippi seized the occasion to denounce the editor as a paid stooge of northern agitators.

Embree's death on December 4, 1820, dramatically disproved the governor's accusation. *The Emancipator* was entirely a one-man operation; when its editor died, so did the newspaper. There was no organization, no staff, and no individual in a position to carry on the financing, writing, and printing of the paper. Embree had managed to run the paper only by neglecting the iron business and that during a critical economic downturn. The Panic of 1819 dried up available cash, commerce was depressed, and banks suspended routine transactions. In Embree's words, business was "unpleasant, precarious, unprofitable." After his brother's death, Elijah revealed the fact that Elihu had run the family business into considerable debt in order to fund his abolitionist crusade.

Embree's devotion to abolitionism also involved grave consequences for his family. On July 10, 1820, his second wife died, after a long, debilitating illness, leaving him a widower with nine children. He raised them as devout Quakers and hoped to send some of his seven daughters to a Friends' school in Philadelphia. His concern for his children's religious instruction and his commitment to abolitionism reflected his desire to atone for his prior lapse of faith. Shortly after his wife's death, he lamented, "A man never fully survives his missteps." As a family friend observed, Embree believed that blacks had been "treated so unjustly, if laying down his own life would gain them their rights, that he would do it instantly." Indeed, the intensity of his individual antislavery efforts may have contributed to his premature death at age thirty-eight after a brief illness. Not only had he neglected the iron business for abolitionism, but the invoice of his personal property taken after his death was so meager as to suggest that he had similarly sacrificed his own private possessions. There were no funds left to send any of his daughters to Philadelphia; relatives and friends aided his orphaned children, some of whom were quite young.

The Emancipator was defunct. Thomas, the father, returned to Tennessee from Ohio with the intent to publish the remaining five issues of the annual subscription but illness and lack of money forced the abandonment of the project without the completion of a single issue. Thomas urged his fellow Quaker, Benjamin Lundy, who published the *Genius of Universal Emancipation* in Mount Pleasant, Ohio, to continue Elihu's work at Jonesborough, using his son's printing tools and subscription list. Lundy moved, however, to Greeneville, Tennessee, in 1822, and his subsequent publication of the *Genius of Universal Emancipation* was not connected with Elihu's *Emancipator* except that they both used the same printing equipment. After two years, Lundy moved to Baltimore, an area he thought more conducive to abolitionism.

National and state newspapers eulogized Elihu Embree and mourned his death. "The loss of this truly good man is indeed a calamity to our country," an East Tennessean obituary commented. Embree's abolitionist activities were indeed praiseworthy but they belied the reality that the organized antislavery movement in Tennessee was always extremely weak. Even *The Emancipator* reflected the lack of solidarity in the antislavery movement. Instead of a collective effort, the paper was the product of one individual's dedicated labor. Embree's wealth derived from manufacturing allowed him to fund the newspaper independently, and the personal quest to atone for his own slaveholding gave him the emotional endurance to persevere alone.

The Tennessee Manumission Society nominally existed until the early 1830s. There was a final petition campaign against slavery in 1834 but it again failed to alter the laws. After 1830 the reaction against immediate abolitionism and the fear of slave insurrection resulted in more repressive black codes; in 1835 leading Nashvilleans had Amos Dresser, an Ohio abolitionist, publicly whipped for the possession of antislavery tracts; and, in the same year, the citizens of Athens, Tennessee, burned abolitionist literature confiscated from the post office. If Embree had lived, he would have found it prudent to move to a more congenial environment, as had his father, Osborn, Rankin, and Lundy. Isolated in the hill country of East Tennessee, the state's abolitionists were never able to mount an effective challenge to the hegemony proslavery forces had over state power.

Bertram Wyatt-Brown

CONSCIENCE AND CAREER

Most abolitionists were evangelicals, but most evangelicals were not abolitionists. Indeed, most antebellum Protestants and their churches staunchly opposed the early immediatists and, more likely than not, endorsed the American Colonization Society. No formula can readily explain why some evangelicals embraced abolitionism while others did not. Nonetheless, Bertram Wyatt-Brown, Milbauer Professor at the University of Florida, clarifies the complexity of motivation by comparing foreign missionaries with abolitionists. He shows that both shared three crucial stages of moral development which were oriented about the internalization of conscience, the experience of conversion, and the choice of career. Though missionaries and abolitionists shared similar psychological predispositions, the timing of their commitment appears most important. The emergence of slavery as the premier domestic issue after 1830 attracted pious young men and women who a decade or two earlier might well have turned to missionary work. In brief, saving heathen abroad lost some of its spiritual appeal in comparison to the new crusade against the sin of slavery at home.

From "Conscience and Career, Missionaries and Abolitionists Compared" from Christine Bolt and Seymour Drescher, *Antislavery, Religion, and Reform: Essays in Memory of Roger Anstey*, Folkestone. Reproduced with the permission of the Copyright Holder.

How easy it is to find fault, . . . with the foreign mission movement. It was an evangelical enterprise as romantic and adventuresome as abolitionism, with which it had closer ties than we have ordinarily thought. Like the teetotalers, prison and asylum advocates, tractarians, and other apostles of repression, the missionaries can be called narrow busybodies who imposed a shabby culture on helpless aborigines and opened the doors for imperialism. Thus, the antislavery humanitarians were allegedly breaking chains while others in far-off places were forging them. Nonetheless, both groups stood for the same things—especially the end of bondage, whether it was suttee or the southern auction block. Because of their doctrinal and social similarities, the missionaries for emancipation and for pagan conversion are worth comparing.

First, neither group was very subtle or circumspect about what it wanted: universal moral discipline and restraint on the one hand and personal autonomy and freedom from ancient sins and passion on the other. Foreign missionaries sought to elevate "heathen" women and other dependents so appallingly maltreated. The abolitionists wished to uplift the "bleeding" slave. Foreign missionaries were probably more condescending toward the natives peoples than abolitionists were in regard to American slaves, but both groups had their egalitarian saints and their racially haughty sinners. Second, the foreign missionaries and emancipationists agreed that literacy should not be used as a means for rulers, priests, and their allies to hold others in the bondage of ignorance. Education, these Christian Yankees insisted, should be available to all, the ordinary people of other continents as well as the blacks at home. Both kinds of reformers hoped to create new Yankeedoms in places of darkness, firmly convinced that their common culture could be exported. Third, from a theological point of view, foreign missionaries and antislavery advocates championed the Second Coming and were naïve enough to think the goals achievable in a matter of years. Despite these similarities, political perspectives of the causes and their leaders have muddled our understanding of who the abolitionists and the foreign missionaries were.

The most important single factor uniting missionary with abolitionist was that most unwelcome New England export: the evangelical conscience. To that purpose, we should start as life does itself—at the beginning. Three crucial areas of moral development were significant: the instilling and growth of conscience in the child; the adolescent problems of religious belief and intellectual ambition; and the stresses of choosing the career in benevolence, when political differentiation seemed to emerge.

The evangelical style of child-raising was an alternative to an older means that relied on shame, open humiliation, and physical pain to curb presumed depravity. The latter doctrine has been associated with Calvinism, but actually the idea that children were all but incorrigible and required stern handling should not be identified too narrowly with any sectarian or theological position. In any case, an enlightened approach to child-rearing had developed by 1800, and those practicing it chiefly belonged to evangelical faiths. The new religious sensibility reflected a concern with the atonement of Christ more than the illimitable sovereignty of God, affection as well as obedience in human relations, the inner life more than the outward appearance, and personal integrity over demands for conformity. . . .

Shame was a device that employed overt exposure to ridicule. In contrast, conscience internalized moral precepts. It also repressed unacceptable impulses and channeled aggressions toward objectives thought socially and personally useful. To accomplish these ends, parents, under religious guidance, learned that explaining the purposes of their decisions and pointing out the consequences for wrongdoing impressed the child. Stirring feelings of anxiety was a part of the disciplinary process, but it contrasted with the uncalculating, inconsistent, reactive style of the past: abrupt demands for total obedience, a heavy beating or ear-boxing, or an unwarranted indulgence to soothe or compensate the child. . . .

Abolitionists, along with other evangelical inheritors, were raised within this framework. To be sure, there were variations, exceptions, and degrees of laxity, strictness, and success. But a similarity of aims, a roughly common understanding of moral boundaries, and a willingness to give attention to the child had evolved. Freedom and discipline, parents and advisors agreed, had to be held in equilibrium. To evangelicals' distress, old ethical standards that revered male honor and glorified male self-indulgences prevailed and even found wide dissemination. Quite correctly, they saw the dangers of temptation that a fast-changing democracy offered their young. Establishing good habits had to begin early. . . .

At the heart of evangelical child-rearing was the role of the mother. The authority for disciplining and making decisions about the children had formerly been in the father's hands. By the end of the American Revolutionary era, the mother had gained the means and the ideology for devoting full attention to child-rearing. Previously she had been preoccupied with such soul-wearying, endless drudgeries as weaving cloth and making soap. But the developing economy provided her not only such comforts as factory textiles but also the time for making plans about child-rearing. Instead of just hastily reacting to the crises of the moment, mothers could concentrate upon becoming professional child-raisers. It was a calling that every evangelical writer in the new Republic assured them was both divinely ordained and patriotic. Through pious clubs called "maternal associations," Sunday school and church sewing societies, and other newly developed organizations, northern mothers, whatever their station, could leave the house to enjoy the exchange of child-rearing ideas and gossip. They could also display an active piety which would instruct their own children. Benevolence, all agreed, should be taught by example as well as by precept. . . .

This self-conscious, inventive role for mothers encouraged the selection of one child or perhaps two for extraordinary attention. Quite early on, the youngster learned that they must begin plans for the future, even though their careers were years away. Kenneth Keniston, the Yale psychologist, has called this emphasis upon the child's moral and career success the creation of "a sense of specialness." In traditional fashion, boys heard about pious and benevolent work for men. . . . More unexpectedly, evangelical mothers sometimes urged daughters to think of serving Jesus as missionary wives. That career combined domesticity with romantic adventure and service to others. . . .

Nonreformers and nonabolitionists—ordinary churchgoers— were raised in the same fashion. The difference was that some children took the lessons of conscience and the burden of inner doubt with unusual seriousness. They were not necessarily prissy or submissive. As a rule, however, the future well-doer was more aware of moral structures than were other youngsters. Theodore Parker, later a leading Garrisonian, offered an insight into his own upbringing. Once, at age five, he nearly killed a turtle. Racing home, he breathlessly asked his mother Hannah why he had not struck it. She exclaimed, " 'Some men call it conscience, but I prefer to call it the voice of God in the soul of man. If you listen and obey it, then it will speak clearer and clearer . . . but if you turn a deaf ear or disobey, then it will fade out . . . and leave you all in the dark and without a guide.' " Parker concluded the recollection, "No event in my life has made so deep an impression upon me."

The tale was not so important as the tendency it represented. Likewise in abolitionist biographies and other sources, there were frequent references to parental kindnesses and sympathies toward a local black, a fugitive slave, or some other victim of prejudice and ridicule. The most impressive example was the early history of Samuel Joseph May, a leading Garrisonian abolitionist and Unitarian clergyman in later years. When he was four, May saw his brother Edward fall from a chair during their barnyard play. A splintered post fatally punctured the six-year-old under the arm. Too young to understand the reality of death, Samuel refused to leave Edward. Stern Calvinists though his Boston parents were, they did not interfere when, as May recalled, "I kissed his cold cheeks and lips, pulled open his eyelids, begged him to speak to me, and cried myself to sleep because he would not." He remained in the room with the body that night until he fell asleep and his parents could at last take him away. After the burial, an uncle took him to the family vault and opened a coffin in which lay another dead sibling. He wanted to show Samuel the corruption of the flesh while assuring the boy that Edward and all the others there entombed enjoyed in heaven an immortality of spirit. For several nights thereafter, Samuel dreamed that Edward came to lie with him as he had in life, declaring that he was happy in his new celestial home. Samuel's fears and grief at last subsided. Two years later, May himself had a severe accident. He fell in the road and struck his head on a rock. When he awoke, he found himself in his house with "a large black woman" looking down at him. She had picked him up and brought him to the house. Agonized with worry and busy washing away the blood, his mother did not even thank the black Samaritan, as it were. The stranger had disappeared, and despite many searches the family never saw her again. No doubt May's later interest in emancipation had much to do with the two incidents of death, guilt, shock, and rescue. But more remarkable was the sensitivity of May's family. Had they not complied with the child's importunings to sleep with his brother, May could well have carried a grim burden of unconscious guilt for his own survival. Instead, their approach to his pain, as much as the black's good deed, prepared him for his eventual antislavery commitment. That reform was dedicated to the memories of his own good fortune and his brother's fate, but it transcended them both. . . .

Even when a mother was affectionate, her nurturing could be offset by the severity of the father. . . . John Greenleaf Whittier vividly recalled seventy years afterward how he had quailed before a weekly trip with his taciturn, unloving father. The Quaker farmer of Massachusetts and his five-year-old son had to climb a steep hill at the top of which a screeching gander always waited. As they approached, the boy grew terrified that the goose would peck at him with a fury to match the squawk. The resentments Whittier felt toward his domineering father prevented him from expressing his fear. He never asked his father for help or sympathy on this or any other occasion. Encouragement would not have been forthcoming. The fretful patriarch, then fifty-three, had already been complaining of his son's unmanly sensitivities and later ridiculed his writing poetry. In Whittier's case, the burden of special holiness and the equally intense agony of introspection, reticence, and suppressed rages, as Perry Miller has noted, lasted nearly a lifetime. Henry C. Wright, the reformer and abolitionist whom Thoreau had found so oppressively intimate, had a similarly taciturn, aloof father, who was a carpenter in western New York. Having lost his mother, whose memory the son romanticized, Henry Wright felt, his perceptive biographer says, as if his throat, in the hands of Seth, his father, "was endlessly vulnerable to Abraham's knife." It would be wrong to assume that the experiences of Whittier and Wright were representative of what happened to others in the abolition cause. Conscience-stricken, even intensely anxious, such figures as these were anything but narcissists, nor were they timid conformists. Their concern for others, not their disappointments with themselves, was to give meaning to their lives.

However much paternal repressiveness affected Whittier, one must be careful to judge each reformer's background separately rather than assume Oedipal longings and resentments as the impetus toward reform. Certainly such tortured struggles were evident in the relationship of Theodore Dwight Weld, a leading abolitionist, and the Reverend Ludovicus Weld, his formidable and unpleasable father. According to Robert Abzug, Weld was torn between a love of order and godly restraint and a sometimes uncontrollable impulse toward freedom and romantic self-fulfillment. Nevertheless, early experiences and their lingering effects varied too much for Freudian generalizations. Childhood hardships and fears came often in many shapes. For instance, William Lloyd Garrison's father, Abijah, a lowly sailor, deserted Fanny Lloyd Garrison, a woman of enormous piety—and girth—leaving her in dire straits. Certainly Abijah bore no resemblance at all to Weld's father. Instead, it was Garrison's mother who dominated her son and warned him constantly of the sins of drink and irresponsibility, a lesson the boy learned well and applied in his later career. . . .

All these examples of familial distress early in childhood could be replicated a thousand times in the lives of people quite outside the antislavery orbit. The illustrations are intriguing, for they are most suggestive about the effects of family troubles upon the way individuals developed. In no sense were they predictive of future careers. They were perhaps a factor in predisposing the child toward some kind of dream of self-sacrifice. Certainly, intense anxieties helped to shape personalities. It should be remembered, however, that Wendell Phillips, the Grimké sisters, the Tappans, William Jay, Elizur Wright, and many others had fathers both loving and successful, supportive and yet strict. Elizur Wright, Jr., one of the early immediatists from the Western Reserve in Ohio, was not unusual in recalling the affectionate nature of his father. After his father, a pious churchman, had died in 1845, has son wrote that Elizur Wright, Sr., "bade me climb the height whereon he stood, and eased its steepness with the kindest smile." Like so many others in that generation of mission-minded New Englanders, the son felt the pressures to conform, to listen to conscience, *and* to find his own way to achievement. No single family problem or childhood distress, no extraordinarily intense antagonism between father and son or between mother and daughter, distinguished all abolitionists from others of similar upbringing and environment. . . .

As one could anticipate, these children, singled out for specifically moral purposes, were often intellectually gifted. Parents encouraged study and reading, for two reasons aside from concern for knowledge. First, reading banked the fires of youthful exuberance and passions; second, being a solitary activity, reading was one way to shield the child from bad influences. In those days churchgoing children could scarcely avoid the usual hazings, but an avid thirst to learn became a form of segregation. Antislavery leaders Theodore Parker, Theodore Weld, and Elijah Lovejoy were all remarkable for their early signs of intellectuality. . . .

Likewise, women in both causes showed uncommon abilities. To be sure, they were not supposed to compete with boys for academic honors or to prepare themselves for independent careers. Nonetheless, many female reform leaders and foreign missionaries showed strong intellects in their formative years. The first women into the foreign mission field, usually as wives of leaders, were also gifted, sometimes even in such unfeminine subjects as mathematics and science. Yet, the road for women was difficult. Even in evangelical households, scholarly competition was meant for boys only. When Elizabeth Cady Stanton, for instance, won academic honors, her father Daniel Cady, grieving for lost sons, exclaimed, "'Ah, you should have been a boy.'" Although he did not wish her to deviate from the submissive role assigned women, he was much less severe with her than was her mother, who deplored Elizabeth's natural intellectual and athletic aggressiveness. . . .

During the higher grades of school, the most significant event in the future abolitionist's or missionary's life was the conversion experience. It was an occasion to be cherished for a lifetime. It marked the beginning not just of manhood but of Christian commitment and a godly career (of some as yet unspecified kind). Some went through the ordeal in conventional fashion, especially when a revival was under way. Then everybody joined in the excitement. Those with special feelings of fervor or declension did not cross the spiritual divide so smoothly. Sensitive souls by inclination, they suffered acutely. . . .

What matters, however, is that the totality of factors pressed the missionaries and abolitionists toward their destiny. *Few men and women of the mission and antislavery causes failed to experience the conversion rite, or came from religiously indifferent households, or grew up with habits quite out of keeping with the evangelical conscience.* Thus, abolitionist Elijah Lovejoy's wanderings were not peculiar to him. Both inside and outside the antislavery circle, others acted similarly, but seldom with such excessive zeal. He walked all the way from Waterville, Maine, to New York City, eating almost nothing. He suffered from headaches, a result of the strains of his soul as much as the rigorous inadequacy of his diet. His pilgrimage was a penance for not professing faith. The transgressions worried his parents and pious brothers for many years. Selfhood, he appeared to say, could not be forced upon him. Eventually, though, he found relief and regeneration. The delay, if not the depth of agony, was one with which any evangelical could sympathize.

Women abolitionists and reformers also had to suffer at this critical juncture. Raised in an unusually high-minded and pious household in South Carolina, Sarah Grimké at thirteen offered herself as godmother for her baby sister Angelina, though she did not feel wholly adequate to the responsibility. As historian Gerda Lerner says, "She was deeply in earnest in her pledge and, years later, remembered the profound emotions which caused her to shut herself in her room after the [baptismal] ceremony and pray to God to make her worthy of the task she had assumed." Susan B. Anthony, another who fought for slaves' and women's rights, mourned over her "hardened heart" and yearned that she might grow "more and more refined until nothing shall remain but perfect purity.". . .

The first crisis of spiritual identity, usually begun and resolved in the teens, did not generally lead to a career decision. One reason was that by the 1820s, New England's sons (and daughters, to some extent) had a variety of options, some requiring additional education. To await further maturing, to provide an emotional resting spot, some of those with a sense of special mission became, for instance, temporary teachers or served as colporteurs for a mission enterprise. . . . Ordinarily there was a second crisis of the spirit in the twenties. Though similar to the first in its gyrations of feeling, the second episode concerned career much more than personal identity. The form was the familiar conviction of sin, emptiness, alienation from God, but the question uppermost was, what am I to do in life? . . . Just as parents had inculcated conscience, so ministers, church elders, and college faculties guided the young person toward a benevolent career during the period between parental authority and adult autonomy. Religious societies and presses churned out hundred of sermons, old works and new, all of which not only demanded belief in a saving Lord but also the witness and sacrifice of spreading the gospel. . . .

Always self-conscious, but forever restless, the products of the evangelical mode of development were well equipped to meet the clearly marked-out goals of New England piety, love, self-reliance, and hatred of sin. They sought the uplift of communities allegedly lacking in those virtues. Certainly there was an almost self-absorbed preoccupation involved, but it was in keeping with the early channelings of conscience and aggression imparted during childhood. "By my influence, with God to direct and bless, Africa may be made to arise from her degradation and shake herself from her chains," mused a seminarian and future abolitionist, Amos A. Phelps. This was American "individualism" at a zenith: the single-handed conversion of a continent. Whatever the cause was to be—missions, antislavery, or some other—the evangelical brought to bear a storehouse of energy. Its source lay in his or her dynamic tensions between love and deprivation, humility and pride, joy and depression, hope and despair. Only in this way can one explain the confidence and determination behind the nineteenth-century reformer and missionary. . . .

In summary, what the missionary and the abolitionist shared often included a common upbringing under strict, orthodox, evangelical parents; a conversion experience of rich personal meaning; a sense of special destiny, the product of compulsive application to study; a later subjection to pious, admired superiors and elder friends who stirred religious ambitions; and finally a decision to seek a risk-taking course for the sake of God and personal fulfillment. The sole distinction, aside from the obvious institutional differences between the causes, was in the matter of politics. One should not, however, overstress the discrepancy. During the 1840s and 1850s, the American Missionary Association, created by abolitionists, served the ambitions of politically minded young evangelicals in the foreign and domestic fields. These pious missionaries were keenly aware of domestic moral troubles, a contrast with the views of their missionary predecessors in the period from 1810 to 1830.

Quite clearly, political interest could well be combined with foreign mission work. The difference between the abolitionist and the foreign missionary might really have reflected only a question of timing and opportunity rather than psychological predisposition. In the years following the War of 1812, political matters were momentarily quiescent. Religious revivals and concerns, on the other hand, seized the public imagination. The brightest and most committed idealists of that era naturally turned to the grand adventure of foreign and domestic missions. The years from 1810 to 1830 were the high-water mark in foreign mission work. After that, however, it gradually became less a leap into the inspiring unknown. Though outstanding leaders—accomplished linguists, teachers, and physicians—continued to enter the mission field in the decades thereafter, the cause was becoming routine and, for some, even unpromising. Guilt for *not* joining fellow seminarians in the pledge to Christianize the heathen became easier to bear. At the same time, in the 1830s and 1840s, attention turned to domestic matters, especially antislavery. . . . The eventual result was that the abolitionist became increasingly man-centered. It was the nature of the cause itself. The foreign missionary, on the other hand, remained God-centered.

In any case, the two causes of foreign missions and antislavery had the same sources of inspiration. Their advocates sought to bring order and healing freedom to those they believed prisoners of slavery, chaos, and blind ignorance. In this effort, discipline and freedom, conscience and career, hope and anxiety were uniquely blended for one generation.

Lawrence J. Friedman

LEWIS TAPPAN'S CIRCLE

Lawrence J. Friedman, a historian at Bowling Green State University in Ohio, coined the phrase "gregarious saints" to refer to disparate tendencies among the first generation of immediate abolitionists. Although intensely concerned with obeying the solitary call of private conscience, they also valued the pious fellowship of their comrades. Friedman identified three major affinity groups of gregarious saints who blended self with community: Garrisonians in Boston, advocating non-resistance; a clique of political abolitionists in central New York, organized around the wealthy landowner Gerrit Smith; and church-oriented abolitionists, led by philanthropist Lewis Tappan in New York City. In this selection, Friedman argues that Tappan's circle of evangelicals was neither "conservative" nor "radical." As soldiers of the Lord, they assailed the proslavery bias in the Protestant denominations, but they also faulted the nonresistants and political abolitionists for abandoning an ecclesiastical approach. Above all, they were devoted Christians who tenaciously believed that the reformation of the churches was the surest path to emancipation.

In his 1933 study, *The Antislavery Impulse,* Gilbert Hobbs Barnes demonstrated for the first time that not all antebellum American abolitionists were "radical" Garrisonians. There were also "conservative" abolitionists like Theodore Weld and James Birney who drew upon reformist aspects of the Finneyite Great Revivals of the 1820s and 1830s. Their aim was not social revolution; instead, they simply sought to make the nation's religious and political institutions unambiguously antislavery. In more recent years, scholars have noted that all "conservative" abolitionists were not the same. Although all "conservatives" were sympathetic with the Liberty Party during the 1840s, a number remained more concerned with reforming evangelical Protestant denominations than building an antislavery political movement. Bertram Wyatt-Brown's 1969 biography, *Lewis Tappan and the Evangelical War*

From Lawrence J. Friedman, "Confidence and Pertinacity in Evangelical Abolitionism: Lewis Tappan's Circle," *American Quarterly,* 31 (1979), 81–106. Reprinted by the permission of the author and The Johns Hopkins University Press.

against Slavery, has been the most sophisticated effort at characterizing these evangelical church-oriented "conservatives." Wyatt-Brown's achievements were two-fold. Differing with Barnes, he demonstrated that evangelical "conservatives" did not restrict their activities to the Midwest; various groups also operated throughout the Northeast. Second, Wyatt-Brown showed how "the evangelicals of [Lewis] Tappan's immediate circle" formed the most influential group of church-centered abolitionists through their dominant role on the American and Foreign Anti-Slavery Society, the American Missionary Association, and the New York City Abolition Society, as well as through their funding of Oberlin and Oneida Institutes—the principal training grounds for evangelical antislavery clergy. But because Wyatt-Brown's focus was biographical, he was unable to provide detailed analysis of the values and interactions within Tappan's immediate circle.

The purpose of this essay is to pick up where Wyatt-Brown left off by exploring this key group of evangelical "conservatives" collectively, and thus to refine even further our understanding of "conservative" church-centered abolitionism. Tappan's circle of evangelical abolitionists included William Jay, Amos A. Phelps, Joshua Leavitt, Simeon Smith Jocelyn, Theodore Dwight Weld, and George Whipple. George Barrell Cheever worked closely if irregularly with the group, while Arthur Tappan withdrew from antislavery activism in the early 1840s. After 1839 it is even difficult to classify Weld as a devoted participant in many group ventures. The finances of these men differed sharply, ranging from the prosperous Tappans and Jay to the chronically impoverished Leavitt, Whipple, and Weld. However, almost all came from old Federalist and Congregationalist families of the Northeast (especially New England). Jay, son of the first Chief Justice, was the group's only Episcopalian. They were all influenced, in varying degrees, by Nathaniel Taylor's modifications of Edwardsean Calvinism along lines of greater human self-sufficiency. In revivalist leader Charles Grandison Finney, they saw the practical expression of Taylor's doctrines. All were active in at least some of the benevolent reform crusades that flourished in the years after the War of 1812, particularly temperance, Bible and tract distribution, and Sabbatarianism. Except for Jay, all worked closely with Congregational and New School Presbyterian churches. Leavitt and

Jocelyn started out as Congregational ministers while Phelps and Cheever continued as Congregationalists of the cloth through their entire careers. All had at least some experience with religious and antislavery journalism. The Tappans were merchants, Jocelyn had worked as an engraver, and Jay was a lawyer and judge. Whipple, Jocelyn, and Weld had had teaching experience. All group members had been cordial with William Lloyd Garrison until the late 1830s. Several moved about, but New York City was usually the center for group activities. To be sure, Phelps usually resided in Boston and Whipple lived in Oberlin until 1847. But the Tappans, Jocelyn, and Cheever resided in New York most of their lives. Jay and Weld dwelled nearby.

Lewis Tappan's immediate circle was therefore bound to the Finneyite revivalist and benevolent reform impulse and was associated with Finneyite elements of Congregationalism and Presbyterianism, particularly in New York City church circles. In addition, all members were urbane and cosmopolitan, and all had at least some experience in religious and antislavery journalism. One may dispute the premise that they constituted a group that worked closely and cooperatively. The independent qualities of all save perhaps Jocelyn might be cited. Weld's contempt for meetings, ceremonies, and organizational activity in general might also be noted. The hostility that arose between Lewis Tappan and Joshua Leavitt over the propriety of political antislavery can be cited. So can the divergent views these men held on the propriety of female officers in the American Anti-Slavery Society. But despite differences over antislavery specifics, they generally enjoyed a smooth and effective working relationship.

One reason for the cohesiveness of the group was that members had accumulated positive experiences associating with each other early in their reform careers. These experiences forged mutual trust and tolerance. Lewis Tappan's very conversion to immediatist abolition, for instance, was due to brother Arthur's "reliable" example, Weld's friendly proddings, and one of Jocelyn's early antislavery orations. Cheever received similar emotional support in the mid-1830s from Lewis Tappan, Weld, and Leavitt as he came to embrace immediatism. Jocelyn could not have undertaken his first major civil rights venture—a black college in New Haven—without the financial and personal support of the

Tappan brothers. Based on successful experience with the Tappans in temperance reform and religious tract distribution in the late 1820s, Leavitt joined with them and with Weld in 1831 to organize the Society for Promoting Manual Labor in Literary Institutions. Whipple and Weld were drawn together as students in Lane Seminary in 1834 when the trustees tried to suppress their abolitionist activities. Leavitt was visiting Lewis Tappan's home in 1834 when an anti-abolition mob attacked the dwelling, and he maintained that this incident initiated his comradeship with the Tappans.

By 1839 mutual interests and frequent contacts among the group had reached the point where they automatically drew together during moments of crisis or in times of social isolation. When Lewis Tappan learned of the arrest of Mendi Africans who had revolted on the slave ship Amistad, for example, he immediately called on Jocelyn and Leavitt, and then on others in his circle, to help him form a defense committee. While in Washington, D.C. in 1842 to campaign against the Congressional Gag Rule and to make Whig legislators more militantly antislavery, Leavitt and Weld spent every evening together reading, writing, and preparing for the next day. On Sundays they often worshipped together at a Negro church. Positive experiences of the past also drew Jocelyn, Whipple, and Lewis Tappan together in the mid-1840s as the principal functionaries of the American Missionary Association's central office. There they mastered the details of each other's lives; each became very dependent on the others and in moments of distress, regularly called on each other.

Working with one another in evangelical reform activity for several decades, the Tappan group developed mutual trusts and dependencies. By 1837 Weld felt that of all antislavery editors, only Leavitt could be depended upon for editorials with a "personal hold" upon "a multitude of persons." Lewis Tappan relied upon Jay for legal guidance on antislavery ventures and felt that Jay's judgment on "reform proprieties" was almost impeccable. Jay was equally trusting of Lewis: "You and I rarely differ in our anti-slavery opinions, & when we do [differ] have too much confidence in each other to think it necessary to conceal our offences." Trusting language characterized much of the correspondence between group members.

The contacts, cooperative ventures, and trusts within the Tappan circle deepened to the point where members articulated strong attachments for one another. Thoughts of group intimacies and friendships caused emotions to seep through the formal and disciplined exteriors of these early Victorian men. In 1869 Whipple reflected on decades of cooperation with his colleagues, particularly with Jocelyn and Lewis Tappan. He found that participation in an "associated capacity" with "the noblest of co-workers" was what made a life of reform worthwhile. On his deathbed, Jay wanted to see and to be remembered by all of the men in the group. All group participants grieved when Jay departed. Whenever his children became seriously ill, Lewis Tappan eagerly sought out those in his circle, particularly Weld and Jocelyn, for sympathy and comfort. By the same token, Tappan was solicitous about the dire economic condition and later the failing health of Phelps. When Phelps died in 1847, Tappan promised to help out the wife and children of "A dear, dear friend."

Jay, Phelps, Leavitt, Jocelyn, Weld, Whipple, and periodically Cheever and Arthur Tappan, were also able to work harmoniously because of Lewis Tappan's managerial skills. To be sure, Lewis Tappan never evoked the near mystical exaltations and fervor from the group that William Lloyd Garrison commanded of his Boston clique of antislavery supporters. Weld once pointed out that Leavitt struck a deeper level of emotion than Tappan ever did within the group. However, Leavitt was often blunt and tactless. In the 1840s he championed the Liberty Party over the church as the proper forum for antislavery operations with a fervor that disenchanted most of the others. He was no group leader. Nor was Weld, who, according to his modern biographers, was neither an unqualified evangelical abolitionist nor deeply involved in evangelical organizational activity. Moreover, what leadership capacities he had were never exhibited within the circle. Henry C. Wright, the Garrisonian, once referred to Phelps as group leader, and Phelps did command the group's trust. However, he usually lived in Boston whereas activities centered in New York City. Moreover, during the 1840s Phelps was too ill to coordinate the functions of any group. Although he died in 1847, the group continued with no apparent interruption.

Although Lewis Tappan was less exciting than Leavitt, Weld,

or Phelps, there is no doubt that he was central administrator-coordinator of most of the projects that the group undertook. During the middle and late 1830s, he was probably the dominant figure on the New York-based Executive Committee of the American Anti-Slavery Society and the Committee's chief spokesman for evangelical abolitionism. He was the primary organizer of the rival American and Foreign Anti-Slavery Society in 1840 and kept it in existence almost single-handedly until 1853. Tappan was also the central policymaker of the American Missionary Association during its early years and assured that the organization remained a voice for evangelical abolitionism. Finally, he was connected with the publication of a dozen newspapers and periodicals in the course of his life; in this capacity he was often able to influence the writings of his friends. Rather than an inspiring leader like Garrison, Tappan was a competent administrator, capable of an enormous work load, and dedicated to improving the efficiency of evangelical reform operations. His comrades respected his capacity to lead them not through innovations or charisma but through administration and coordination.

One basic element in Lewis Tappan's style was the capacity to share policymaking. As long as Phelps was alive, Tappan called upon him to help formulate and implement policies. Indeed, he was probably as much influenced by Phelps as Phelps was affected by him. He consulted with Jay as frequently, and his trust and respect for Jay deepened as time passed. Moreover, as Tappan admitted to James Birney, he was willing to set aside his personal preferences if those he trusted disagreed with him on a particular issue. Tappan's skill was also facilitated by his tolerant and gentle manner. For example, his reprimands of Jocelyn for tardiness in preparing an A.M.A. annual report and of Cheever for corporate membership in the "proslavery" American Board of Commissioners for Foreign Missions were mild, indirect, and cordial. He counseled "sweetness of disposition" and "good temper & discretion" as the way through which group members could be most effective. Finally, Tappan's generosity with his funds helped him to continue over decades as the central administrator of group affairs. All except the wealthy Jay received Tappan's financial aid during times of need. He funded much of Phelps' foreign travel, provided support for Leavitt so that he could go to Washington to work with Congressional antislavery insurgents, helped Jocelyn's son out of a financial jam, and provided economic counsel and assistance to Weld.

Through certain common social characteristics, personal bonds, and effective leadership, then, a small but united Tappanite group carried on and surmounted internal disagreements with no great difficulty. From the 1830s to the Civil War, while group members were active in antislavery and other evangelical reform ventures, they retained an inner calm and confidence which also helped to promote stable group operations. . . .

Although they assumed leadership roles in the American Peace Society and the American Missionary Association while they crusaded for Christian self-help values, members of the Tappan group saw their abolitionism inextricably tied to the nation's churches. Since churches and church-linked missionary societies were the agencies that promoted morality on earth, slavery would fall once parishioners and clergy recognized the sins of bondage. Only Weld was skeptical about lodging the entire antislavery cause in the churches.

Between 1837 and 1848 this strategy was challenged on two fronts—first by growing anti-church, anti-institutional espousals by several leading Garrisonians and then by Liberty Party men who sought to move beyond the churches into a brand of abolitionism that focused upon parties and electoral politics. In the face of both challenges, the Tappan men deepened their commitment to church antislavery. And they dealt with both not by desperate and dogmatic rear-guard "conservative" positions but by calmly trusting that God would set things right and by renewing their faith in the values of Christian self-help. The Tappan circle met its major internal abolitionist challenges just as it had dealt with the peace and missionary society issues. The period of crises concluded in the late 1840s with all of them committed to directing their evangelical crusade through the churches. Adversity invoked a two-provision belief system that held them to their established antislavery course.

Save for Weld, who refused to be "poisoned" by the "fierce feud" with the Garrisonians, all of the Tappan men participated in the group's first major conflict with other abolitionists. Most often, they attacked Garrison and his followers for trying to attach "extraneous issues" to the functions of the American Anti-Slavery Society. In June of 1839 Lewis Tappan stated the matter succinctly in his diary:

> Garrison and others have grown lukewarm on the anti-slavery subject & have loaded the cause with their no-government—woman's rights—non-resistant &c until we have got among breakers. Garrison told me 2 1/2 years ago that there were subjects he considered paramount to the anti-slavery cause, to which he meant to devote his attention chiefly. It is a sad mistake to make it instrumental in carrying on other matters.

On other occasions, Lewis publicly reiterated this charge. The Garrisonians' endorsement of women's rights, no-government, anti-Sabbatarianism, and other issues signified that they were abandoning or at least slackening their efforts on behalf of the slave. This was intolerable. Just as he criticized the benevolent societies and churches for antislavery vacillation, Lewis attacked the Garrisonians. Phelps, Jay, Leavitt, Arthur Tappan, and even Weld voiced these same apprehensions. Most disliked several of the new causes the Garrisonians were embracing, but they felt that the multi-issue Garrisonian approach was most dangerous because it waivered in the crusade against slavery. After all, slavery was the institution most antithetical to God's will and to Christian self-help virtues. All energies had to be channeled toward its elimination. . . .

At base, when the Tappan men attacked Garrisonianism, they were defending the order-rendering God they held dear. The apparent Garrisonian rejection of such a deity assaulted their theologies, their psychologies, and their ideals—the sources of their antislavery activism. Thus, the traditional characterization of the Tappanite-Garrisonian dispute of 1837–1840—a contest between "conservative" and "radical" abolitionists—does not take Lewis Tappan's men on their own terms. The Tappanites did not see themselves as "conservatives" struggling to derail a more militant form of antislavery activism. Rather, they saw themselves as the abolitionists who remained committed to God, to the Bible, to the churches, and to the emancipation of black bondsmen; their Garrisonian opposition had lost sight of both Christianity and the slave. Garrisonians were not viewed as "radicals" so much as infidels who had abandoned antislavery.

During these confrontations with the Garrisonians, Tappan's circle never questioned their commitment to church-centered abolitionism. If anything, the apparent Garrisonian infidelity caused them to cling even more ardently to their values. They emerged from the battles having formed the American and Foreign Anti-Slavery Society—an organization directed by Lewis Tappan and committed to evangelical churches as the directive arm for antislavery missions. Between early 1839 and late 1843 they faced their second major internal abolitionist challenge—from men like James Birney, Alvan Stewart, and their own Joshua Leavitt—to deemphasize evangelical church-centered abolitionism for a political party approach to antislavery. The episode concluded with most of the Tappan men temporarily supporting the antislavery Liberty Party while continuing to rely on churches and church-linked missionary work.

To assess this third party controversy, it is important to recognize that in 1839 Tappan's circle participated in the same sorts of political activities as the founders of the Liberty Party—church prayer for better rulers, circulation of antislavery petitions, and interrogation of political candidates. Although only Leavitt took part in the Party's formation, most Tappanites voted for Liberty candidates whenever they appeared on the ballot. Thus, most Tappan circle men differed from party founders in only one particular—the relevance of more than ballot box support for Liberty candidates. Only Leavitt was willing to participate in Party operations and to publicly support Party platforms and candidates. The Tappan brothers, Phelps, Jay, Jocelyn, Whipple, Weld, and Cheever was not initially Liberty Party publicists. . . .

Although the Liberty Party was of short duration, the Tappan group's flirtation with political party activism was even shorter. In 1849 Whipple noted why he could not vote much less campaign for Free Soil candidates: "I do not wish to justify voting for men who do not regard the claims of God and the rights of suffering humanity." To vote Free Soil was "to sin against God and incur his displeasure." "My heart was never in the Liberty Party instrument," Weld claimed. Anybody who had entered politics "weakened his whole moral spontaneity by the contact and appliances of a political career." "To what lengths will party men go!" Lewis Tappan proclaimed. Ever since the formation of the Liberty Party, "attention to the political duties of Anti-Slavery men have prevented due attention to the moral & religious aspects of the cause." For Cheever, any political party was deficient in "heartfelt, eternal hostility against slavery as sin, as reprobated and forbidden of God. . . ." Jay, too, was apprehensive about ever again engaging in party politics, for none of the antebellum parties had the moral decency to embrace the principles of "the Washington School."

In 1847 Garrison's friend Edmund Quincy privately referred to the Tappan circle as "The religionists, who set up the [Liberty] party as a cover for their own retreat back to the world. . . ." Quincy was far off the mark. Aside from Leavitt, Tappan circle participants were apprehensive about the Liberty Party as an abandonment of church-centered abolitionism and only campaigned for Liberty men by 1843 when convinced otherwise. Moreover, as the Liberty party began to merge with discontented Democrats and Whigs, these apprehensions were rekindled, and Leavitt could not effectively draw them into the new Free Soil coalition. Whereas Leavitt himself may have been "retreating" from the old Tappan brand of antislavery, the rest of the Tappan men held firm. Contrary to both Quincy and several modern historians, they were never really "absorbed" by the Liberty or Free Soil movements much less by the Republican Party. By the end of the 1840s they stood for the same beliefs and values that characterized them at the end of the 1830s—supreme confidence in an order-rendering God and the Christian self-made man, with church-missionary abolitionism the best way to universalize God's will.

Neither Garrisonians nor Liberty Party challenges, then, had shaken the Tappan men from what they had always held most dear. It is as erroneous to call them "conservatives" for temporarily supporting the Liberty Party as it is to accord them this label for disputing with the Garrisonians. In their own eyes, the men of Lewis Tappan's immediate circle were neither "conservatives" nor "radicals" but soldiers of the Lord and missionaries for Christian self-help virtues. The world might change about them—the benevolent societies might vacillate on the slavery issue, the Garrisonians might embrace ungodly doctrines, and colleagues like Leavitt might lose sight of God's directives through party politics—but they held firm to the assumptions and values that they had always embraced, forever confident that God would set things right.

Thus the Tappanites remained relatively unchanged by people and circumstances about them. They knew what they wanted and they were always confident that God would order the world in accord with their values. They saw no need to cater to the sinful ways of other mortals. They constructed a psychological buffer that made them persistent in their chosen course while almost immune to outward events. Sometimes this buffer made them bold and innovative reformers, as when they assumed leadership roles and formulated ideas for the unpopular antebellum peace movement or when they threatened to destroy the benevolent society network by forming the rival American Missionary Association. But at other times, as in their dealing with the Garrisonians and the Liberty Party, they defended their church-centered abolitionism and were unresponsive to changes within the broader antislavery movement. The Tappan circle's confidence in an order-rendering God and in Christian self-help therefore promoted insensitivity and rigidity, but it also made for pertinacity and innovation.

Lewis Perry

ABOLITIONISM AND ANARCHY

Disillusioned with endemic antiabolitionism in American society, William Lloyd Garrison and his circle formed the New England Non-Resistance Society in 1838. A type of Christian anarchism or antinomianism, nonresistance condemned all physical coercion because it interposed a human agency between the individual and the deity. The brutality of slavery and war were merely extreme examples of illegitimate force on which the institutions of church and state were based. Nonresistants demanded the end of human government and its replacement by the millennial kingdom of God. Their belief in human perfectibility assumed that a harmonious and just society would ensue as redeemed individuals placed themselves directly under divine authority. As a "come-outer," Garrison urged the sanctified to cease participation

From Lewis Perry, *Radical Abolitionism: Anarchy and the Government of God in Antislavery Thought* (Ithaca: Cornell University Press, 1973), 298–301. Reprinted by permission of the author.

in both politics and the church, a view that outraged evangelical abolitionists and supporters of the Liberty party. In this selection, Lewis Perry, Andrew Jackson Professor at Vanderbilt University, explains the tensions inherent in nonresistant thought.

. . . abolitionists tended toward anarchism because of their opposition in principle to slavery. . . . When abolitionists took an anarchistic position they tended to argue in this form: whoever does not go all the way with us is, in effect, in league with slavery. Slavery became a paradigm of human authority, of any state in which the standing of one man with respect to another was secured by force. The only consistent antislavery, then, was anarchism. Even in this abstract analysis, however, there appeared one important source of ambivalence. In one sense slavery was wrong because it was the government of man by force, but in another sense it was wrong because it was a government of insufficient force. That is, government by force did not work. It did not keep the peace. It led to the multiplying use of force, not to anarchism in the good sense of harmonious self-government but to anarchy in the bad sense of lawlessness and pandemonium.

This ambivalence becomes more understandable when we study the New England Non-Resistance Society. Originating within an antiwar movement, this society insisted on the Christian doctrine that violence should never be resisted with violence. Just as anarchism alone consistently opposed slavery, it was said that no opposition to war would be consistent and uncompromising unless it repudiated all manifestations of force. It does not seem strange that it was the abolitionists, of all the opponents of war, who seceded into anarchism. But the origins of nonresistance were slightly more complicated. In the background were millenarian and perfectionist strains of thought within revivalism that had been best articulated by John Humphrey Noyes. When they broke out from the narrowness of the peace movement, abolitionists were responding to the perfectionist claim that any human government was a challenge to the commanding authority of God. To end war and slavery—to end anarchy in the bad sense of lawlessness—the guiding strategy was to abolish human government and to institute the government of God. The precept of nonviolence had been construed narrowly by the Quakers as they moderated the ecstasies of the Reformation; now that same precept had led others back into its radical past.

In a word, nonresistance was millennial. The millennium, variously as it may be conceived in detail, is the government of God. It has also been useful to call nonresistance antinomian in order to indicate that its view of the progress of the millennium precluded support for intermediary authorities between God and the individual moral agent. Attacks on governors, soldiers, and religious officials were not extraneous to the attack on slaveholding, as Garrison's critics charged, once it was felt that the true objective was the millennium. All human authorities were extraneous to that exalted period to come.

The most important source of ambivalence, then, was this antinomian emphasis on the pre-emptive sovereignty of God. Until the time of the millennium, it could reasonably be asked, would not the renunciation of human authorities contribute to that very lawlessness to which the millennium was theoretically opposed? There were a few coherent answers to this question—particularly in Adin Ballou's faith that the means of introducing the millennium must not contradict the end for which they were supposedly designed. But the point is that such answers were few and were disregarded. For the most part, nonresistant abolitionism sought to be both a harbinger of the millennium and a secular reform movement. When come-outers and no-organizationists pursued the antinomian argument to what appear to be quite logical conclusions, the leading Garrisonians were appalled. In the ensuing struggle the heart of New England abolitionism was rent, but the errors of the no-organizationists could not be explained. Faced with the possibility that a temporal reform movement, however dedicated to ending slavery in the South, might well be a violation of God's authority over individuals, the Garrisonians assailed those who brought the possibility to light. At this point a potential contradiction was made real and irremediable. Thereafter abolitionists were less certain of their attitude toward human authorities, and the millennium came to seem less imminent.

In the 1850s the anarchistic denunciation of force was silenced. . . . The silencing was due less to influences outside the movement than to internal contradictions—the very contradictions just summarized. In the first place, a secular reform concerned with slavery had to assign some role to the slave. From a millennial perspective it might have been possible to argue that perfect love would vanquish the masters, that an immediate assertion of liberation would loose little tactical violence, or that in this vale of woes chattel slavery was no worse than any other bondage. But these viewpoints were not accessible to a secular reform movement: the problem was that whites owned Negroes, not that man was alienated from his true ruler. When nonresistance turned to the subject of the rights and duties of the slave, it doffed any pretense of millenarianism. It exonerated the slave of guilt in possible acts of violence, and ultimately it exhorted him to violence thus excused.

Second, and more significantly, the sovereignty of God implied the right of private judgment on the part of every individual moral agent. And this right entailed responsibility to act out whatever was privately judged to be true and holy. The right of private judgment theoretically did not extend to goals (these were still tacitly assumed to be millennial, insofar as anything made sense any more); it extended only to the choice of alternative means. Nevertheless, the general goal of ending force became less important than the specific goal of ending one manifestation of force: slavery. In terms of the antislavery struggle this meant that nonresistants could beseech others to take up arms in the cause of the slave. They could finally solicit the government to obey its best lights and to end slavery by force, which had once seemed a contradiction in terms. Now antislavery entered into an awkward, contradictory partnership in that very work. . . .

Comments on other movements, distinct from nonresistance but related to antislavery, serve to fill out the argument. Come-outerism and no-organizationism clarified the paradox of antinomian abolitionism: law and order could be established only by terminating human efforts to enforce these virtues. Political abolitionism, on the other hand, feared the antinomianism of the Garrisonians. But the fact that it was political did not mean that it compromised principles or believed in governmental coercion as the remedy for sin. On the contrary, it agreed with the Garrisonians that an effective end to slavery had to be voluntary. It prized independent political action chiefly as a method of registering individual moral commitments. Independent parties and local congregations were, in other words, vanguards of the millennium, exerting moral influence but eschewing secular compulsions. Political abolitionists, then, yearned to build some institutions in the vastness between man and the divine sovereign. But although they feared antinomianism, they drew many of the same conclusions from evangelicalism as did the Garrisonians.

. . . anarchism seemed a complete failure in its own time. The Civil War was taken to be hideous proof that nonresistance was out of phase with reality. God waged the Civil War; maybe thereafter would come a dispensation when men could bring on the millennium by ending war and government as well as slavery. Of course that time did not come. By the century's end, Tolstoy was frustrated to discover that scarcely an American remembered that any abolitionists had been anarchists.

Louis S. Gerteis

MORALITY AND UTILITY

The abolitionist argument for the moral autonomy of the individual was complemented by a similar economic rationale. The fusion of what Louis S. Gerteis, a historian at the University of Missouri, St. Louis, calls morality and utility represented the growing acceptance in the North of a liberal bourgeois agenda. It was felt that slavery degraded the work ethic and retarded social progress. Abolitionists celebrated the virtues of free labor, with its emphasis on personal freedom in the capitalist marketplace. Thus free labor negated slavery, and, as English utilitarians put it, would secure "the greatest good for the greatest number," the ideal of nineteenth-century middle-class democracy. In liberal thought, economic freedom meant self-ownership, the ability to exchange labor for wages. Economic freedom also stressed the harmony of capital and labor and the values of private ownership of wealth, social mobility, and personal initiative. Although abolitionists sought to liberate slave labor, they overlooked the plight of "wage slaves"—northern operatives— buffeted by low pay, long hours, and little control over the workplace.

Reprinted from *Morality and Utility in Antislavery Reform*, by Louis S. Gerteis. Copyright © 1987 by the University of North Carolina Press. Used by permission of the author and publisher.

From the early 1830s through the abolition of slavery during the Civil War, American antislavery reformers pressed their demands for freedom with a sense of urgency that contrasted sharply with older projections of slavery's gradual decline. In this new mood, the practice of slaveholding collided violently and, it seemed, unavoidably with American republican values. With remarkable suddenness, and with a sense of exhilaration that prompted determined and even heroic action, reformers shed the traditional restraints of gradualism to demand the immediate abolition of slavery as a clear and present danger to the republic.

Bolstered by the successes of British abolitionists, American antislavery reformers drew particular strength from the altruism of their cause. If, in the broadest sense, their agitations must be understood in relationship to what David Brion Davis describes as "the triumphant hegemony of a capitalist world view and particularly to capitalist views of labor," their cause also challenged capitalist complicity in slavery and disrupted profitable economic ties between slave masters and allied merchants and manufacturers. Antislavery reformers had no discernible immediate economic advantages to gain from slavery's demise. There is every reason to accept the sincerity of their concern with the plight of the slave and the despotism of slavery. As Eric Foner observes, "It will not do to defang the abolitionist crusade: it was indeed a radical impulse, challenging fundamental aspects of American life."

Demands for immediate abolition during the mid-nineteenth century marked a departure from past practices but not a rejection of traditional antislavery convictions. Nineteenth-century reformers continued to insist, in the manner of Adam Smith and the American revolutionary generation, that slavery could not survive in a modern society. But the urgency of their attack on slavery reflected conditions and perceptions unique to their era. Looking on slavery through the newly mounted lens of utilitarian political economy, reformers joined with John Stuart Mill in England and Henry C. Carey in America in identifying objective forces of progress that were sweeping slavery aside and leaving the South's "peculiar institution" a relic of a barbarous past—if it managed to survive at all. The reformers' sense of urgency, then, expressed a new confidence in their own historical destiny and responsibility.

These self-conscious agents of progress attacked slavery at its economic, moral, legal, and political base. By questioning the right of southern masters to hold their laborers as property, antislavery reformers rejected the traditional accommodations that associated slavery with the developing capitalist world view. The clash of interests sparked by antislavery reform and the expectations the reformers raised for the postemancipation South and nation form the central themes of this study.

Two terms . . . require definition and discussion at the outset. The first, "utilitarianism," refers to the doctrines of political economy and the related ethical theories most directly associated with Mill and with his mentor Jeremy Bentham. My interest is not with the theory of utilitarianism but with its American applications. In any case, the term's meaning remains the same: that men act and interact in society to maximize their individual pleasure and that the greatest happiness for the greatest number in the long run (that is, the highest social good) will be achieved in the pursuit of individual self-interest. As a theory of political economy, utilitarianism offered an objective guide to moral action which challenged traditional notions of Christian philanthropy at the same time that it projected the perfectibility of human society. By the 1850s, utilitarianism subsumed older and narrower laissez-faire doctrines and became incorporated into the optimistic language of political liberalism, which invoked state powers to promote individual autonomy and the liberty to pursue material gain. It was in the aggressive pursuit of a liberal state, moreover, that the compatibility of slavery with American republican values came directly into question. In the antebellum rhetoric of antislavery reform, the fight against slavery pitted right against wrong, civilization against barbarism, liberty against despotism. The inexorable advance of freedom defined the rise and fall of nations. As a slaveholding nation, America could not advance although the path of potential progress remained clear. The Declaration of Independence proclaimed the equality of man, and antislavery reformers took it to be their historical task to advance this standard of liberty, extending the principle of equality to the enslaved laborers of the South. At the very least, utilitarianism required nominal freedom and equality for all.

The second term that requires definition and discussion refers to the social basis of utilitarianism and political liberalism—that is, to a developing middle class. The formation, influence, and social function of an American middle class continues to be a matter of historical investigation and debate. In the familiar consensus analysis of the 1940s and 1950s, the absence of a landed aristocracy in America and the wide distribution of property in the form of land made the vast majority of Americans independent producers and middle class in temperament. Political liberalism, bland but serene, seemed to suffuse the nation's public life. More recent concerns with the social transformation of early industrial society (and particularly with the emergence of an American working class) depict a more turbulent reality. The world of the independent producer, particularly the artisan, was in turmoil during the first half of the nineteenth century. Prosperous master craftsmen emerged as employers of wage labor, and journeymen artisans (once relatively young as a group and hopeful of becoming independent producers in their own right) grew increasingly dependent as wage earners. Out of this social flux emerged a middle class, distinguished by property and social values from the workers they employed and separated by their modest wealth and uncertain social standing from the established elites whose economic and political power they challenged.

The relationship between antislavery reform and developing middle-class concerns is itself a topic of historiographical debate. Neither the antislavery struggle nor the multitude of moral reforms that swept across the expanding North during the 1830s and 1840s necessarily defined the interests of a new middle class of manufacturers and entrepreneurs. But in both cases—in the increasingly secular concerns of antislavery reform and in the perfectionist enthusiasms of evangelical Protestantism—reform appealed strongly to elements of the middle class and expressed itself in terms of middle-class interests and values. To speak of the antislavery movement as middle class in character is not to reduce the antislavery impulse to a pursuit of narrow economic interests. Nor does such a discussion require that antislavery reform receive universal or exclusive support from the middle class. Certainly one would expect the most fervent and in social terms the most radical expressions of antislavery sentiment (the "come-outers," for example) to raise resentments even in the absence of diverging interests. Indeed, abolitionism's capacity to outrage public opinion remains its most striking characteristic. Nevertheless, using the reformers' perceptions of their own interests and goals both as a point of departure and of reference, the social concerns of antislavery reform come into focus: middle-class reformers had good reason to champion individual autonomy and self-control through temperance and other moral reforms, and they had good reason as well to grow increasingly hostile toward an expanding slaveholding interest.

The relationship between antislavery reform and antebellum workingmen's movements underlies any discussion of the social significance of the slavery issue in the industrializing North. The capacity of some antislavery reformers to identify the oppression of "wage slavery" has suggested to some historians the existence of an antislavery tradition distinct from the free labor and free market concerns of middle-class reformers. Certainly the victory of Union forces over the rebellious South during the Civil War involved more than middle-class hostility to the slave power. Nor did a patriotic response to the Union call to arms necessarily subordinate workingmen's interests and goals to a middle-class pursuit of nationalism. Nevertheless, reliable evidence of an antislavery tradition independent of middle-class goals has yet to be presented. In this regard, it might prove useful to distinguish the war from antislavery reform and to recognize that the war—not antislavery reform—produced a collective experience (on both sides of the contest) that may have added new strength to postwar challenges to the consolidation of industrial capitalism.

At a time when the historical profession held abolitionists in very low esteem, Richard Hofstadter observed that "[Wendell] Phillips was in some ways more sophisticated than those who condemn him." When Phillips spoke of the advancing influence of the northern middle class, he perceived himself to be allied with an emerging social order resting on equitable relations between capital and labor. He and reformers generally may have deceived themselves into thinking that they were central to the new industrial order, but their understanding of the process of historical change required neither self-deception nor cynicism. In the postwar era, it is true, utilitarian principles led most antislavery reformers toward the stern liberal orthodoxy of Edwin L. Godkin, or to the somewhat more ambivalent Mugwump style of Charles Francis Adams. But utilitarianism also sustained visions of social harmony and human perfection which the dominant drift toward Social Darwinism could not entirely contain. These visions led some reformers (Phillips among them) to champion cooperativist and socialist remedies in the manner of the English Fabians to the class divisions of industrial America. Whatever individual scholars make of the character and purpose of antislavery reform, the reformers' capacity to question the foundations of social order, to oppose established interests, and (when necessary) to resist the authority of the state continue to merit study.

It is an unavoidable aspect of antislavery reform that the modern concept of race emerged as the antislavery struggle advanced. To be sure, antislavery reformers labored to overturn discriminatory laws and restrictions as they resisted slavery itself. In this struggle, they denounced all barriers of class and caste as the tyranny of past ages and identified progress in human affairs with the advancement of individual liberty and equality. Moreover, the antislavery concern with autonomous moral uplift paralleled and in some ways encouraged the self-help arguments of northern black leaders during the antebellum decades. But antislavery reform also advanced comfortably with developing doctrines of white superiority and expressions of the white man's burden among the dark-skinned peoples of the world. When Frederick Douglass concluded his autobiography in 1892, the concepts of race and of American destiny could not be separated. Douglass looked back over the era of antislavery reform with pride in the accomplishments of his active life, accomplishments which "servitude, persecution, false friends, desertion, and depreciation" could not expunge.

Douglass understood that the antislavery cause in America did not wholly embrace the black struggle for freedom, although the destruction of slavery certainly altered the conditions of that struggle in the North as well as in the South. In the 1850s, when Douglass observed that immigrant laborers displaced northern blacks from traditional employments as servants and menial laborers, he witnessed the liberating and limiting character of the utilitarian view of progress. "The old employments . . . are gradually, and it may be inevitably, passing into other hands," Douglass noted. It was not entirely bad that they did. "White men are becoming house servants, cooks and stewards, common laborers and flunkies to our gentry," he continued. The increasing numbers of the white laboring poor "proved that if we cannot rise to the whites, the whites can fall to us." This, too, reflected the meaning of progress in antislavery reform.

In the distinct but interrelated spheres of political economy, law, mass politics, and moral reform, a middle-class pursuit of free labor and free market relations transformed the republican values of the Revolution. Free labor republicanism, in turn, sustained reformers in their opposition to slavery as a system of despotic class relations resting on the absorption of labor by capital. Conversely, freedom and democracy required the independence and harmony of capital and labor. In political terms, the advancement of antislavery reform demanded a substantial unity among the "producing classes" of the North, a unity of employer and wage earner which reformers hoped to forge in mass politics. Accordingly, although antislavery reformers identified over-whelmingly with the anti-Jackson sentiments of the Whig party—and with the Yankee Calvinist values Whiggery championed—the triumph of their reforms depended upon a political victory over the defenders of the traditional order, including the defenders of traditional political accommodations of slaveholding interests. Antislavery reform never entirely shed its New England Whig bias, but reformers identified sufficiently with mass politics to drive the old elite from the field or, at least, to force it to forge accommodations with the new managers of party politics. In the moral sphere, reformers combined the postmillennialist and perfectionist doctrines of the Second Great Awakening with middle-class drives to release individual energies and to promote social order and productive labor through self-restraint. Secular and spiritual visions of progress merged as morality and utility outlined a single course of human endeavor.

Jean Fagan Yellin

SOJOURNER TRUTH AND HARRIET JACOBS

In this selection about two African-American women, Jean Fagan Yellin, Distinguished Professor at Pace University, analyzes the tension between racial and gender issues in abolitionism. Various depictions of the emblem of a kneeling female slave (see the frontispiece from *The Abolitionists*) imploring "Am I Not a Woman and a Sister?" were widely disseminated as antislavery mementos. With the Grimké sisters' challenge to patriarchy during their sensational speaking tour of 1837, discourse about the definition of womanhood and sisterhood as well as the meaning of self-emancipation and slave emancipation became prominent among antislavery feminists. As white women identified their own subordination metaphorically with slave women, they confused the distinction between literal bondage and their own plight. Professor Yellin discusses the effort of Sojourner Truth and Harriet Jacobs to authenticate the condition of African-American women.

Enslaved women were the cause. Their presence had jolted free women, forcing them to examine the condition of slaves in relation to their own situation, to take seriously the double inquiry, Am I Not a Woman and a Sister? As free black and white antislavery feminists used the discourse deriving from antislavery emblems to explore issues of race and gender as well as of condition, they recreated themselves as liberated Women and Sisters. Concurrently, black ex-slaves were also using these emblems as they created their own structures of true womanhood and inscribed themselves the subjects of their own discourse.

Not surprisingly, determining the authenticity of the speeches and writings of ex-slaves presents problems. Because Sojourner Truth was illiterate, her words have come down to us—if at all—as transcribed by others. The varied ways that her language has been rendered suggest the enormous influence of her transcribers in shaping the texts we have today. Harriet Jacobs's sensational slave

From Jean Fagan Yellin, *Women and Sister: The Antislavery Feminists in American Culture* (New Haven, Conn.: Yale University Press, 1989), 77–96. Reprinted by permission of Yale University Press.

narrative, *Incidents in the Life of a Slave Girl: Written by Herself,* which was accepted in her day as her own work, became in our century a questionable text assigned to L. Maria Child, who was named on the title page as editor. Only now that Jacobs has been established as the author of *Incidents* can it be examined seriously as the narrative of a black woman who had been held in slavery. Sojourner Truth's speeches—however mutilated in transcription— and Harriet Jacobs's book—however shaped to appeal to her target audience of free white women—bring us as close as we can come to the words of African American women held in slavery.

Angelina Grimké's central insight was that the antislavery emblem figured the condition of free women. She believed that in a patriarchal America where slavery was institutionalized, all women were in a sense slaves. Grimké had focused on her own shock of recognition, on her sense that she was figuratively an enslaved and enchained victim. L. Maria Child had written fiction identifying a powerless female victim as representative of all slaves. But the enchained oppressed women who inhabit the sentences of Sojourner Truth and Harriet Jacobs were seen differently.

Sojourner Truth and Harriet Jacobs understood the difference between being legally chattel and legally free. Excluded from the patriarchal definition of true womanhood because of their race and their condition, they approached this definition not as a category of nature, but as a cultural construct that functioned to justify their oppression. Their life experience in a system that denied their very humanity enabled them to penetrate the myths obscuring the political implications of the patriarchal ideology of true womanhood. They developed a definitive critique of that ideology that constituted a unique challenge to it.

The life experience of Jacobs and Truth also enabled them to unmask the racial implications of alternative models of the true woman as Woman and Sister. Free antislavery feminists found it liberating to relate the antislavery emblem to their own condition. Angelina Grimké, applying the terms of this emblem to her own life, had been able to recognize and acknowledge her oppression and to begin her struggle for self-emancipation. The abolitionist discourse encoded in the antislavery emblems structured the free antislavery feminists' discourse and dramatized their oppression as women in a patriarchal society.

But by conflating the oppression of women who were enslaved and the oppression of women who were free, by collapsing the literal enslavement of (conventionally) black women into the figurative enslavement that they felt they suffered, white free antislavery feminists obscured the crucial differences between the experience of women who were held as chattel and their own experience. Confusion resulted. On one hand, the free women misinterpreted the situation of slave women, and on the other, they misinterpreted their own: they were not, after all, literally in irons. Their appropriation of the emblems of antislavery discourse masked the very real differences between the oppression of black slave women and free white women in America—and the very real differences in the character of the struggle against these oppressions.

The speeches and writings of black women who had been held in slavery testify that they did not, however, confuse the experience of free women with their experience as female slaves. Nor did they confuse the free women's struggle for self-liberation from a metaphorical slavery with their own struggle for self-liberation from slavery. For them, the discourse of antislavery feminism became not liberating but confining when it colored the self-liberated Woman and Sister white and reassigned the role of the passive victim, which the patriarchy traditionally had reserved for white women, to women who were black.

Transforming themselves from the objects of the discourse of others into the subjects of their own discourse, these women who had been held in slavery refined the antislavery feminists' definitions of womanhood. Jacobs, like Grimké, recounts in her writings the initial shock of awareness that came when she realized that she was a slave. Instead of expending energy on surprise and focusing on her recognition of powerlessness, however, she centers on ways to counter her oppression. Where Grimké had attempted to devise a new definition of womanhood to express her needs and goals, Sojourner Truth uses her everyday experience as the norm. These former slaves present themselves not as powerless, but as powerful; not as passive, but as active. Characterizing their situation as a war, they present themselves engaged in struggles for freedom, and they successfully invent new identities and new communities, emerging as self-liberated liberating women, tried by fire. On paper, they create what Henry David Thoreau had demanded of every writer: "a simple and sincere account of their own lives." Inscribing themselves as black women who have survived through struggle, they use the first person to discuss their female humanity, their womanhood, and to articulate their efforts to expand female siblingship into a political sisterhood of black and white women. They urge this sisterhood to follow their lead into the public arena to oppose slavery, racism, and patriarchy. Recasting the free antislavery feminists' motto Am I Not a Woman and a Sister? into an even more potent text, these female survivors of slavery compress its formal double inquiries into a vernacular question that functions as an assertion: "A'n't I a woman?"

In her *Narrative,* Sojourner Truth repeatedly addresses the issue of selfhood in her discussions of names. Born Isabella, a slave, she was legally property. In 1827, the year before emancipation in New York, she escaped from her owner, found refuge with the nearby Van Wageners, and assumed their name. As Isabella Van Wagener, she initiated the legal proceedings that rescued her son from Alabama, supported her youngest children working as a domestic in New York City, bore public witness as a mystic on the streets of Manhattan, and joined a religious commune. Then in 1843, the Spirit commanded her to travel and preach, and she announced herself Sojourner Truth.

Her speech at the 1851 Akron Women's Rights Convention articulates her awareness of her power. In a noisy atmosphere in which hostile white ministers, who were trying to take over the meeting, spouted biblical strictures against females participating in public life, a number of the convention participants opposed giving a black woman the floor. They feared being identified "with abolition and niggers." The chair had to plead for silence as Sojourner Truth stood, tall and black, to deliver a speech that redefined womanhood. Her subject was power: the lack of power that men ascribe to womankind and the presence of her own power and the power of all women.

With a manner her audience called magical, she countered the ideas of the white male representatives of the clerical establishment: "That man over there says that women need to be helped into carriages, and lifted over ditches, and to have the best place everywhere. . . . Nobody ever helps me into carriages, or over mud puddles, or gives me any best place!" Instead, she proposed a redefinition of womanhood based on her own experience. In doing so, she transformed the formal antislavery inquiry circling the abolitionist emblem into a revolutionary chorus: "A'n't I a woman?"

Standing before the white audience of fearful white women and hostile white men, she commanded, "Look at me!" Directing their eyes—not to the breasts and hips with which the patriarchy defines womanhood—but to her arm, she defined herself as an oppressed producer: "I have ploughed, and planted, and gathered into barns, and no man could head me! And a'n't I a woman? I could work as much and eat as much as a man—when I could get it—and bear de lash as well! And a'n't I a woman?" She next characterized herself as an oppressed reproducer, a mother whose children had been used as commodities: "I have borne thirteen children, and seen them most all sold off to slavery." And she defined herself as God's creature, as a suffering Christian: "when I cried out with my mother's grief, none but Jesus heard me! And a'n't I a woman?". . .

Sojourner Truth articulated her autonomy in all major ways but one. Conspicuously absent from her speeches, her *Narrative,* and her *Book of Life* is any discussion of sexuality. Forbidden to female speakers and writers in America throughout the nineteenth century and most of the twentieth, this tabooed subject is central to Harriet Jacobs's pseudonymous slave narrative, *Incidents in the Life of a Slave Girl.*

Incidents counters racist endorsements of slavery, and racist condemnations of it, by presenting Linda Brent, a narrator who assumes responsibility for her own actions. In and through her first-person discourse, Jacobs's pseudonymous narrator demonstrates that she is one of God's moral creatures. She focuses on her struggle against her oppression as a sexual object and as a mother. Like Sojourner Truth, Jacobs's narrator was excluded from traditional definitions of true womanhood because of her color— which, to racist white Americans, identified her as less than human, as a female whose enslaved condition was a natural consequence of her inferior race. Like other female slaves identified as her mother's daughter and forbidden the legal status of wife, Brent was required to obey neither a father nor a husband, but an owner.

In childhood the light-skinned Linda Brent, whose mother died young, was gently treated by her first mistress whose mother had died young, was taught to read and sew; later, in her second mistress's household, she was raised among the children in the family. But she was a slave nonetheless, and she quickly learned, "that which commands admiration in the white woman only hastens the degradation of the female slave." During adolescence, Linda is denied the treatment of a true woman. Instead of her sexual "purity" being insisted upon, she is made to understand that her virginity will not be tolerated.

Her lecherous middle-aged master, whom she calls Dr. Flint, forbids her to marry the young black man she loves and demands that she instead submit to him. His jealous wife, instead of rushing to her defense, treats her as a sexual rival. Linda Brent feels threatened and isolated. Too embarrassed to confide in her grandmother (a freed woman who was her major emotional support), desperate to deny her master's claim that she must comply with his demands, and determined to exert some control over her sexual experience, she tries to utilize the sexuality her master covets as a defense against him. Brent involves herself in a secret liaison with a young white neighbor. When her master orders her to move into the house where she is to live as his concubine, she announces that she is pregnant. As she anticipated, Dr. Flint feels cheated of her virginity and no longer wants her.

Pregnancy outside wedlock presented a serious problem in nineteenth-century American life and fiction. Its treatment in *Incidents,* however, is unusual. Popularly, the cult of motherhood enshrined the relationship of a mother and child only if the mother was first a wife; in popular fiction, pregnant girls found their way to the riverbank and drowned themselves and their unborn babes. Although Linda Brent presents her sexual history as a confession, she counters this condemnation of unwed motherhood: initially she views her pregnancy not as a problem but as a solution, thinking it will save her from further sexual harassment by her master. Later, by repeatedly characterizing her baby as a "tie to life," she implicitly criticizes the notion that extramarital sex and illegitimacy involve sin and death. Brent writes that she lives for her beloved children and that her determined efforts to win them freedom and a home give her existence meaning. . . .

Confessing her sexual history, Linda Brent defines her reader as a woman who endorses patriarchal patterns and believes that females must not engage in sex outside of marriage. Pleading with this reader not to judge her too harshly, the narrator plays the role of a supplicant and, apologizing for her transgressions from this standard, apparently endorses it.

> Pity me, and pardon me, O virtuous reader! You never knew what it is to be a slave; to be entirely unprotected by law or custom; to have the laws reduce you to the condition of a chattel, entirely subject to the will of another. You never exhausted your ingenuity in avoiding the snares, and eluding the power of a hated tyrant; you never shuddered at the sound of his footsteps, and trembled within hearing of his voice.

Yet by repeating "you never," the narrator also invites a reading that emphasizes the reader's ignorance of the circumstances and minimizes her fitness as a judge. In accord with this, at the conclusion of the passage, instead of awaiting her reader's verdict Linda Brent assumes a judge's role and pronounces judgment on herself. "I know I did wrong. No one can feel it more sensibly than I do. The painful and humiliating memory will haunt me to my dying day."

Later, Linda Brent negates any possible resemblance between herself and the figure of a passive victim by recalling that her motivations for establishing the sexual liaison with the father of her children were "revenge . . . calculations of interest . . . flattered vanity . . . and sincere gratitude for kindness." Further, she says that "I knew nothing would enrage Dr. Flint so much as to know that I favored another; and it was something to triumph over my tyrant even in that small way." Brent assumes full responsibility for transgressing patriarchal standards and involving herself in the longstanding relationship that produced her two children. "I will not try to screen myself behind the plea of compulsion from a master; for it was not so. Neither can I plead ignorance or thoughtlessness. . . . I knew what I did, and I did it with deliberate calculation."

Then, in what appears to be a major reversal, she uses the present tense to assert an alternative standard of female sexual behavior: "Still, in looking back, calmly, on the events of my life, I feel that the slave woman ought not to be judged by the same standard as others." By proposing that patriarchal strictures on women's behavior are not applicable to slave women, Brent reveals these strictures as arbitrary and conventional, not natural and inevitable. This makes possible a discussion of alternative sexual standards for women. It is a long step from her statement to the proposition that free women, to the extent that they are coerced by men, should also be spared condemnation for untraditional sexual behavior. And it is another long step to the proposition that if enslaved women should not be judged solely in terms of their sexual behavior, but on a variety of grounds (as men are), then free women should also be judged on multiple grounds. Yet, in politicizing her sexual experience and in moving toward these logical extensions of Brent's brief statement, *Incidents* moves beyond the limits of nineteenth-century polite discourse and toward modern feminism.

It is not surprising that Jacobs's narrator did not extend to free women her reevaluation of female sexual behavior or that she could not consistently reject her condemnation as a woman who had deviated from accepted sexual patterns. In her rebellion against slavery, she was bolstered by a fully developed ideology of antislavery and antiracism that was endorsed by much of her functional community. But there was no comparable articulation of an antisexist ideology in nineteenth-century America to support her challenge to patriarchal views of women's sexual behavior. When Jacobs wrote, free women who were feminists were promoting an end to the double standard by urging that men, like women, remain virginal before marriage and monogamous afterward. Some reformers such as Child, who publicized the plight of prostitutes and other sexually nonconforming women, condemned the patriarchy for punishing its female victims. Abolitionists denounced the sexual abuse of slave women and exposed the hypocrisy of the southern patriarchy, which demanded that free women conform to the model of virginity before marriage and monogamy afterward while simultaneously denying slave women either virginity or legal marriage. Brent's condemnation by her grandmother suggests that a slave woman who transgressed patriarchal norms was vulnerable to censure even within the black community.

Because Linda Brent does not sustain and develop her

assertion of sexual autonomy, the conflict over her sexual behavior remains dramatically unresolved until near the end of *Incidents*. In a chapter called "The Confession," Brent reveals her sexual history to her young daughter and receives full and complete acceptance. This exoneration solves the problem caused by her grandmother's initial harsh judgment and reestablishes the generational community of black women.

The narrator handles her struggle for freedom differently. Discussing emancipation, she addresses an audience that she assumes shares her conviction that mothers are entitled to use any and every means to free their children. Nevertheless, Brent writes that years after escaping to the North, she rejected the offer of her employer, Mrs. Bruce, to purchase her.

> The more my mind had become enlightened, the more difficult it was for me to consider myself an article of property; and to pay money to those who had so grievously oppressed me seemed like taking from my sufferings the glory of triumph. I wrote to Mrs. Bruce, thanking her, but saying that being sold from one owner to another seemed too much like slavery; that such a great obligation could not be easily cancelled; and that I preferred to go to my brother in California.

Despite Brent's wishes, Mrs. Bruce purchases and frees her, and her children are finally safe. The narrator, however, expresses relief—not triumph. Further, it appears that the successful realization of freedom, her primary goal, may have negated the possibility of achieving her secondary objective, a home for her children. The means by which Brent is emancipated apparently place her under such a "great obligation" to Mrs. Bruce that she feels she cannot leave to establish her own home, though she still longs "for a hearthstone of my own . . . for my children's sake more than for my own."

Thus suddenly, after establishing Linda Brent as a self-liberated liberator, in its final pages *Incidents* suggests the pattern of the double antislavery emblem in which the activity of the white female emancipator renders the black woman passive. In a letter . . . quoted in the appendix of *Incidents,* Jacobs expressed the frustration she felt after being freed by purchase: "I served for my liberty as faithfully as Jacob served for Rachel. At the end, he had large possessions; but I was robbed of my victory; I was obliged to resign my crown, to rid myself of a tyrant." Deeply disappointed, yet feeling that "since I have no fear of my name coming before those whom I have lived in dread of I cannot be happy without trying to be useful in some way," Jacobs wrote her book to further the antislavery cause. Like other slave narrators, she gained her triumph in and through the process of recreating herself as the subject of her own discourse.

In *Incidents*, by redefining womanhood in terms of her own life, a "slave mother" directly challenged white patriarchal notions that denied her the status of a true woman. By shaping her sexual and maternal experience into autobiography, Jacobs's Linda Brent articulates structures of female individuality and female community that counter patriarchal definitions of true womanhood. In the process, she also challenges an easy acceptance of the notion that, in nineteenth-century patriarchal racist America, the condition of a free white woman could be equated with the condition of a black slave woman. The black female slave narrator of *Incidents* addresses herself to an audience of free white women readers precisely because their lives are so different from hers that she feels compelled to tell them her story.

Jacobs's narrative and Sojourner Truth's speeches sharpened the antebellum debate over definitions of true womanhood by presenting a critique of patriarchal definitions that restricted true womanhood to free white women. They also presented a critique of those antislavery-feminist definitions that envisioned free white women as the potential liberators of oppressed passive black slaves or that, alternatively, collapsed the oppression of black slave women into the oppression of free white women and presumed to speak for the slave. Inscribing their life experience within the antislavery-feminist discourse structured by the antislavery tokens, these former slaves translated the figure of the Woman and Sister into the vernacular. In doing so, they reinvented womanhood.

Richard O. Curry

RIGHTEOUS VIOLENCE

At first abolitionists thought they could convert the slaveholders through moral suasion. By 1860 most abolitionists, including nonresistants, endorsed the use of righteous violence against the slave power. Richard O. Curry, professor emeritus of history at the University of Connecticut, agues that abolitionists held an ambivalent attitude toward nonviolence from the beginning. Divine wrath, they believed, threatened to punish a sinful nation. The assumption of a higher law and the right of private judgment provided a ready means to justify the use of force. With the escalation of sectional confrontation during the 1850s, the failure of moral suasion was apparent, and violence begat violence. Ultimately most abolitionists were committed nationalists who viewed the Civil War as a divine scourge necessary to purge a guilty land of the sin of slavery.

Historian Alice Felt Tyler once used the expression "Freedom's Ferment" to characterize the antebellum period in American history. It was an apt phrase referring to the multitude of reform movements, religious enthusiasms, and social experiments which transformed American culture in fundamentally important ways. The modern abolitionist movement emerged out of this cauldron of ferment—a movement which called for immediate repentance from the sin of slavery, and denounced the South's peculiar institution in thunderous, vituperative terms. The abolitionists' rhetoric called down upon their heads mobs in the North and threats of reprisal in the South and ultimately of secession if slavery was not granted absolute security by the North. But northern abolitionists were not only courageous but unrelenting in condemning slavery as sin and calling for the elevation of black people to an intellectual, moral, and political equality with whites.

In essence the sin of slavery was not simply the brutalization and exploitation of one human being by another. It also stemmed from the fact that enslavement prevented black people from being

From Richard O. Curry, "Ambivalence, Ambiguity, and Contradiction: Garrisonian Abolitionists and Nonviolence," *The Journal of Libertarian Studies*, 6:3–4 (Summer/Fall 1982), 217–226. Reprinted by permission of the publisher.

"free moral agents." As the constitution of the Lane Seminary Antislavery Society phrased it, God created the black man as "a moral agent, the keeper of his own happiness, the executive of his own powers, the accountable arbiter of his own choice." Slavery "stifle[d] the moral affections, repress[ed] the innate longings of the spirit, paralyze[d] conscience, turn[ed] hope to despair and kill[ed] the soul." But if most early immediate abolitionists advocated the use of moral suasion to bring about the repentance of slaveholders, they nevertheless warned that if slaveholders did not take heed by voluntarily emancipating their slaves, an angry God would visit his wrath on a sinful nation—the end result of which would be violence, bloodshed, and civil war. As the constitution of Lane's Antislavery Society warned, slavery "aroused feelings of desperation and revenge, provoke[d] insurrection and periled public safety." It "fomented division and alienation in our public councils and put in jeopardy the existence of the union," and it paralyzed "all missionary effort" and "expose[d] the nation to the awful judgment of God."

In sum, there was a degree of ambiguity or ambivalence in the commitment of many abolitionists to nonviolence from the outset. Even so, it is clear that the principles of nonviolence were still the dominant abolitionist credo in the 1830's and early 1840's. But between the Mexican War of 1846–1848 and the secession of the South in the winter of 1860–1861, pacifism declined in importance, and the call for a holy war against the evil of slavery increased in some abolitionist circles. One of [the] major tasks here, therefore, is to explain in comprehensive terms why nonviolent principles gradually lost ground to the idea of waging a jihad against sin.

Before attempting that, however, we should first examine the nature of the abolitionist commitment to moral suasion and pacifism, particularly that of the Garrisonian or "ultra" wing of the abolitionist movement. The Garrisonians, unlike other abolitionists after 1837, not only attacked the institution of slavery but challenged the legitimacy of all human institutions, including civil government. In order to understand what is known as Garrisonian nonresistance, we must analyze the implications of the work of historian Lewis Perry. . . . As Perry phrases it: "Some abolitionists had come to believe that the Biblical injunctions against violence meant that Christians had to renounce all manifestations of force, including human government; this is the belief we call nonresistance."

While such a view contains anarchistic overtones, Garrisonian nonresistants resented the charges of "no-governmentism" attributed to them, and "insisted that they were striving for, and placing themselves under the only true and effective government, the government of God. They maintained that they opposed not government, but human pretensions to govern." By becoming regenerate, men would become free of ordinary shackles and restraints and develop noncoercive, spontaneous, voluntary relationships that not only would lead to harmony, but would usher in the millennium, the kingdom of God on earth. As Perry concludes, "With their minds set on the government of God it was possible for abolitionists to seek an end to slavery, to call for governments of perfect moral purity or to say . . . that human government was no more necessary than sin."

There is, however, still another aspect of nonresistant anarchism that needs to be stressed—the potential for internalized "social control." Henry Clarke Wright, the chief theoretician of nonresistance, argued (in Perry's words) that "if one is owned by God and therefore free of usurped coercive authorities—controls are internalized." As Wright phrased it, "The action of each human body must be controlled by a *power within it*—or by a power without it—by an Interior or by an Exterior power." The potential for individual self-control was not appreciated by contemporary opponents who viewed the extreme libertarianism of nonresistance as dangerously disruptive to social stability because of its strong indictment of institutions such as civil government. Although Wright was a "belligerent nonresistant, a combative, divisive figure," he also urged "mankind to be calm and harmonious." In Wright's view, nonresistance was more than a pacifist doctrine. He was self-conscious enough to realize that "it was a form of restraint as well as a form of expression: it represented his own victory over murderous feelings" which empowered him through professions of pacifism and love "to show the blood on his brother's hand and prove his own innocence." In contrast to some anarchists and pacifists, Wright did not view human nature as benign. As Wright explained, "combativeness and destructiveness are essential parts of our nature, that our guilt lies not in the possession, but in the abuse of these propensities; and they are to be regulated and not destroyed." The key was to seek "vengeance" not against individuals, but rather against principles and institutions that were corrupt.

If . . . contradictions, ambiguities, and ambivalence regarding violence were present in nonresistant abolitionist thought from the outset, we are nevertheless faced with explaining more precisely why it was not until the period between the Mexican War and John Brown's Raid on Harpers Ferry in 1859 that abolitionist acquiescence in or militant advocacy of "righteous violence" became dominant, if not universal.

In part, abolitionist receptivity to violent means can be explained as a "stimulus-response" reaction to the growing sectional crisis over slavery and slavery expansion. Numerous abolitionists, while condemning the Mexican War, nevertheless expressed the hope that the American Army would incur heavy losses and be repelled by Santa Anna and his legions. The strengthened Fugitive Slave Law of 1850 also escalated demands for physical opposition. As the Garrisonian Samuel J. May exhorted: "If you are fully persuaded that it would be right for you to maim or kill the kidnapper who had laid hands upon your wife, son or daughter, or should be attempting to drag yourself away to be enslaved, I see not how you can excuse yourself from helping by the same degree of violence, to rescue the fugitive slave from the like outrage." And Frederick Douglass, who had earlier broken with the Garrisonian circle and abandoned pacifist principles, stated in 1852 that "the only way to make the Fugitive Slave Law a dead letter [is] to make a half dozen or more dead kidnappers." When guerilla warfare broke out in "Bleeding Kansas" in mid-1850's and nonresistant Charles Stearns wrote to Garrison that if "nonresistance is not a safe principle it is not a true one," Garrison staunchly responded that Stearns had been frightened out of his commitment to pacifism. But Garrison's close colleague, Wendell Phillips— revealing the conflict that had developed between his "head" and his "heart" (that is, his intellect and his emotions)—agreed with Stearns. "I believe in moral suasion," Phillips said. "I believe the age of bullets is over. I believe the age of ideas is come. . . . Yet, let me say in passing, that I think you can make a better use of iron than forging it into chains. If you must have metal, put it into Sharp's rifles."

It was John Brown's raid, however, that produced the greatest reaction, the largest number of defections from pacifism. Lydia Maria Child declared: "All I know, or care to know, is that his example stirred me up to consecrate myself with renewed earnestness to the righteous cause for which he had died so bravely." And Henry Clarke Wright, undoubtedly the most brilliant nonresistant theorist, recanted in 1859 when he proclaimed that "resistance to slaveholders and slavehunters is obedience to God, and a sacred Duty to man" and that "it is the right and duty of the North . . . to instigate the slaves to insurrection."

Although the "stimulus-response" phenomenon goes far toward explaining the abandonment of nonviolence among an increasing number of abolitionists, there had to have been . . . ambivalent feelings toward violence in the first place. But there was also an important ideological component in abolitionist thought, an intellectual loophole, which permitted nonresistants who had not themselves abandoned the principles of nonviolence to acquiesce in or condone violence on the part of others. This, of course, was the nonresistants' emphasis upon the idea of private judgment or individual accountability to God. In essence, Garrisonian emphasis upon the uncontested sovereignty of God meant that the individual must follow his own best light. An explicit statement of this doctrine was made by Bronson Alcott in 1839 when he said:

> What guide have I but my conscience: Church and State are responsible to *me*; not I to them. They cease to deserve our veneration from the moment they violate our consciences. We then protest against them. I believe that this is what is now going on. . . . I look upon the Non-Resistance Society as an assertion of the right to self-government. Why should I employ a church to write my creed or a state to govern me? Why not write my own creed? Why not govern myself?

In other words, nonresistants emphasized the contrast between their ideal of noncoercion in all human affairs with the violent reality of American society. This distinction allowed them to condemn violence in the abstract while spurring those who in good conscience advocated violence to employ physical resistance on behalf of the just end of the abolition of slavery. As William Lloyd Garrison put it, "We are taking the American people on their own ground and judging of them by their own standard." The right of private judgment thus allowed nonresistants a brilliant, if not very logically consistent, agitational tactic: on the one hand they condemned violence, but on the other supported its use against slavery. As Garrison argued to the unconvinced pacifist Adin Ballou during the Civil War, "Although nonresistance holds human life in all cases inviolable, yet it is perfectly consistent for those professing it to petition, advise and strenuously urge a pro-war government to abolish slavery solely by the war-power."

In addition, there are still other factors which help to explain the repudiation of pacifism by an increasing number of nonresistant abolitionists. The use of moral suasion in the 1830's and early 1840's (which was accompanied by millennial expectations of creating God's kingdom here on Earth) simply had not worked. In the minds of abolitionists, the "slave power" was not in decline, but was advancing aggressively on all fronts. Nor had they succeeded in influencing most of the nation's churches and benevolent societies to adopt an antislavery stance. Lack of apparent success caused among abolitionists feelings of failure and powerlessness, or what historian Lawrence J. Friedman has called a sense of "fragmented personal selfhood." The resort to violence transformed their original missionary impulse based on moral suasion into a crusade for righteous violence, a Manichean quest to destroy evil. . . .

The outbreak of war itself convinced still other nonresistants to abandon their pacifist principles. When confronted by charges that the Civil War was not a war to free the slaves, abolitionists nevertheless expressed their hope and belief that in time the war could be transformed into a righteous crusade to destroy evil. In the spirit of "The Battle Hymn of the Republic," Garrisonian Lydia Maria Child was "convinced that this is the great battle of Armageddon between the Angels of Freedom and the Demons of Despotism." Abolitionists saw the war as a heavenly retribution on a sinful people. To regain divine favor, Americans would have to undergo a bloody expiation, and if they proved worthy they could remake the nation into a model Christian republic that would be an example to the world. Nonresistants viewed slavery as the example par excellence of sinful coercion, and by the advent of the Civil War it became clear that most desired slavery's extinction even at the cost of a national bloodletting. The nonresistant Stephen Foster had earlier pointed out the direction that much abolitionist sentiment would follow when he militantly commented on the Fugitive Slave Law that he would "rather a hundred lives should be sacrificed than that one fugitive should be carried back to bondage."

In conclusion, it must be said that, if the concept of righteous violence became the dominant view of nonresistants, a minority still clung tenaciously to their original pacifist beliefs. Adin Ballou, the founder of the nonresistant Hopedale Community, was perhaps the most prominent among them. In response to Henry Ward Beecher's charge that nonresistants were cowards, Ballou asked if it was not "absurd twaddle" for Christians to argue that it was moral to kill their enemies if it was done "in pure love, with holy affection, for the sake of justice." The most significant group of nonresistants who conscientiously objected to the war were young, second generation Garrisonians, including Ezra Heywood, Francis and Wendell Phillips Garrison, Alfred Love, John Wesley Pratt, and Moncure Conway. With quintessential nonresistant logic, Heywood declared that the draft law must be disobeyed because it was "plainly in conflict with divine law." Although William Lloyd Garrison supported the war effort and conscription, he argued that non-voting conscientious objectors, whether church members or not, should be exempted from military service. It is true that Garrison respected his son George's personal decision to enlist in the army, but his ideological sympathy was clearly with his sons Francis and Wendell Phillips who were conscientious objectors.

The case of Moncure Conway, scion of a Virginia slaveholding family, is instructive because it illustrates that William Lloyd Garrison and Wendell Phillips and most other nonresistants valued their commitment to the Union war effort before their peace principles. When on a mission to England to stir up British abolitionist sentiment in favor of the Union cause, Conway startled his compatriots with his proposal to the Confederate commissioner, James M. Mason, that if the South would emancipate their slaves, the "abolitionists and antislavery leaders of the Northern States shall immediately oppose the further prosecution of the war on the part of the United States government, and, since they hold the balance of power, will certainly cause the war to cease by the immediate withdrawal of every kind of support from it and with its secession a restoration of peace and the independence of the South." Conway's statement raised a furor in both American government and abolitionist circles. In a somewhat exaggerated response Wendell Phillips remarked: "Moncure Conway does not represent one single man on this side of the Atlantic."

What Conway had not understood was that the Garrisonian slogan of the 1850's—"No Union with Slaveholders"—was not simply a device to exonerate themselves from personal complicity with sin, but a political tactic to counter southern threats of secession. In the final analysis, many abolitionists were also committed nationalists, believers in an American nation endowed with a unique mission in the world. . . .

III

Civil War and

Reconstruction

Primary Sources

Abraham Lincoln

FINAL EMANCIPATION PROCLAMATION (1863)

Military and political necessity, not moral suasion, brought emancipation. By 1862 Congress had abolished slavery in the District of Columbia and the federal territories and, in the Confiscation Acts, had freed the slaves of rebels, though these latter measures had little enforcement power. With the partial victory at Antietam after a series of military setbacks, President Abraham Lincoln (1809–1865) issued the Preliminary Emancipation Proclamation on September 22, 1862, as a war measure against the Confederacy. He hoped not only to weaken and diplomatically isolate the Confederacy but also to placate Radical Republicans in their demand for emancipation and recruitment of black troops. On January 1, 1863, the decree nominally freed slaves in areas in open rebellion, but left bondage intact in the loyal border states and in regions under Union occupation. Although abolitionists welcomed the fact that the war to save the Union was now inextricably linked to the eradication of slavery, they objected to the decree's limitations. They also remained suspicious of a cautious president who favored gradual, compensated emancipation coupled with voluntary colonization of free blacks outside the United States.

Whereas on the 22d day of September, A.D. 1862, a proclamation was issued by the President of the United States, containing, among other things, the following, to wit:

That on the 1st day of January, A.D. 1863, all persons held as slaves within any State or designated part of a State the people whereof shall then be in rebellion against the United States shall be then, thenceforward, and forever free; and the executive government of the United States, including the military and naval

From John G. Nicolay and John Hay, *Abraham Lincoln: A History* (New York: The Century Company, 1890), 422–428.

authority thereof, will recognize and maintain the freedom of such persons and will do no act or acts to repress such persons, or any of them, in any efforts they may make for their actual freedom.

That the Executive will on the 1st day of January aforesaid, by proclamation designate the States and parts of States, if any, in which the people thereof, respectively, shall then be in rebellion against the United States; and the fact that any State or the people thereof shall on that day be in good faith represented in the Congress of the United States by members chosen thereto at elections wherein a majority of the qualified voters of such States shall have participated shall, in the absence of strong countervailing testimony, be deemed conclusive evidence that such State and the people thereof are not then in rebellion against the United States.

Now, therefore, I, Abraham Lincoln, President of the United States, by virtue of the power in me vested as Commander in Chief of the Army and Navy of the United States in time of actual armed rebellion against the authority and Government of the United States, and as a fit and necessary war measure for suppressing said rebellion, do, on this 1st day of January, A.D. 1863, and in accordance with my purpose so to do, publicly proclaimed for the full period of one hundred days from the day first above mentioned, order and designate as the States and parts of States wherein the people thereof, respectively, are this day in rebellion against the United States the following, to wit:

Arkansas, Texas, Louisiana (except the parishes of St. Bernard, Plaquemines, Jefferson, St. John, St. Charles, St. James, Ascension, Assumption, Terrebonne, Lafourche, St. Mary, St. Martin, and Orleans, including the city of New Orleans), Mississippi, Alabama, Florida, Georgia, South Carolina, North Carolina, and Virginia (except the forty-eight counties designated as West Virginia, and also the counties of Berkeley, Accomac, Northampton, Elizabeth City, York, Princess Anne, and Norfolk, including the cities of Norfolk and Portsmouth), and which excepted parts are for the present left precisely as if this proclamation were not issued.

And by virtue of the power and for the purpose aforesaid, I do order and declare that all persons held as slaves within said designated States and parts of States are and henceforward shall be free, and that the executive government of the United States, including the military and naval authorities thereof, will recognize and maintain the freedom of said persons.

And I hereby enjoin upon the people so declared to be free to abstain from all violence, unless in necessary self-defense; and I recommend to them that in all cases when allowed they labor faithfully for reasonable wages.

And I further declare and make known that such persons of suitable condition will be received into the armed service of the United States to garrison forts, positions, stations, and other places and to man vessels of all sorts in said service.

And upon this act, sincerely believed to be an act of justice, warranted by the Constitution upon military necessity, I invoke the considerate judgment of mankind and the gracious favor of Almighty God. . . .

Charlotte Forten Grimké

RECONSTRUCTION IN SOUTH CAROLINA (1863)

On October 22, 1862, Charlotte Forten left New York City for the Sea Islands of South Carolina, which had been seized early in the Civil War by Union forces. Abolitionists had formed freedman's aid societies to uplift the ex-slaves, and the Port Royal Relief Association of Philadelphia sent her into the occupied South as the first black teacher on St. Helena Island. She was from one of Philadelphia's most prominent African-American families: her grandfather, James Forten, had helped to organize the 1817 protest against the Colonization Society, and his children (Margaretta, Sarah, Harriet, and Robert) were all leading abolitionists. A cultivated woman who wrote poetry, played the piano, and spoke French fluently, Charlotte Forten taught "contraband" slaves in a one-room schoolhouse for some eighteen months. Although her elite Yankee culture distanced her from the illiterate field-workers, she

From Brenda Stevenson, ed., *The Journals of Charlotte Forten Grimké* (New York: Oxford University Press, 1988), 442–445. Reprinted by permission of Howard University—Spingam-Moorhead Research Center.

genuinely admired their resilience and defiance of their masters. These excepts from her private journal describe her experiences, including a meeting with Harriet Tubman, who served the army there as scout, nurse, and cook. In 1878, Forten married the Reverend Francis Grimké, a former slave whose father was Henry Grimké, a Charleston planter and brother of abolitionists Sarah Grimké and Angelina Grimké Weld. In keeping with their principles, the two Grimké sisters had extended a helping hand to their biracial nephew.

Saturday, January 31

. . . In B.[eaufort] we spent nearly all our time at Harriet Tubman's otherwise [*sic*] "Moses." She is a wonderful woman—a real heroine. Has helped off a large number of slaves, after taking her own freedom. She told us that she used to hide them in the woods during the day and go around to get provisions for them. Once she had with her a man named Joe, for whom a reward of $1500 was offered. Frequently, in different places she found handbills exactly describing him, but at last they reached in safety the Suspension Bridge over the Falls and found themselves in Canada. Until then, she said, Joe had been very silent. In vain had she called his attention to the glory of the Falls. He sat perfectly still—moody, it seemed, and w'ld not even glance at them. But when she said, "Now we are in Can.[ada]" he sprang to his feet—with a great shout and sang and clapped his hands in a perfect delirium of joy. So when they got out, and he first touched *free* soil, he shouted and hurrahed "as if he were crazy"—she said. How exciting it was to hear her tell the story. And to hear her sing the very scraps of jubilant hymns that he sang. She said the ladies crowded around them, and some laughed and some cried. My own eyes were full as I listened to her—the heroic woman! A reward of $10,000 was offered for her by the Southerners, and her friends deemed it best that she sh'ld, for a time find refuge in Can.[ada]. And she did so, but only for a short time. She came back and was soon at the good brave work again. She is living in B.[eaufort] now; keeping an eating house. But she wants to go North, and will probably do so ere long. I am glad I saw her—*very* glad. . . .

Saturday, February 7

One day this week Tina, an excellent woman from Palawana came in, and told us a very interesting story about two girls, one about ten and the other fifteen, who having been taken by their master up into the country about the time of the "Gun Shoot," determined to try to get back to their parents who had been left on this island. They stole away at night, and travelled through woods and swamps, for two days without eating. Sometimes their strength w'ld fail and they w'ld sink down in the swamps, and think they c'ld go no further, but they had brave little hearts, and struggled on, till at last they reached Port Royal Ferry. There they were seen by a boat-load of people who had also made their escape. The boat was too full to take them but the people, as soon as they reached these islands, told the father of the children, who immediately hastened to the Ferry for them. The poor little creatures were almost wild with joy, despite their exhausted state, when they saw their father coming to them. When they were brought to their mother she fell down "jus' as if she was dead" as Tina expressed it. She was so overpowered with joy. Both children are living on Balta now. They are said to be very clever. I want to see the heroic little creatures.

Another day, one of the black soldiers came in and gave us *his* account of the Expedition. No words of mine . . . can give you any account of the state of exaltation and enthusiasm that he was in. He was eager for another chance at "de Secesh." I asked him what he w'ld do if his master and others sh'ld come back and try to reenslave him. "I'd fight un Miss, I'd fight un till I turned to dust!" He was especially delighted at the ire which the sight of the black troops excited in the minds of certain Secesh women whom they saw. These vented their spleen by calling the men "baboons dressed in soldiers' clothes, and telling them that they ought to be at work in their masters' rice swamps, and that they ought to be lashed to death." "And what did you say to them?" I asked. "Oh miss, we only tell us 'Hole your tongue, and dry up,! You see we wusn't feared of *dem, dey cldn't hurt us now.* Whew! didn't we laugh to see dem so mad!" The spirit of resistance to the Secesh is strong in these men.

Frederick Douglass

"MEN OF COLOR, TO ARMS!" (1863)

With the Emancipation Proclamation, the federal government openly sought the enlistment of black troops. African-American leaders, who had lobbied Lincoln for such a measure, hailed the opportunity. In this enthusiastic call-to-arms published in his Rochester newspaper, Frederick Douglass (1817–1895) invokes the militant tradition of Nat Turner, Denmark Vesey, Shields Green, and John Anthony Copeland. The 54th Regiment of Massachusetts Volunteer Infantry, the first black unit mobilized in the North, included more than 100 members recruited by Douglass, including his sons Lewis and Charles. Those joining Douglass as recruiters included Henry Highland Garnet, Martin Delaney, and Charles Lenox Remond. Although racially segregated and commanded by white officers, the nearly 180,000 black soldiers in the Union army exhibited great dedication and were instrumental in defeating the Confederacy.

Born a slave in Maryland, Douglass first defied the law by learning to read and write. He fled north in 1838 and established himself in New Bedford, Massachusetts, where in 1841 he began lecturing for that state's antislavery society. In 1845 he published a famous narrative about his enslavement and two years later co-founded the antislavery newspaper *The North Star*. A brilliant orator, Douglass was the foremost black spokesman of the nineteenth century.

When first the rebel cannon shattered the walls of Sumter and drove away its starving garrison, I predicted that the war then and there inaugurated would not be fought out entirely by white men. Every month's experience during these weary years has confirmed that opinion. A war undertaken and brazenly carried on for the perpetual enslavement of colored men, calls logically and loudly for colored men to help suppress it. Only a moderate share of sagacity was needed to see that the arm of the slave was the best defense against the arm of the slaveholder. Hence with every reverse to the national arms, with every exulting shout of victory raised by the

Reproduced with permission of Macmillan Publishing Company from *Life and Times of Frederick Douglass* by Frederick Douglass. (New York: Collier Books/Macmillan, 1926), 339–341.

slaveholding rebels, I have implored the imperiled nation to unchain against her foes, her powerful black hand.

Slowly and reluctantly that appeal is beginning to be heeded. Stop not now to complain that it was not heeded sooner. That it should not, may or it may not have been best. This is not the time to discuss that question. Leave it to the future. When the war is over, the country is saved, peace is established, and the black man's rights are secured, as they will be, history with an impartial hand will dispose of that and sundry other questions. Action! Action! not criticism, is the plain duty of this hour. Words are now useful only as they stimulate to blows. The office of speech now is only to point out when, where, and how to strike to the best advantage.

There is no time to delay. The tide is at its flood that leads on to fortune. From East to West, from North to South, the sky is written all over, "Now or Never." "Liberty won by white men would lose half its luster." "Who would be free themselves must strike the blow." "Better even die free, than to live slaves." This is the sentiment of every brave colored man amongst us.

There are weak and cowardly men in all nations. We have them amongst us. They tell you this is the "white man's war"; that you will be no "better off after than before the war"; that the getting of you into the army is to "sacrifice you on the first opportunity." Believe them not; cowards themselves, they do not wish to have their cowardice shamed by your brave example. Leave them to their timidity, or to whatever motive may hold them back.

I have not thought lightly of the words I am now addressing you. The counsel I give comes of close observation of the great struggle now in progress, and of the deep conviction that this is your hour and mine. In good earnest then, and after the best deliberation, I now for the first time during this war feel at liberty to call and counsel you to arms.

By every consideration which binds you to your enslaved fellow-countrymen, and the peace and welfare of your country; by every aspiration which you cherish for the freedom and equality of yourselves and your children; by all the ties of blood and identity which make us one with the brave black men now fighting our battles in Louisiana and in South Carolina, I urge you to fly to arms, and smite with death the power that would bury the government and your liberty in the same hopeless grave.

I wish I could tell you that the State of New York calls you to this high honor. For the moment her constituted authorities are silent on the subject. They will speak by and by, and doubtless on the right side; but we are not compelled to wait for her. We can get at the throat of treason and slavery through the State of Massachusetts. She was first in the War of Independence; first to break the chains of her slaves; first to make the black man equal before the law; first to admit colored children to her common schools, and she was first to answer with her blood the alarm cry of the nation, when its capital was menaced by rebels. You know her patriotic governor, and you know Charles Sumner. I need not add more.

Massachusetts now welcomes you to arms as soldiers. She has but a small colored population from which to recruit. She has full leave of the general government to send one regiment to the war, and she has undertaken to do it. Go quickly and help fill up the first colored regiment from the North. I am authorized to assure you that you will receive the same wages, the same rations, the same equipments, the same protection, the same treatment, and the same bounty, secured to the white soldiers. You will be led by able and skillful officers, men who will take especial pride in your efficiency and success. They will be quick to accord to you all the honor you shall merit by your valor, and see that your rights and feelings are respected by other soldiers. I have assured myself on these points, and can speak with authority.

More than twenty years of unswerving devotion to our common cause may give me some humble claim to be trusted at this momentous crisis. I will not argue. To do so implies hesitation and doubt, and you do not hesitate. You do not doubt. The day dawns; the morning star is bright upon the horizon! The iron gate of our prison stands half open. One gallant rush from the North will fling it wide open, while four millions of our brothers and sisters shall march out into liberty. The chance is now given you to end in a day the bondage of centuries, and to rise in one bound from social degradation to the plane of common equality with all other varieties of men.

Remember Denmark Vesey of Charleston; remember Nathaniel Turner of Southampton; remember Shields Green and Copeland, who followed noble John Brown, and fell as glorious martyrs for the cause of the slave. Remember that in a contest with oppression, the Almighty has no attribute which can take sides with oppressors.

The case is before you. This is our golden opportunity. Let us accept it, and forever wipe out the dark reproaches unsparingly hurled against us by our enemies. Let us win for ourselves the gratitude of our country, and the best blessings of our posterity through all time. The nucleus of this first regiment is now in camp at Readville, a short distance from Boston. I will undertake to forward to Boston all persons adjudged fit to be mustered into the regiment who shall apply to me at anytime within the next two weeks.

Charles Lenox Remond and William Lloyd Garrison

DEBATE OVER THE DISSOLUTION OF THE AMERICAN ANTI-SLAVERY SOCIETY (1865)

With state ratification of the Thirteenth Amendment appearing certain, delegates to the annual convention of the American Anti-Slavery Society during May 9–10, 1865, debated if the national organization should be dissolved, its mission accomplished. William Lloyd Garrison, its president, thought so. Abolitionists should now mingle, he urged, "with the great mass of our fellow-citizens" in new organizations for the cause of black suffrage. He believed that racial attitudes had been transformed and that white citizens would "speedily give the colored man all his rights."

Charles Lenox Remond (1810–1873) disagreed. Born in Salem, Massachusetts, he was the first black agent of the Massachusetts Anti-Slavery Society and a recruiter for the 54th Massachusetts Regiment. Along with other black abolitionists and a faction organized around Wendell Phillips, Remond argued that white supremacy was alive and

From *The Liberator*, 35 (May 26–June 2, 1865), 81–82.

well in the North as well as in the South. In a telling comment, he observed that it was "utterly impossible" for his white colleagues "fully to understand the black man's case in this nation." The struggle against racism, he urged, could best be waged by the existing organization. The resolution calling for dissolution was defeated by a vote of 118 to 48. The presidency was again offered to Garrison, but he declined and was succeeded by his rival, Phillips. This selection emphasizes differences between black and white abolitionists.

C. L. Remond—I differ very materially from the friend who has just taken his seat. If I understand the Declaration of Sentiments and the Constitution, the object of this Society includes the very point to which our friend Mr. Keese refers, for the emancipation of the slave and the elevation of the free people of color were the original objects of the American Anti-Slavery Society. The work now being done in every part of our country for the enslaved and the nominally free, comes strictly and logically within the purposes of this Society.

Now, I am not among the number who would retain for a moment any one of the members or officers of the Society against his or her wish; for I hold that the man or the woman who remains reluctantly within its pale is of no service to our cause at this critical moment, and it strikes me they have but little to do but ask to be excused. I cannot understand the necessity for disbanding the Society, especially since it is doubtful in my own mind whether a new Society could be got into full play before some valuable hours, days, and perhaps months shall be lost to us.

Now, while I am upon the platform, allow me to remark, once for all, that if I understand its spirit, it is, that individual judgment shall remain inviolate upon it; and if I shall differ in my remarks from my friend Mr. Garrison, or any other member of the Society, I protest against the imputation, that the colored man who differs from his old and tried friends becomes an ingrate. Sir, if there is one work which I hate next to slavery, it is ingratitude; still, I hold that, as colored men or as white men, we may differ from these old friends without being liable to that charge.

Now, sir, how does the case stand in this country? It is assumed (and I do not know that I object to the assumption, only when things are brought to a very fine point, as they are sometimes here) that our white friends understand the black man's case; that they have so often put their souls in his stead, that it cannot be otherwise. To a great extent, this is true; but in many particulars it is not true. Now, while I defer to some and reverence others—and I hope no man can prove himself more grateful than I feel towards our friends—I do assume here that it is utterly impossible for any of our white friends, however much they may have tried, fully to understand the black man's case in this nation. I think I could name one or two men, perhaps a dozen here, who get very near to it, but not exactly "on the square," so to say. Our friend Mr. Garrison told us today, that antislavery being the order of things, there is no further necessity for antislavery work. Why, sir, if my friend should go out upon the highways and byways here, and put the very question which he has assumed as a foregone conclusion, he would find himself so utterly overwhelmed with opposition that he would hardly understand himself. I deny, from beginning to end, that antislavery, according to this platform, characterizes any State in this country. I deny, without fear of successful contradiction, that the antislavery which takes its color from this platform has a majority in the nation at the present time. Put the question nakedly to the American people today, whether they are prepared for the entire and full recognition of the colored man's equality in this country, and you would be voted down ten to one. This being true, I cannot sit here and hear these assertions and assumptions without raising my protest against them.

While coming through in the cars last evening (I give this as an isolated case), I gave the conductor my ticket, as the other passengers did. When the others gave up their tickets, he handed them checks. He gave me no check, and I asked him if he did not intend to. He turned round, and gave me to understand that my black face was check enough. Again: I was going to a meeting of our friends in Salem last week, to consult in reference to the question of free suffrage, and schools for the black man, and during my walk from my home to the Lyceum Hall, I heard the expressions, "D—d nigger on the stomach," "d—d nigger on the brain," etc., etc. Such expressions were never more rife in our country than at the present moment. And yet we are to understand that antislavery is the order of the day! Sir, it is not true.

But I will not occupy the time further, except to say, that

standing as we do at this moment between the fires of rebellion in the South, and this hatred of the colored man in the North, I hope nothing will be done within this Society that shall look like a betrayal of our movement. I know how much our friends have been tried, how much they have sacrificed; and I do not blame those who are growing old, like myself, for their desire to retire. Still, sir, this retirement may be done in a way that shall cause great harm to our cause, and great harm to the colored people throughout the country. I hope, therefore, that this Society may be continued, and if its present officers desire to retire, we will endeavor to succeed them with others. . . .

Mr. Garrison—(Referring to a remark made by Mr. Remond)—I do not ask the Society to *permit* me to retire. That is language I do not understand on this platform. I shall retire when I think proper, and I shall think proper to do so at the end of this anniversary.

I think I am competent to interpret the language of the Declaration of Sentiments, if any man living be. I was the author of it; and, unless I have grown demented, I ought to know what I meant, and what this Society meant in using that language. This Society is "The American *Anti-Slavery* Society." That was the object. The thought never entered my mind then, nor has it at any time since, that when slavery had received its death-wound, there would be any disposition or occasion to continue the Anti-Slavery Society a moment longer. But, of course, in looking over the country, we saw the free colored people more or less laboring under disabilities, and suffering from injustice, and we declared that, incidentally, we did not mean to overlook them, but should vindicate their rights, and endeavor to get justice done to them. The point is here. We organized expressly for the abolition of slavery; we called our Society an *Anti-Slavery* Society. The other work was incidental. Now, I believe slavery is abolished in this country; abolished constitutionally; abolished by a decree of this nation, never to be reversed (applause); and, therefore, that it is ludicrous for us, a mere handful of people, with little means, with no agents in the field, no longer separate, and swallowed up in the great ocean of popular feeling against slavery, to assume that we are of special importance, and that we ought not to dissolve our association, under such circumstances, lest the nation should go to ruin! I will not be guilty of any such absurdity.

But is this to retire from the field of labor in regard to whatever is to be done in putting down prejudice, and giving the colored man his political rights? I hold all such representations, come from what quarter they may, to be slanderous. No man thinks of doing it; no officer of this Society, who is to retire, proposes to give himself up to idleness, or to abate his testimony against the proscription of men on account of their color. It is part of our nature, it is part of our duty to each other as fellow-men, it is part of our obligation to God, to denounce everywhere all proscription on account of the manner in which it has pleased God to make His children. We, however, are not distinctive on this question of elevating the colored people. If we were, then there might be an argument, not for perpetuating the American *Anti-Slavery* Society, with no slavery to abolish, but for organizing a special movement, whereby we should seek the moral and political elevation of the emancipated. But we are no longer, I say, peculiar in this respect; we have the million with us. I hold the speech of my friend, Mr. Remond, to be a caricature of this nation, in its present attitude, and a perversion of the views and feelings of those who are about to retire from this Society. We mingle now, thank God! with the great mass of our fellow-citizens. I have only to go before any loyal audience that may be gathered for the discussion of this question, and assert that it is the right of the colored man to vote, to have the verdict given there, as it was given here today, strongly in favor of the measure. The newspaper press of the country—the loyal press—is almost universally, I think, friendly to the measure; at any rate, we, a handful of Abolitionists, are not the special champions of that movement. Let us mingle with the mass, then, and endeavor to work with the mass, and not affect isolation or singularity, nor assume to say, "Stand by, we are holier than you," when we are no better. I maintain, therefore, that what was put into the Declaration of Sentiments, in reference to the elevation of the free people of color, was incidental to the grand object—the abolition of slavery. Slavery being abolished, the change that has done that work is a change that will cooperate with us, and speedily give the colored man all his rights. . . .

U. S. Constitution

THIRTEENTH, FOURTEENTH, AND FIFTEENTH AMENDMENTS (1865, 1868, 1870)

The three Reconstruction amendments to the Constitution, the first amendments to be added since 1804, sought to reshape Southern society. A massive petition drive by the Woman's Loyal League, organized by antislavery feminists Elizabeth Cady Stanton and Susan B. Anthony on behalf of the Thirteenth Amendment, helped to gain its adoption. The amendment secured universal, immediate, uncompensated emancipation, long a goal of abolitionists.

The Fourteenth Amendment, a compromise between Moderate and Radical Republicans in the special joint committee on Reconstruction, only partly satisfied abolitionists. Representative Thaddeus Stevens's proposal for confiscation and redistribution of Confederate land, for example, was rejected as too extreme. The less controversial first section nullified the *Dred Scott* decision (1857) by extending citizenship as well as equality under the law to African-Americans, pledges that the civil rights movement of the twentieth century struggled to uphold. The complex but inoperative second section encouraged Southern states to enfranchise black men with the threat of otherwise reducing their membership in Congress. The sensitive issue of Northern restrictions on the black vote was expediently ignored. The third and fourth sections, respectively, barred prominent rebels from political office and repudiated the Confederate war debt. The Military Reconstruction Act of 1867 required Southern states to approve the Fourteenth Amendment.

With the ratification of the Fifteenth Amendment, the American Anti-Slavery Society, at the direction of its president Wendell Phillips, dissolved in April 1870, declaring that black male suffrage was "the capstone and completion of our movement." For all practical purposes, abolitionism as an organized movement was over. In addition, the failure of most abolitionists to endorse the vote for women in the Fourteenth and Fifteenth Amendments outraged Stanton and Anthony, who in turn launched an independent feminist crusade. Indeed, the negative and limited wording of the Fifteenth Amendment accommodated Northern states that prohibited women, Chinese, and other groups from voting.

'rom the U.S. Constitution.

Amendment XIII

[Adopted 1865]

Section 1 Neither slavery nor involuntary servitude, except as a punishment for crime whereof the party shall have been duly convicted, shall exist within the United States, or any place subject to their jurisdiction.

Section 2 Congress shall have power to enforce this article by appropriate legislation.

Amendment XIV

[Adopted 1868]

Section 1 All persons born or naturalized in the United States, and subject to the jurisdiction thereof, are citizens of the United States and of the State wherein they reside. No State shall make or enforce any law which shall abridge the privileges or immunities of citizens of the United States; nor shall any State deprive any person of life, liberty, or property, without due process of law; nor deny to any person within its jurisdiction the equal protection of the laws.

Section 2 Representatives shall be apportioned among the several States according to their respective numbers, counting the whole number of persons in each State, excluding Indians not taxed. But when the right to vote at any election for the choice of Electors for President and Vice-President of the United States, Representatives in Congress, the executive and judicial officers of a State, or the members of the legislature thereof, is denied to any of the male inhabitants of such State, being twenty-one years of age and citizens of the United States, or in any way abridged, except for participation in rebellion, or other crime, the basis of representation therein shall be reduced in the proportion which the number of such male citizens shall bear to the whole number of male citizens twenty-one years of age in such State.

Section 3 No person shall be a Senator or Representative in Congress, or Elector of President and Vice-President, or hold any office, civil or military, under the United States, or under any State, who, having previously taken an oath, as a member of Congress, or as an officer of the United States, or as a member of any State legislature, or as an executive or judicial officer of any State, to support the Constitution of the United States, shall have engaged in insurrection or rebellion against the same, or given aid or comfort to the enemies thereof. Congress may, by a vote of two-thirds of each house, remove such disability.

Section 4   The validity of the public debt of the United States, authorized by law, including debts incurred for payment of pensions and bounties for services in suppressing insurrection or rebellion, shall not be questioned. But neither the United States nor any State shall assume or pay any debt or obligation incurred in aid of insurrection or rebellion against the United States, or any claim for the loss of emancipation of any slave; but all such debts, obligations, and claims shall be held illegal and void.

Section 5   The Congress shall have power to enforce, by appropriate legislation, the provisions of this article.

Amendment XV

[Adopted 1870]

Section 1   The right of citizens of the United States to vote shall not be denied or abridged by the United States or by any State on account of race, color, or previous condition of servitude.

Section 2   The Congress shall have power to enforce this article by appropriate legislation.

Secondary Sources

Eric Foner

THE COMING OF EMANCIPATION

As Union troops marched south, 400,000 slaves sought refuge behind their lines. Others stopped work on their masters' farms and plantations; some became insubordinate and defiant. Although armed insurrection did not occur as It had in Haiti, slaves seized the opportunity of the Civil War to subvert the system that oppressed them. Eric Foner, DeWitt Clinton Professor at Columbia University, argues that the Confiscation Acts and Emancipation Proclamation were more reactions to the collapse of slavery than to its cause. African-Americans were agents of historical change who transformed a war to save the Union into a war of liberation. In addition, the military service of the 180,000 black soldiers had important implications for peacetime. Men who had fought for freedom, who had protested low pay, and who had aspired to the rank of commissioned officers were not likely to accept racial subordination as natural and inevitable.

On January 1, 1863, after a winter storm swept up the east coast of the United States, the sun rose in a cloudless sky over Washington, D.C. At the White House, Abraham Lincoln spent most of the day welcoming guests to the traditional New Year's reception. Finally, in the late afternoon, as he had pledged to do 100 days before, the President retired to his office to sign the Emancipation Proclamation. Excluded from its purview were the 450,000 slaves in Delaware, Kentucky, Maryland, and Missouri (border slave states that remained within the Union), 275,000 in Union-occupied Tennessee, and tens of thousands more in portions of Louisiana and Virginia under the control of federal armies. But, the Proclamation decreed, the remainder of the nation's slave population, well over 3 million men, women, and children, "are and henceforth shall be free."

Throughout the North and the Union-occupied South, January 1 was a day of celebration. An immense gathering, including black and white abolitionist leaders, stood vigil at Boston's Tremont Temple, awaiting word that the Proclamation had been signed. It was nearly midnight when the news arrived; wild cheering followed, and a black preacher led the throng in singing "Sound the loud timbrel o'er Egypt's dark sea, Jehovah hath triumphed, his people are free." At a camp for fugitive slaves in the nation's capital, a black man "testified" about the sale, years before, of his daughter, exclaiming, "Now, no more dat! . . . Dey can't sell my wife and child any more, bless de Lord!" Farther south, at Beaufort, an enclave of federal control off the South Carolina coast, there were prayers and speeches and the freedmen sang "My Country 'Tis of Thee." To Charlotte Forten, a young black woman who had journeyed from her native Philadelphia to teach the former slaves, "it all seemed . . . like a brilliant dream." Even in areas exempted from the Proclamation, blacks celebrated, realizing that if slavery perished in Mississippi and South Carolina, it could hardly survive in Kentucky, Tennessee, and a few parishes of Louisiana.

Nearly two and a half centuries had passed since twenty black men and women were landed in Virginia from a Dutch ship. From this tiny seed had grown the poisoned fruit of plantation slavery, which, in profound and contradictory ways, shaped the course of American development. Even as slavery mocked the ideals of a nation supposedly dedicated to liberty and equality, slave labor played an indispensable part in its rapid growth, expanding westward with the young republic, producing the cotton that fueled the early industrial revolution. In the South, slavery spawned a distinctive regional ruling class (an "aristocracy without nobility" one Southern-born writer called it) and powerfully shaped the economy, race relations, politics, religion, and the law. Its influence was pervasive: "Nothing escaped, nothing and no one." In the North, where slavery had been abolished during and after the American Revolution, emerged abolition, the greatest protest movement of the age. The slavery question divided the nation's churches, sundered political ties between the sections, and finally shattered the bonds of Union. On the principle of opposing the further expansion of slavery, a new political party rose to power in the 1850s, placing in the White House a son of the slave state Kentucky, who had grown to manhood on the free Illinois prairies and believed the United States could not endure forever half slave and half free. In the crisis that followed Lincoln's election, eleven slave states seceded from the Union, precipitating in 1861 the bloodiest war the Western Hemisphere has ever known.

To those who had led the movement for abolition, and to slaves throughout the South, the Emancipation Proclamation not only culminated decades of struggle but evoked Christian visions of resurrection and redemption, of an era of unbounded progress for a nation purged at last of the sin of slavery. Even the staid editors of the *New York Times* believed it marked a watershed in American life, "an era in the history . . . of this country and the world." For emancipation meant more than the end of a labor system, more even than the uncompensated liquidation of the nation's largest concentration of private property ("the most stupendous act of sequestration in the history of Anglo-Saxon jurisprudence," as Charles and Mary Beard described it). The demise of slavery inevitably threw open the most basic questions of the polity, economy, and society. Begun to preserve the Union, the Civil War now portended a far-reaching transformation in Southern life and a redefinition of the place of blacks in American society and of the very meaning of freedom in the American republic.

In one sense, however, the Proclamation only confirmed what was already happening on farms and plantations throughout the South. War, it has been said, is the midwife of revolution, and well before 1863 the disintegration of slavery had begun. Whatever politicians and military commanders might decree, slaves saw the war as heralding the long-awaited end of bondage. Three years into the conflict, Gen. William T. Sherman encountered a black Georgian who summed up the slaves' understanding of the war from its outset: "He said . . . he had been looking for the 'angel of the Lord' ever since he was knee-high, and, though we professed to be fighting for the Union, he supposed that slavery was the cause, and that our success was to be his freedom." Based on this conviction, the slaves took actions that propelled a reluctant white America down the road to abolition.

As the Union Army occupied territory on the periphery of the Confederacy, first in Virginia, then in Tennessee, Louisiana, and elsewhere, slaves by the thousands headed for the Union lines. Union enclaves like Fortress Monroe, Beaufort, and New Orleans became havens for runaway slaves and bases for expeditions into the interior that further disrupted the plantation regime. Even in the heart of the Confederacy, far from Union lines, the conflict undermined the South's "peculiar institution." Their "grapevine telegraph" kept many slaves remarkably well informed about the war's progress. In one part of Mississippi, slaves even organized Lincoln's Legal Loyal League to spread word of the Emancipation Proclamation. Southern armies impressed tens of thousands of slaves into service as laborers, taking them far from their home plantations, offering opportunities for escape, and widening the horizons of those who returned home. The drain of white men into military service left plantations under the control of planters' wives and elderly and infirm men, whose authority slaves increasingly felt able to challenge. Reports of "demoralized" and "insubordinate" behavior multiplied throughout the South. Six months after the war began, slaves in one Kentucky town marched through the streets at night, shouting hurrahs for Lincoln.

But generally, it was the arrival of federal soldiers that spelled havoc for the slave regime, for blacks quickly grasped that the presence of occupying troops destroyed the coercive power of both the individual master and the slaveholding community. A Virginia coachman, informed by soldiers in 1862 that he was free, "went straight to his master's chamber, dressed himself in his best clothes, put on his best watch and chain . . . and insolently informed him that he might for the future drive his own coach." On Magnolia plantation in Louisiana, the arrival of the Union Army in 1862 sparked a work stoppage and worse: "We have a terrible state of affairs here negroes refusing to work. . . . The negroes have erected a gallows in the quarters and give as an excuse for it that they are told they must drive their master . . . off the plantation hang their master etc. and that then they will be free." Here in the sugar country, where large gangs of slaves labored in some of the South's most wretched conditions, blacks sacked planters' homes and, months before the Emancipation Proclamation, refused to work unless paid wages. Slavery, wrote a Northern reporter in November 1862, "is forever destroyed and worthless, no matter what Mr. Lincoln or anyone else may say on the subject."

"Meanwhile," in the words of W. E. B. Du Bois, "with per-plexed and laggard steps, the United States government followed in the footsteps of the black slave." The slaves' determination to seize the opportunity presented by the war initially proved an embarr-assment to the Lincoln administration and a burden to the army. Lincoln fully appreciated, as he would observe in his second in-augural address, that slavery was "somehow" the cause of the war. But he also understood the vital importance of keeping the border slave states in the Union, generating support among the broadest constituency in the North, and weakening the Confederacy by holding out to irresolute Southerners the possibility that they could return to the Union with their property, including slaves, intact. In 1861 the restoration of the Union, not emancipation, was the cause that generated the widest support for the war effort.

Thus, in the early days of the war, the administration insisted that slavery had little to do with the conflict. When Congress assembled in special session in July 1861, one of its first acts was to pass, nearly unanimously, the Crittenden Resolution, affirming that the "established institutions" of the seceding states were not to be a military target. Throughout 1861, army commanders ordered their camps closed to fugitive slaves and some actually returned them to their owners, a policy that caused Gov. John A. Andrew to protest: "Massachusetts does not send her citizens forth to become the hunters of men." Yet as the Confederacy set slaves to work as military laborers, and the presence of Union soldiers precipitated large-scale desertion of the plantations, the early policy quickly unraveled. Increasingly, military authorities adopted the plan, inaugurated in Virginia by Gen. Benjamin F. Butler, of designating fugitive slaves as "contraband of war." Instead of being either emancipated or returned to their owners, they would be employed as laborers for the Union armies.

Then, too, an influential segment of the Northern public—abolitionists and Radical Republicans—recognized that secession offered a golden opportunity to strike a fatal blow at slavery. "We have entered upon a struggle," wrote a Massachusetts abolitionist four days after the firing on Fort Sumter, "which ought not to be allowed to end until the Slave Power is completely subjugated, and *emancipation made certain*." Black abolitionist Frederick Douglass repeatedly called for the liberation and arming of the slaves, insisting from the outset, "The Negro is the key of the situation—the pivot upon which the whole rebellion turns." Carl Schurz, who had fled his native Germany after the abortive revolution of 1848 and emerged as a leading antislavery lecturer in the 1850s, later remarked that emancipation would have come "even if there had not been a single abolitionist in America before the war." But the pressure of antislavery men and women had its impact. With traditional policies unable to produce victory, abolitionists and Radicals offered a coherent analysis of the conflict and a plausible means of weakening the rebellion. Most of all, they kept at the forefront of Northern politics the question of the struggle's ultimate purpose.

The steps by which Congress and the President moved toward abolition have often been chronicled. As the danger of secession by the border states receded, the collapse of slavery accelerated, and the manpower needs of the Union armies increased, pressure mounted for emancipation. In March 1862, Congress enacted an article of war expressly prohibiting the army from returning fugitives to their masters. Then came abolition in the District of Columbia (with compensation for loyal owners) and the territories, followed by the Second Confiscation Act, liberating slaves who resided in Union-occupied territory or escaped to Union lines, if their masters were disloyal.

Seeking to hold the political middle ground, even as that ground shifted to the left, Lincoln searched for a formula that would initiate the emancipation process but not alienate conservatives and Southern Unionists. First, he urged the border states to adopt measures for gradual, compensated emancipation, promising generous financial aid from the federal government. But he found no takers, even in tiny Delaware with fewer than 2,000 slaves. In a widely publicized conference, Lincoln urged Northern black leaders to support the colonization of freedmen in Central America or the Caribbean, insisting "there is an unwillingness on the part of our people, harsh as it may be for you colored people to remain with us." Whether his embrace of colonization stemmed from genuine conviction, uncharacteristic naïveté, or political calculation (an attempt to neutralize fears that emancipation would produce an influx of blacks into the free states), Lincoln's plans came to naught. But to the very end of 1862, he held out the possibility of compensation and colonization, raising both ideas in his December message to Congress, and adding a thinly veiled suggestion that Northern states possessed the authority to exclude freedmen from their territory. As late as December, the President signed an agreement with an entrepreneur of dubious character for the settlement of 5,000 blacks on an island off Haiti. (Four hundred hapless souls did in fact reach Île à Vache; those fortunate enough to survive returned to the United States in 1864.)

It is tempting to interpret the evolution of Lincoln's policy as the vacillation of a man desperate to avoid the role history had thrust upon him. This, however, would be unfair, for Lincoln genuinely abhorred slavery. He shared, it is true, many of the racial prejudices of his time and accepted without dissent the racial discriminations so widespread in both sections. But Frederick Douglass, who had encountered racism even within abolitionist ranks, considered Lincoln a fundamentally decent individual. "He treated me as a man," Douglass remarked in 1864, "he did not let me feel for a moment that there was any difference in the color of our skins." It is probably most accurate to say that Lincoln, neither an egalitarian in a modern sense nor a man paralyzed, like so many of his contemporaries, by racial fears and prejudices, did not approach any policy, even emancipation, primarily in terms of its impact upon blacks; for him, winning the war always remained paramount. The Emancipation Proclamation itself, with its exemption of Union-held areas, reflected not only Lincoln's effort to make emancipation legally unassailable, but also his determination to retain the backing of the millions of Northerners who cared little about abolition but might support an act essential to military victory.

Most important of all, however, Lincoln understood that the war had created a fluid situation that placed a premium upon flexibility and made far-reaching change inevitable. As Wisconsin Sen. Timothy O. Howe explained in December 1861, change had become the order of the day: "Don't anchor yourself to any policy. Don't tie up to any platform. The very foundations of the Government are cracking. . . . No mere policy or platform can outlast this storm." The Proclamation represented a turning point in national policy as well as in the character of the war. For the first time tying Union success to abolition—a commitment from which Lincoln never retreated—it ignored entirely both compensation and colonization, and for the first time authorized the large-scale enlistment of black soldiers. In effect, it transformed a war of armies into a conflict of societies, ensuring that Union victory would produce a social revolution within the South. In such a struggle, compromise was impossible; the war must now continue until the unconditional surrender of one side or the other. Even in areas exempted from the Proclamation, the Union Army henceforth acted as a liberating force. Indeed, a federal army officer in Tennessee flatly declared in 1863: "Slavery is dead; that is the first thing. That is what we all begin with here, who know the state of affairs." In December 1861 Lincoln had admonished Congress that the Civil War must not degenerate into "a violent and remorseless revolutionary struggle." The Emancipation Proclamation announced that this was precisely what it must become.

Of the Proclamation's provisions, few were more radical in their implications or more essential to breathing life into the promise of emancipation than the massive enrollment of blacks into military service. Preliminary steps had been taken in 1862, since as the army moved into the South, it required a seemingly endless stream of laborers to construct fortifications and additional soldiers to guard its ever-lengthening supply lines. The reservoir of black manpower could not be ignored, but it was only with the Emancipation Proclamation that the enlistment of blacks began in earnest. Massachusetts Governor Andrew commissioned a group of prominent black abolitionists to tour the North for recruits, and other Northern governors quickly followed suit. In the South, especially in the Mississippi Valley under the direction of Gen. Lorenzo Thomas, former slaves by the thousands were enlisted. By the war's end, some 180,000 blacks had served in the Union Army—over one fifth of the nation's adult male black population under age forty-five. The highest percentage originated in the border states, where enlistment was, for most of the war, the only route to freedom. Nearly 60 percent of eligible Kentucky blacks served in the armed forces. Here, military service pushed the Union's commitment to abolition beyond the terms of the Proclamation to embrace, first, black soldiers, and, shortly before the war's end, their families as well. Well before its legal demise, slavery in the border states had been fatally undermined by the enlistment of black men in the army.

Within the army, black soldiers were anything but equal to white. Organized into segregated regiments, they often found themselves subjected to abuse from white officers. Initially, black enlistment was intended to free whites for combat; accordingly, black recruits received less pay than white and were assigned largely to fatigue duty, construction work, and menial labor, with few opportunities to demonstrate their martial talents. Even after proving themselves in battle, blacks could not advance into the ranks of commissioned officers until 1865. In the end, only about 100 (including chaplains and surgeons) obtained commissions.

Nonetheless, black soldiers played a crucial role not only in winning the Civil War, but in defining the war's consequences. Their service helped transform the nation's treatment of blacks and blacks' conception of themselves. The "logical result" of their military service, one Senator observed in 1864, was that "the black man is henceforth to assume a new *status* among us." For the first time in American history, large numbers of blacks were treated as equals before the law—if only military law. In army courts blacks could testify against whites (something unheard of throughout the South and in many Northern states), and former slaves for the first time saw the impersonal sovereignty of the law supersede the personal authority of a master. The galling issue of unequal pay sparked a movement that familiarized former slaves with the process of petition and protest, and resulted in a signal victory when Congress in 1864 enacted a measure for equality in pay, bounties, and other compensation. It was in the army that large numbers of former slaves first learned to read and write, either from teachers employed by Northern aid societies or in classrooms and literary clubs established and funded by the soldiers themselves. "A large portion of the regiment have been going to school during the winter months," wrote a black sergeant from Virginia in March 1865. "Surely this is a mighty and progressive age in which we live."

From Oliver Cromwell's New Model Army to the militias raised during the American Revolution to guerrilla armies of our own day, military service has often been a politicizing and radicalizing experience. Lincoln's "thinking bayonets" (his term for

Union soldiers) debated among themselves the issues of war and emancipation. As the army penetrated the heart of the Deep South and encountered the full reality of plantation slavery, soldiers became imbued with abolition sentiment. "Since I am here," one Democratic colonel wrote from Louisiana, "I have learned and seen . . . what the horrors of slavery was. . . . Never hereafter will I either speak or vote in favor of slavery." For black troops, particularly the vast majority just emerging from slavery, the army's impact was especially profound. "No negro who has ever been a soldier," wrote a Northern official in 1865, "can again be imposed upon; they have learnt what it is to be free and they will infuse their feelings into others." Black troops flaunted their contempt for symbols of bondage, and relished the opportunity to exert authority over Southern whites. One soldier celebrated his ability to walk "fearlessly and boldly through the streets [of New Orleans] . . . without being required to take off his cap at every step." Another, recognizing his former master among a group of military prisoners, exclaimed: "Hello massa; bottom rail top dis time!"

For black soldiers, military service meant more than the opportunity to help save the Union, more even than their own freedom and the destruction of slavery as an institution. For men of talent and ambition, the army flung open a door to advancement and respectability. From the army would come many of the black political leaders of Reconstruction, including at least forty-one delegates to state constitutional conventions, sixty-four legislators, three lieutenant governors, and four Congressmen. One group of discharged black soldiers formed "the Council" after the war to collect information on the condition of Louisiana's freedmen, "look after their contracts" with white employers, and explain their legal rights. In time, the black contribution to the Union war effort would fade from the nation's collective memory, but it remained a vital part of the black community's sense of its own history. "They say," an Alabama planter reported in 1867, "the Yankees never could have whipped the South without the aid of the negroes." Here was a crucial justification for blacks' self-confident claim to equal citizenship during Reconstruction, a claim anticipated in the soldiers' long battle for equal pay during the war. At the Arkansas constitutional convention of 1868, former slave William Murphey held his silence for weeks, in deference to more accomplished white delegates (who, he pointed out, "have obtained the means of education by the black man's sweat"). But when some of these delegates questioned blacks' right to the suffrage, Murphey felt compelled to protest: "Has not the man who conquers upon the field of battle, grained any rights? Have we gained none by the sacrifice of our brethren?"

The Emancipation Proclamation and the presence of black troops ensured that, in the last two years of the war, Union soldiers acted as an army of liberation. As the Civil War drew to a close, the disintegration of slavery accelerated, even as masters clung tenaciously to the institution. Early in 1865, slaves were still being brought and sold in areas as yet unoccupied by Northern troops. By then, however, more than 1 million blacks were within Union lines inside the Confederacy, and another 700,000 lived in states of the border and Upper South where slavery was dead or dying. Even in Confederate territory, planters were negotiating wage and share agreements to induce their increasingly recalcitrant laborers to return to the fields. Seemingly minor incidents told of slavery's death throes, for example, the Mississippi black who responded early in 1865 to a planter's salutation "Howdy, Uncle" with an angry "Call me Mister." By 1865, no matter who won the Civil War, slavery was doomed.

For upholders of the South's "peculiar institution," the Civil War was a terrible moment of truth. The most perceptive among them suddenly realized they had never really known their slaves at all. "I believed that these people were content, happy, and attached to their masters," South Carolina rice planter A. L. Taveau confessed two months after the war's close. But if this were the case, why did the slaves desert their masters "in [their] moment of need and flock to an enemy, whom they did not know?" Blacks, Taveau now understood, had, for generations, been "looking for the Man of Universal Freedom."

James Brewer Stewart

THE CLASH BETWEEN PHILLIPS AND GARRISON

In this selection, James Brewer Stewart, a historian at Macalester College, shows that antagonistic agendas for social change during the Civil War severed a long friendship between Wendell Phillips (1811–1884) and William Lloyd Garrison (1805–1879) and polarized other abolitionists. By the early 1860s Garrison's quest for social approval and his strong nationalism had made him a staunch supporter of Lincoln and led him to bask in official recognition as the vindicated prophet of emancipation. With the approaching end of slavery, Garrison called for the dissolution of the antislavery societies and the organization of freedman aid organizations that would provide a moral and religious foundation for freedom.

Phillips objected. A dissident Boston Brahmin and Harvard Law School graduate, he was a prominent abolitionist and brilliant orator. Instead of following Lincoln and his moderate policies, Phillips endorsed John C. Fremont for the Republican presidential nomination in 1864. Fremont, he believed, would enact a federal program of military occupation and land redistribution in the South as well as civil rights, suffrage, and education for the ex-slaves. Phillips's personal ambition and political approach alienated Garrison. Their clash factionalized the Massachusetts Anti-Slavery Society and the American Anti-Slavery Society; the Garrisonians then abandoned both organizations to Phillips and his allies.

On December 4, 1863, members of the American Anti-Slavery Society convened in Philadelphia to mark three decades of activity. It was a time to reflect and celebrate. Garrison presided, and Samuel J. May, J. Miller McKim, and other veterans made speeches in which they cast their thoughts back to the 1830s, when they had been young and their movement small and despised. Now, vindication sat on the platform in the person of Senator Henry Wilson of Massachusetts, who told the abolitionists how great an inspiration the cause had been to him as he promised to work to

From *Wendell Phillips: Liberty's Hero* by James Brewer Stewart, Copyright © 1986 by Louisiana State University Press. Used with permission.

"break the last fetter of the last slave." Then as Garrison read their names, charter members of the society arose to great applause. Wendell Phillips did not add to the cheering, however, for he was in New York City's Cooper Institute, assailing Lincoln's Reconstruction plans before a distinguished audience of Republicans. As Garrison well knew, Phillips had boycotted the festival to protest disagreements with its sponsors.

From the first, Civil War had brought confusion to the American Anti-Slavery Society, for dozens of prominent people joined the organization they had denounced for so long. Some, including Elizur Wright, Jr., Lewis Tappan, Gerrit Smith, and Frederick Douglass, had returned from the Liberty party and its successors, and others, such as George B. Cheever and Henry Ward Beecher, were great evangelical preachers. Still others, seasoned politicians like Senator Wilson, George W. Julian, and John A. Andrew, had furnished the best proof of all that the old disunionist community of saints was rapidly vanishing, but in a way that could only make many longtime Garrisonians rejoice. Since the war was leading the North to abolition, it was not time, some of these veterans had concluded, to lay the cause aside. As early as 1862, Maria Weston Chapman, the Weston sisters, and J. Miller McKim had resigned from the American Anti-Society and had called instead for missionary efforts to former slaves.

Then Lincoln issued his Emancipation Proclamation, and Garrison declared his eagerness to dissolve the society, despite Phillips' immediate objection that the nation needed the abolitionists now more than ever. In January, 1863, for example, Garrison hinted at an antislavery gathering that final victory lay just ahead. Phillips praised Garrison's "encouraging faith" in "the progress of the antislavery idea," but he went on to lament the weaknesses of the Emancipation Proclamation and the need to stand by Lincoln for two more years. Phillips heaped praise on John C. Fremont and Benjamin F. Butler, the military governor of Union-occupied New Orleans, whose stringent policies were protecting blacks and repressing white obstructionists. These were men Lincoln ought to emulate. The Fosters and Charles L. Remond, displaying less diplomacy than Phillips, then pointedly reminded Garrison of the original Declaration of Sentiments of the American Anti-Slavery Society, specifically the clauses that bound abolitionists to eradicate not just chattel slavery but white racism itself across the land. This part of the abolitionists' work was far from complete. Thus, when Garrison again spoke in favor of dissolution, during the anniversary celebration in Philadelphia, Foster and Frederick Douglass were already well prepared. Denouncing Lincoln's proclamation as the product of expediency, they warned Garrison that white supremacy reigned as widely as ever in American political culture. As Douglass put it, abolitionists must never disband until "the black man of the South, and the black man of the North, shall have been admitted fully and completely into the body politic of America." He was clearly reflecting the sentiments of the conspicuously absent Wendell Phillips as well.

Just prior to this Philadelphia meeting, Lincoln had outlined some of his Reconstruction plans, which seemed to Phillips to reconfirm the folly of Garrison's call for dissolution. The president offered pardons to all who would swear loyalty to a Union without slavery, excluding only the most prominent Confederates; and he suggested that any rebel state should be readmitted when one-tenth of its 1860 population had taken this oath and had established an acceptable new state government. As to race relations, Lincoln insisted only that there be no more slavery; other "temporary arrangements" would be acceptable. Southern whites, understanding Lincoln's willingness to let them manage the freedmen alone, perhaps through peonage or apprentice systems, of course felt no compulsion to grant civil and political rights. Lincoln, moreover, had seemingly excluded Congress from the Reconstruction process. Charles Sumner, Ben Wade, and the rest were, presumably, to have no voice in determining readmission policy.

Some took Lincoln's statements as pragmatic efforts to weaken the rebellion and placate the border states, not as fixed policy. To Phillips, however, they seemed to fit a distressing pattern in which his own impact was hard to document. In 1863, for example, Lincoln had undercut Benjamin Butler's iron rule over "disloyal" whites in New Orleans by appointing Nathaniel P. Banks, an old Cotton Whig, as military governor of Louisiana. Banks had then conducted elections under the state's antebellum constitution that returned power to the old planter classes and had instituted a labor system that forced former slaves to work under restrictive labor contracts. Some abolitionists, Garrison among them, had justified Banks's regime as necessary to bring social order to chaotic Louisiana. Phillips, however, and the black abolitionists who had flooded Washington with protest petitions saw it as slavery in disguise. "What you call the freedom of Louisiana is 'Banks' freedom,' and it is no freedom to me," Phillips had declared, insisting on the contrary that no class or race was safe, "no freedom real . . . which does not place in the hands of the man himself the power to protect his own rights." As the Christian paternalist Garrison supported Lincoln and Banks, the Radical Republican Phillips began demanding that black men be granted independent citizenship, "in accord with our philosophy of government since the 4th day of July 1776." He now feared that Lincoln meant to extend his Louisiana policies throughout the rebel states.

After meeting with the president again early in 1863, Phillips came away certain that Lincoln had personally confirmed all such misgivings. In deciding to revisit the White House, Phillips had hoped to persuade Lincoln to appoint an antislavery leader like Fremont to administer subjugated areas of North Carolina. Instead, Lincoln had installed a unionist from that state, Edward N. Stanly, a former slaveholder who had once threatened Joshua Giddings with physical assault on the floor of the House of Representatives. Little wonder, then, that Phillips much preferred denouncing Lincoln at Republican gatherings to contemplating "victory" and retirement with Garrison. As his debates with abolitionist colleagues grew sharper, Phillips' attacks on Lincoln and his demands for reconstructing the South also became more wide-ranging.

In his speech before the New York City Republicans at the Cooper Institute Phillips rehearsed all his disagreements with the president. If he began rather mildly, it was only because he wished to develop many more fundamental criticisms. He could grant, he said, that the president was a "growing man, with his face zionward," but Lincoln's greatest merit, in Phillips' view, was that his obstinacy was weaker than "the force of events and the public pressure which crush it." In short, Lincoln could be pushed by abolitionist agitation, but even such pressure would not prevent the catastrophe Phillips foresaw should the president proceed as he wished with Reconstruction. Great secessionist planters would regain control over the South's economy, its politics, and its black labor force, reinstituting slavery under one guise or another and leaving the freedmen as helpless as they had been in 1860. Lincoln, according to Phillips, proposed that "we should stand and see the freedmen, whose arms helped us to victory, robbed of their liberty at the sight of its reality. Mr. Lincoln is a very prudent man, people say. Well, prudence is a worthy virtue, except when exercised at other people's expense."

As Phillips next detailed what he believed could be a truly effective Reconstruction policy, some of his reasons for boycotting Garrison's victory celebration suddenly became clear. Slavery would never truly be destroyed, he insisted, until the federal government "crumbled up the nobles' estates into small farms" and put them "into the hands of the negroes and white men who fought for [them]." Only by redistributing rebel lands and by subjecting the South to military occupation could a truly victorious North expect to "plant a union as sure to grow as an acorn to become an oak," said Phillips. "Plant two hundred thousand negro farmers, and by their side two hundred thousand white soldiers, and I will risk the South, Davis and all."

But confiscation would be only the first step. White Americans must never forget that they had "robbed four million men and their ancestors for seventy years" by practicing slavery. Every black had more than earned from them the "substantial protection in all his rights." And so Phillips returned to his lifelong reliance on the power of the state to institute a sweeping agenda of nationally legislated black equality. He called for the enactment of two constitutional amendments, one prohibiting slavery and the other providing that "no state shall make any distinction among its citizens on account of race or color." Then he demanded even more, proposing federal laws that guaranteed land and public education for every former slave. "The nation owes the negro not merely freedom," Phillips insisted. "It owes him land; it owes him education also. It is a debt that will disgrace us before the people if we do not pay it." Anything less, he warned, would lead to another fatal compromise similar to those of 1787 or 1850, exactly the direction in which Lincoln's plans inevitably led. "The President's plan is not feasible," Phillips warned, "and ends in shame or defeat. . . . A union so reconstructed would be sure not to work. Such a peace would be war in disguise." The great struggle between antagonistic nations that Phillips had spoken of so often would certainly continue, he believed, until the North realized that the slaves, to be truly free, must be protected with preferential legislation. And to achieve these goals, Phillips vowed finally, he would never rest until the nation had a president better than Lincoln, "someone whose character this war has brought to the surface. . . . In other words, until either Butler or Fremont mans the guns."

If Phillips had not quite made a presidential endorsement, he had certainly highlighted his disagreement with Garrison. He had also unveiled the rudiments of southern Reconstruction policies that he would ceaselessly reiterate during the next six years. Fremont (Phillips' new hope for achieving his sweeping objectives) and Lincoln (Garrison's agent of vindication) now represented opposite political poles for feuding abolitionists, and as they began to gravitate toward one leader or the other, division within the movement quickly grew. The wide differences now separating Phillips from Garrison also became dramatically public when the Massachusetts Anti-Slavery Society met in January, 1864.

In this first face-to-face debate with Garrison, Phillips delivered blunt warnings about the white South's intransigence, the importance of the upcoming presidential elections, and the dangers he saw in supporting Lincoln. Lincoln, a bigot, "does not recognize the negro as a man; he does not blot out races," Phillips charged, calling once more for laws that would revolutionize southern society—land redistribution, black suffrage, compulsory education, and an amendment banning racial discrimination. "As the educational apparatus of New England follows close behind the garrison," Phillips rhapsodized, technology and moral enlightenment would reshape the slaveocracy in the image of Massachusetts. "The moment we get an acre, we set a school house on it. God speed New England! and next door to it we set up a spinning machine; and next to that we plant in the sweat of each man's brow the harvest he is to gather and eat. Civilization taking possession of the recovered states!"

Lincoln wanted to stifle the liberating spread of free-labor civilization before it even began, Phillips asserted in conclusion, and he put forward a resolution condemning the president's haste to fabricate a "sham peace" that would return embittered whites to power and "leave the negro in a condition little better than slavery." Garrison then leapt to his feet and offered his own motion, which endorsed Lincoln's reelection and disagreed vehemently with Phillips' assessment. "Now Sir," said Garrison, "I do not believe a word of it, and cannot vote for it. . . . In my judgment, the reelection of Lincoln would be the safest and wisest course." When the vote was finally taken, Phillips' resolution prevailed by a three-to-two margin. The Massachusetts Anti-Slavery Society was now on record in opposition to Lincoln's second term, in favor of social revolution in the South, and controlled by a majority loyal to Wendell Phillips.

The victory itself actually meant far less than the dynamics that lay behind it. Garrison, in defending Lincoln, had rejected all that Phillips was seeking in his quest to create a republican South and to fulfill his vision of a nation whose laws secured harmony and freedom for all its races and classes. Phillips' own personal liberator seemed instead to favor replacing the crusade for equality with an "old clothes movement" that would "dish out thin soup" to the freedmen and hand their liberties to vengeful planters. Abolitionists would argue interminably over the next year as Garrison and his supporters prepared to leave the movement. Nothing anyone said, however, modified the fundamental clash of assumptions that Garrison and Phillips explored in this first exchange. A young abolitionist who listened to them argue sensed quite correctly that "something terrible" lay behind the more obvious points in Phillips' and Garrison's exchanges.

Garrison, to be sure, felt he had persuasive grounds for resenting Phillips' charge of abandoning the freedman. Like Quincy, the Westons, the Mays, Maria Chapman, and Oliver Johnson, Garrison believed that he was remaining truly faithful to one of abolitionism's oldest tenets. As a founder of the American Anti-Slavery Society, he had long ago declared it his obligation to prepare blacks for freedom by furnishing Christian assistance. Paternalism it certainly was, but Garrison believed it his duty to aid those whom society had so grievously wronged. From his perspective, Phillips' exclusive emphasis on legislation seemed dangerous. After all the statutes had been enacted, he feared, freedmen would still be left with no cultural or religious supports for their freedom. Phillips, in turn, regarded Garrison's quest for vindication as a serious threat not only to black emancipation but also to his self-conceived political role, which was continuing to expand as rapidly as debate over Reconstruction itself.

Having fashioned himself for decades to be a latter-day Edmund Burke, Phillips finally had begun to achieve the national stature he had dreamed about as a college student and even before. He had demonstrated that he was a newsmaker of indisputable authority, a radical spokesman for powerful constituencies, and he had taken pains to develop connections with influential politicians. Yet Lincoln seemed impervious to his influence. Now Garrison was joining the president to stand directly against all that Phillips wished to achieve. Content with the person in office, Garrison felt placidly removed from political struggle. Phillips, by contrast, was becoming ever more deeply enmeshed in partisan activities, seeking to translate his indisputably great influence into explicit political control. To those ends, he sought out Benjamin Butler as confidant and assured Sumner and George W. Julian that he intended "to work with your gang" to ripen "public opinion sufficient to control legislative action in . . . reconstruction." Little wonder, then, that Phillips felt his anger grow as Garrison challenged his loftiest social visions and most private political ambitions.

Major newspapers soon began speculating about an open break, while abolitionists tried to minimize the conflict. Garrison and Oliver Johnson wrote conciliatory editorials, asserting that "no schism exists in, or impends over, the Anti-Slavery body." Yet in the weeks before issuing these denials, Johnson had editorialized that the antislavery societies must disband as soon as the states ratified the Thirteenth Amendment. He, McKim, Quincy, and Samuel J. May also assured Garrison that Phillips was behaving irresponsibly, and Ann Warren Weston bluntly conveyed the same opinion to Ann Phillips. Phillips, meanwhile, received assurances of support from the predictable sources—the Fosters, Pillsbury, Henry Wright, and most of the female and black abolitionists. Personal relations were souring quickly. Phillips, for instance, hedged when invited to a recognition celebration for Garrison. "Give me a few days to consider when I return from a talking tour," he requested.

Although he protested privately that he still loved Garrison like a "dear brother," when he had ended his trip, he did not attend Garrison's party. Moreover, on that talking tour Phillips announced that John C. Fremont, not Lincoln, should bear the Republican party standard in 1864. Shortly thereafter, when the American Anti-Slavery Society gathered in New York City, Phillips was ready with still more anti-Lincoln resolutions. Garrison, of course, issued his familiar protest, but the society, by a small margin, voted against Lincoln's renomination. Twice now Phillips had demonstrated that he, not Garrison, controlled the antislavery societies.

John C. Fremont looked upon these developments with hope, for he wanted the nomination and had support in Congress. In late 1863, Fremont visited Boston, bought a summer home near the Phillips' place in Nahant, and delivered a stirring speech at the Music Hall. Phillips sat behind him on the platform, and enjoyed another friendly talk with Jessie Fremont. In May, 1864, when insurgent Republicans called for an independent nominating convention and demanded a platform of black suffrage and southern land redistribution, Phillips' interest in the candidacy of the "Pathfinder" had grown considerably. The convention was scheduled to meet in Cleveland before either of the two major parties selected its candidates.

Hoping to create upheaval in the politics that so baffled him and eager to secure his influence with Lincoln's possible replacement, Phillips endorsed the convention and put Fremont forward as his own nominee. "If Mr. Lincoln is reelected, I do not expect to see the union reconstructed in my day," he declared. "If I turn to General Fremont, I see a man whose first act was to use the freedom of the negro as his weapon." Phillips next traveled to Vermont to drum up anti-Lincoln delegates for the Republican nominating convention in Baltimore. Finally, as if to show everyone how completely he had abandoned his long-cherished independence, Phillips even appeared at his neighborhood Republican caucus, where he offered anti-Lincoln resolutions that party regulars roundly rejected. Then, in late May, the insurgent Cleveland convention met, adopted a platform of legal equality and land confiscation, and nominated Fremont. Meanwhile, at the Republican convention in Baltimore, Garrison was ushered to the speaker's platform as the delegates wildly cheered. Enjoying yet another moment of vindication, he wrote, "Even my friend Phillips would have been highly gratified with the tone and spirit of the convention." Now that he and Phillips were looking in such opposite political directions, Garrison could not have misspoken more completely.

Though Phillips plunged into electioneering with a will, he failed to transform himself into an effective political strategist. Actually believing that Fremont could win in a three-way election, he thought, at the least, that the Cleveland convention would frighten the Republicans so badly that they would abandon Lincoln for someone more radical. He even dreamed for a time that Fremont would become a "nucleus to which breaking parties may gravitate" as the entire structure of partisan politics collapsed. Soon, however, Phillips saw his naïve hopes deflated. Instead of expanding his role in politics and reshaping the Republican party, he was charged with abetting prosouthern "copperheads." Fremont, as Lincoln's supporters pointed out, would draw votes away from the wartime president even as his commander, Ulysses S. Grant, prepared to move south. Both the *Liberator* and the *Standard* therefore editorialized persuasively that Fremont's radical supporters were actually crippling the war to end slavery, and even close advisers like Aaron Powell urged Phillips to give Fremont up as "the smallest specimen of manhood he had ever attempted to associate with." Pillsbury wrote him even more bluntly: "To speak for [the] Cleveland [convention] up here, or indeed anywhere," he reported from New Hampshire, "is to class yourself with the copperheads." Phillips soon found himself forced to rebut charges that he had become the unwitting cat's-paw of the slave power, and Garrison, of course, delighted in his opponent's discomfiture.

As the summer wore on, Phillips grew increasingly irritated and confused. On the other hand, he insisted to detractors like Samuel May, Jr., that supporting Fremont had not really undermined his political independence. "Soon I shall find occasion to say why I shall remain a reformer—not a politician—still (as in 1843) prefer[ing] *justice* to the *union*." But to supporters like Elizabeth Cady Stanton he voiced a revealingly contradictory lament: "I wish I had more influence with F[remont] and some men less. But I believe in *him*." Wendell Phillips Garrison, Phillips' namesake, resolved his own divided family loyalties by lashing out at his second parent. "You surrendered your dignity and your independent position for a paltry equivalent," he wrote. By endorsing Fremont, the young Garrison lectured, "you left Olympus for a caucus." These words, of course, as Phillips surely appreciated, echoed his own assessment of Daniel Webster's political bankruptcy in 1850. He replied in patient tones but implausibly, for he insisted that he was now no less his own political man than he had been in the 1840s. William Lloyd Garrison and his confederates wrote to each other in the meantime, lamenting poor Wendell's behavior. By June, Garrison knew "that our society must be rent asunder. . . . I fear that P[hillips] has made up his mind to leave us. He is evidently in a heated state."

Garrison's was a noteworthy understatement. As Phillips' abolitionist friendships crumbled, so did his political aspirations, and he lashed out furiously at Garrison, now a "lost leader," and his followers. *Standard* editor Oliver Johnson became his target for special vehemence. Phillips claimed that Johnson's editorials criticizing Fremont had transformed the official voice of the American Anti-Slavery Society into a Lincoln campaign sheet. Johnson struck to his position, however, and was supported by the society's Executive Committee. When negotiations failed, the Phillips camp withdrew financial support for the paper. Phillips, Pillsbury, and others also prevented income from the Hovey Fund, an abolitionist bequest for freedman aid, from falling into Garrison's hands, and by now everyone had become so upset that the Executive Committee canceled the American Anti-Slavery Society's usual round of summer meetings. The Fremont campaign meanwhile became mired in confusion as Sherman's army moved decisively upon Atlanta and military triumph made Lincoln politically invincible. Fremont hurriedly withdrew his name from contention, spurning Phillips' last-minute pleas that he remain in the race.

Lincoln easily won the general election. The vast body of abolitionists, many of Phillips' usual supporters among them, rejoiced at the outcome even as the politically frustrated orator delivered a bitter post-election denunciation of the president at the Tremont Temple. His own association with Fremont had only hastened the collapse of abolitionist unity and cast doubt on his own political position. Indeed, from every perspective, Phillips' engagement in presidential politics could only be judged a debacle. In the aftermath nothing remained for him but to write Benjamin Butler sourly of his fears about the "too-hasty-peacemaker-on-any-terms" that the people had returned to the White House. Meanwhile, he tried to bolster his morale by believing that abolitionists could actually put aside their differences and "rally together to claim of the Republican party their performance of their pledge" of passing an emancipation amendment. This vain hope represented Phillips' sincere gesture to the memory of a fellowship, now shattered, that had sustained his spirit and confirmed his social visions for nearly thirty years. Never did he reveal his deeper feelings about his many broken friendships; it was too painful a subject for him to address openly.

Had even the slightest grounds remained for reconciliation, Garrison dashed them in January, 1865, when he announced to a meeting of the Massachusetts Anti-Slavery Society that the enfranchisement of the freedmen, though proper, must not be imposed on the South. Phillips, as usual, had readied a counterresolution that "no emancipation can be effectual, no freedom real" until universal male suffrage was enshrined as constitutional writ. Moreover, Phillips maintained, defeated states must be forced by Congress to enact black enfranchisement before being readmitted to the Union, lest white obstructionism prevent subsequent ratification of a suffrage amendment. After savage exchanges among Stephen Foster, Quincy, and Garrison, the competing resolutions were put to the vote, and Phillips won overwhelmingly. Even before the balloting, however, Garrison stalked out, leaving Phillips to remark magnanimously: "Whatever, therefore, may be the conclusion of the debate, I recognize the same leading mind at the head of the antislavery struggle. . . . In time to come we shall need, find and welcome the same leader." There could be no denying that Garrison had lost badly. Twice now, the Massachusetts Anti-Slavery Society had rejected his views, concurring with Phillips instead that the franchise was crucial to all aspects of postwar reform.

Once war had broken out, Phillips, as we have seen, had greatly expanded his demands for legislated equality, insisting that a powerful central government must develop laws to reshape the

South as a showplace of republican culture. In such a program, Garrison's states' rights notions obviously had no place. But despite his acquisition of power and his ever-growing reliance on state authority, Phillips harbored no fewer inherent suspicions of governments and political parties in 1864 than he had in 1844. He still believed that original sin held sway over human nature, officeholders still betrayed their constituents, governments still inherently tended toward despotism, and laws by themselves offered no automatic guarantees of liberty. Voters, however, most certainly did. At this point, Garrison's opposition to the national franchise constituted a declaration of total war against all that Phillips envisioned for America's reconstruction.

Waldo E. Martin, Jr.

FREDERICK DOUGLASS, ABOLITIONIST AND FEMINIST

During the Woman's Rights Convention at Seneca Falls, New York, in 1848, Frederick Douglass (1817–1895) seconded Elizabeth Cady Stanton's call for the female franchise. He remained a dedicated feminist throughout his long abolitionist career. Nonetheless, issues of race and gender greatly complicated efforts of reformers to forge a united front. Douglass joined forces with feminists in 1866 to form the Equal Rights Association dedicated to universal suffrage, but his priorities differed from those of Stanton, Susan B. Anthony, and their circle. Given the limited political possibilities of Reconstruction, he thought that black male suffrage must take precedence over women's vote, which was an even less popular cause with the male electorate. Stanton and Anthony were thus alienated from their abolitionist allies, such as Douglass, who endorsed black male suffrage over universal suffrage. The contention led in 1869 to two rival groups: Stanton's and Anthony's National Woman Suffrage Association (which at times reverted to racial recrimination) and the rival American Woman Suffrage Association (which endorsed the Fifteenth Amendment) led by Lucy Stone, Elizabeth Blackwell, and Julia Ward Howe. The 1869 rift over issues of gender and race was reminiscent of the abolitionist schism of 1837–1840. The author of this selection, Waldo E. Martin, Jr., teaches history at the University of California, Berkeley.

During the Civil War, abolitionist-feminists, regardless of their stand on the priority between abolitionism (or black liberation) and woman's liberation, sloughed aside their differences and focused squarely on the issue of the slave's emancipation. In the closing months of the war, Douglass reiterated his support for universal suffrage, but added that he believed the related, though separable, issues of black male suffrage and woman suffrage rested upon different bases. Douglass joined forces with feminist-abolitionists in 1866 to form an Equal Rights Association dedicated to universal suffrage. Again, he emphasized his belief that the black man's claim to the vote was more urgent than woman's. An increasingly ardent Republican, more and more he interpreted the Negro's future advancement as inextricably tied to the Negro's allegiance to the Republican party. Black male suffrage, he believed, represented a necessary Republican strategy to enhance its constituency, notably in the South. Most important, black male suffrage signified an integral step toward black liberation: making the political system more responsive to its black constituency. Unlike Stanton and Anthony who believed the Republican party's Reconstruction strategy should endorse the highly principled ground of universal suffrage, Douglass believed that black male suffrage represented a necessary and more viable first step toward universal suffrage. Douglass's priority, black male suffrage, clashed with that of Stanton and Anthony, woman suffrage. The Equal Rights Association institutionalized that clash.

Douglass's willingness to subordinate woman's suffrage to black male suffrage during Reconstruction revealed several things. First, it showed his tendency to view the antiracist component of his human rights philosophy as more important than its antisexist component. He thus identified primarily with the black liberation struggle and secondarily with the woman liberation struggle. Second, it evinced his ostensible rationale for subordinating woman's cause to the Negro's cause. Whereas for women the vote was "a desirable matter," for black men it was "a question of life and death." Whereas men were "compelled to protect . . . women" out of "politeness and affection," most whites hated blacks "and in proportion to the measure of the dislike is the necessity of defence before and in the law." Third, it illustrated the ineluctable male bias limiting his feminism. In part, then, Douglass's acceptance of the black man's vote, without the vote for woman, represented a compromise with, and tacit approval of, male supremacy.

Douglass, along with Gerrit Smith, Wendell Phillips, Lydia Maria Child, and Frances Ellen Harper, led those feminists who saw the woman's need for the vote as secondary to that of black men. Furthermore, they maintained that the prospects for eventually achieving woman suffrage were best working through the liberal, progressive wing of the Republican party. Stanton, Anthony, and Olympia Brown led those feminists who viewed woman's need for the vote as primary, arguing that even the liberal, progressive wing of the Republican party remained insufficiently committed to woman suffrage. As a result, they sought allies outside of what they construed to be an unsympathetic and unresponsive Republican party. These alliances were typically unstable and unsuccessful, for the other parties did not share the fervent singular commitment of the Stanton contingent to woman suffrage. This was particularly true in the cases of the attempted alliances between 1868 and 1869 with the National Labor Union and the Working Women's Association. In the latter case, the middle-class bias of the Stanton group helped to undermine the alliance. Another problem in both cases was the tricky question of manipulation. In both cases, the high-handed way in which the Stanton faction tried to graft their key concerns onto the key concerns of each group left them quite vulnerable to the charge of manipulation.

They attempted another series of more dubious alliances with racist Democrats, including James Brook, New York publisher and congressman, and Samuel S. Cox, Ohio journalist and congressman. Neither man evinced a cogent commitment to woman suffrage. Similarly, George Train, the eccentric railroad promoter, financier, woman suffragist, and racist, who initially helped to sponsor the *Revolution,* Stanton and Anthony's feminist newspaper, was another important ally. This series of alliances alienated innumerable anti-racists, notably Douglass, and actually gave the Stanton faction only marginal aid.

Congress ratified the Fifteenth Amendment guaranteeing black male suffrage on 25 February 1869. In early May, the Equal Rights Association met. Before the convention could respond directly to Stanton's keynote address calling for the association to dedicate itself to a sixteenth amendment enfranchising women, the problems of racism and priority between black male suffrage and woman suffrage touched off a series of heated exchanges. Stephen Foster accused Stanton and Anthony of racism because of their slurs against black men and their hostility to the Fifteenth Amendment. He maintained that their refusal to support the Fifteenth Amendment unless it included women represented a violation of Equal Rights Association principles and that they should consequently resign their offices.

Douglass supported Stanton's call to rally around a sixteenth amendment enfranchising women. Yet, the racist rhetoric she and her supporters exploited deeply upset him. Much of it, he observed, clearly aimed at vilifying black men—specifically, questioning their fitness to vote—sought to undermine congressional and public support for the Fifteenth Amendment. Indeed, as early as 1854, he had detected racism in Stanton's ardent feminism. In that year, he had supported a woman's rights pamphlet she prepared, but found it necessary to reject its assumption of the superiority of white women to Negroes. Arguing on behalf of the legal rights of white women, Stanton had remarked: "We are . . . moral, virtuous, and intelligent, and in all respects quite equal to the proud white man himself; and yet by your laws, we are classed with idiots, lunatics, and Negroes." This racist logic highly offended Douglass, who, like Stanton, did not relish being legally classified with "idiots" and "lunatics." He totally rejected as elitist and racist nonsense, therefore, her argument that somehow the political rights of white women rested on a firmer basis than those of black men. He noted: "We are willing to allow and contend that woman has as good a right as we have to the exercise of suffrage, but we can't grant even as a matter of rhetoric or argument, that she has a better" right.

The blatant racism of Stanton's feminism persisted. In a letter to the *National Anti-Slavery Standard,* 30 December 1865, she blasted the notion that Reconstruction should be "the Negro's Hour" alone. The nation's "representative women" had labored arduously for the freedom of the Negro, she maintained. "So long as he was lowest in the scale of being we were willing to press his claims; but now, as the celestial gate to civil rights is slowly moving on its hinges, it becomes a serious question whether we had better stand aside and see 'Sambo' walk into the Kingdom first." While willing to exploit "the strong arm and blue uniform of the black soldier" toward securing universal suffrage, she nevertheless saw the Negro as her racial and social inferior. She further argued that if the freedwomen were not enfranchised along with the freedmen, the former will have gone from one form of slavery to another. "In fact," she claimed, "it is better to be the slave of an educated white man, than of a degraded, ignorant black one."

Racism was not unusual, moreover, in the *Revolution*, which began publication in 1868. In fact, the publication of Train's blatantly antiblack male suffrage column, "That Infamous Fifteenth Amendment," in the *Revolution* sparked the charges of racism against the Stanton faction at the 1869 Equal Rights Convention. For Foster and Douglass, both of whom found the Train article pernicious, it did not matter that Train had disassociated himself from the journal. The article had been published and neither Stanton nor her supporters had repudiated Train, his arguments, and his racism. Douglass acknowledged his deep admiration for Stanton's work on behalf of "woman's rights and equal rights," but countered that he found her apparent approval of Train's article and similar ones deeply disturbing. He found particularly repugnant references to blacks throughout the *Revolution* "as 'Sambo,' . . . the gardener, . . . the bootblack, and the daughters of Jefferson and Washington."

Douglass's disaffection with the Stanton contingent within the Equal Rights Association centered not only on their exploitation of racism, but also on their intentionally destructive opposition to the Fifteenth Amendment because it did not include women. He thought their position strikingly ungenerous, especially because as white women their male relatives voted. Of course for the Stanton group, this was precisely the issue: only the male relatives of white women voted. For Douglass, on the contrary, the issue remained the overwhelmingly more urgent necessity of black male enfranchisement. He reiterated before the convention that:

With us, the matter is a question of life and death, at least, in fifteen States of the Union. When women, because they are women, are hunted down through . . . New York and New Orleans; when they are dragged from their houses and hung upon lampposts; when their children are torn from their arms, and their brains dashed out upon the pavement; when they are objects of insult and outrage at every turn; when they are in danger of having their homes burnt down over their heads; when their children are not allowed to enter schools; then they will have an urgency to obtain the ballot equal to our own.

To a voice which asked—"Is that not true about black women?"—Douglass responded· "Yes, yes, yes; it is true of the black woman, but not because she is a woman, but because she is black."

Douglass thought generous and proper the position of Julia Ward Howe, white feminist, social reformer, and author. At the Boston convention of the Equal Rights Association the year before, she had acknowledged: "I am willing that the Negro shall get the ballot before me." Once black male suffrage became law, Douglass unequivocally embraced woman suffrage as the next step in the struggle for universal suffrage. In the heat of the battle for priority between woman suffrage and black male suffrage, however, he had sometimes fallen prey to the pervasive male supremacist notion that at least woman's interests were indirectly represented through their natural and affectionate ties with men. Clearly, neither black women nor black men possessed any comparable mode of indirect representation. If black men got the vote, though, black women, too, would gain this indirect representation. But when the Fifteenth Amendment passed, there was no longer any need for Douglass to rationalize his elevation of the black male vote above woman's vote. Consequently, he no longer used the common antifeminist smoke screen of indirect representation.

Anthony had forcefully criticized the antifeminist bias of Douglass's indirect representation rationale. She suggested that it merely reinforced male supremacy. At the time, she observed of Douglass's stirring remarks before the final Equal Rights Association meeting in 1869 that the men rather than the women had clapped when he subordinated woman suffrage to black male suffrage. "There is not the woman born who desires to eat the bread of dependence," she argued, "no matter whether it be from the hand of father, husband, or brother; for any one who does so eat her bread places herself in the power of the person from whom she takes it." When Anthony suggested that Douglass would rather be a man than to "exchange his sex and take the place of Elizabeth Cady Stanton," Douglass implicitly agreed, asking sarcastically if woman suffrage would "change the nature of our sexes?" Douglass's question sidestepped the issue of sexism. It suggested, nonetheless, the preference, quite understandable from the male perspective, to face sexism from the vantage point of male dominance as opposed to that of female subordination.

Stone's "middle principle," which recognized woman's superior claim to the vote and the black man's superior practical need for it, eschewed the vulgar racism in the attacks of the Stanton faction on black men. She could forgive Douglass for his error of placing black male suffrage above woman suffrage "because he felt as he spoke." In her "middle principle," she soft-pedaled her theoretical contention that woman suffrage was ultimately "more imperative." Instead, she insisted that "we are lost if we turn away from the 'middle principle' and argue for one class." Ironically, however, she felt compelled to argue for woman's cause in response to Douglass's graphic description of southern racist oppression. She stressed the parallels between sexual and racial oppression. She contended that when Douglass spoke of "what the Ku Kluxes did all over the South," he failed to mention that northern "Ku Kluxes"—fathers—had total legal control over the custody of their children. Consequently, "any father—he might be the most brutal man that ever existed—" could separate a mother and child as effectively as a slave auctioneer on the block. Only in Kansas did mothers have legal recourse to claim their own children against such tyrants. Stone thus concluded that woman as well as the Negro faced "an ocean of wrongs too deep for any plummet." Indeed, she argued, "there are two great oceans; in the one is the black man, and in the other is the woman." The black woman apparently straddled these "two great oceans."

Because black women battled both racism and sexism, the issues of which battle took precedence in their own lives and which battle should take precedence in the black liberation struggle most directly affected them. Most black feminists, women included, apparently shared Douglass's point of view that the struggle against racism was paramount. Nevertheless, the issue of the priority between the grand principle of universal suffrage, encompassing woman suffrage and black male suffrage, and the compromise principle of black male suffrage alone, split black feminists as it did the Equal Rights Association, in which several actively participated. Robert Purvis, Charles Lenox Remond, Sojourner Truth, and Francis Watkins Harper—besides Douglass—were active participants. Purvis, Remond, and Truth pressed for universal suffrage as the priority, while Douglass and Harper pressed for black male suffrage as the priority. Unlike the Stanton faction that favored universal suffrage, preeminently woman suffrage, and opposed the Fifteenth Amendment for its failure to include women, black feminists also criticized that failure, but supported the amendment nonetheless as an important advance in the recognition of black rights. This closing of the black feminist ranks in support of the Fifteenth Amendment suggested that they perceived the struggle against racism as the priority. Speaking as black women as well as feminists, Harper supported this rationale, while Truth asserted that the battle against sexism was equally as important and necessitated at least equal commitment.

The demise of the short-lived Equal Rights Association in 1869 led to the formation that same year of rival woman suffrage organizations: the American Woman Suffrage Association headed by Stone, Blackwell, and Howe; and the National Woman Suffrage Association headed by Stanton and Anthony. Naturally enough, Douglass favored and worked closely with the former, which, unlike the latter, both supported the Fifteenth Amendment and agreed to male participation. In 1873, the Stanton group still alienated Douglass and his cohorts with "their flings at the Negro and the constant parading him before their conventions as an ignorant monster possessing the ballot, while they are denied it." Besides racism, these attacks revealed, Douglass maintained, "an aristocratic feeling" based on the status and superior education of these women.

By 1876, however, Douglass and the Stanton faction agreed upon a truce and united to work together for woman suffrage. Still, both parties remained sensitive to recent conflicts and did not apologize for past disagreements. A spirit of compromise prevailed in 1890 when the rival woman suffrage organizations finally merged. With Douglass and Stanton, as with their respective factions, though, now that the Fifteenth Amendment was law, the dilemma of the priority between black male suffrage and woman suffrage was moot. Between 1876 and his death nineteen years later, Douglass's feminist awareness deepened as he became increasingly attuned to woman's need for self-definition, her need to lead her own cause, as well as the impenetrable depths of sexism. These were clearly the key developments in Douglass's mature, post–1876 feminism.

The struggle for woman's rights, Douglass perceived, was a social reform movement with revolutionary ramifications. If fully realized, the social, political, and economic position of woman—in fact her basic cultural and historical position—could never be the same. He likened the achievement of sexual equality to "a revolution, the most strange, radical, and stupendous that the world has ever witnessed. It would equal and surpass the great struggle under Martin Luther for religious liberty." Like most feminists, nonetheless, his belief in the traditional nineteenth-century notions of woman's primary roles being familial and domestic circumscribed that understanding. Inadequate to the revolutionary task of total black liberation, even the most radical philosophy and pursuit of social reform were also inadequate to the revolutionary task of woman's total emancipation.

According to Douglass, male supremacy had complex roots: universal, historical, and cultural. Instead of fully detailing and exploring these roots, though, he generally described them. He spoke, for instance, of male supremacy being based upon "usage, custom, and deeply rooted prejudices" and "the universality of man's rule over woman." An unconscionable wrong and logical fallacy, male supremacy, he contended, was "too transparent to need refutation." Its origins, ideology, and reality revealed "strongly opposing forces"; "time-hallowed abuses"; "deeply entrenched error"; "world-wide usage"; "the settled judgment of mankind." As with slavery and racism, sexism poisoned social relations. He reiterated constantly, in reference to serious social evils, that "relations of long standing beget a character in the parties to them in favor of their continuance." This strong tradition of male supremacy worked especially against the vital feminist goal of woman suffrage. Douglass observed that "man has been so long the King and woman the subject—man has been so long accustomed to command and woman to obey—that both parties to the relation have been hardened into their respective places, and thus has been piled up a mountain of iron against woman's enfranchisement."

Douglass was very sensitive to the problem of male bias. Personally and ideologically, however, he never fully resolved it. He excoriated man for viewing and treating woman "as his drudge, or a convenient piece of household furniture." This blatant chauvinism constituted "striking evidence of his mental imbecility and moral depravity." Unlike such "open, undisguised, and palpable evils" as "war, intemperance, and slavery" which "the best feelings of human nature revolt at," the undeniable evil of sexism, from the perspective of male dominance, remained quite ambiguous, if not imperceptible. Douglass noted, consequently, that most men thought everything just fine with woman's condition. "She had no rights denied, no wrongs to redress." They likewise believed that "she herself had no suspicion but that all was going well with her. She floated along on the tide as her mother and grandmother had done before her as in a dream of Paradise. Her wrongs if she had any, were too occult to be seen, and too light to be felt." Although reinforcing male supremacy, the stifling impediments of male bias and false female consciousness, Douglass claimed, "did not appeal or delay the word and work" of woman suffrage which went forth, regardless.

The ironic antifeminist substratum of Douglass's feminism was most evident in the beginning stages of his feminist work. During this period, he tended to interpret certain aspects of woman's dependence on man as acceptable. He alleged, for example, that woman voted indirectly through her influence over her male relations. He also tended to be insensitive to the justifiable fears of many female feminist colleagues concerning male dominance within women's organizations, suggesting that these women felt unable to compete equally with men for positions within them. This feeling, Douglass implied, smacked of an acceptance of the notion of woman's inherent inferiority. The motivation and reasoning of his collegial feminist antagonists, however, were different. More personally and clearly than Douglass, they perceived the machinations of male dominance. The more important issue for them remained male supremacy, even among their male colleagues, rather than evidence of adherence to female inferiority among themselves.

Notably after his conflicts with the Stanton-Anthony faction over, first, the relative priority of woman suffrage and black male suffrage, and second, support for the Fifteenth Amendment, Douglass displayed a greater sensitivity to woman's inherent need for self-definition, self-direction, and self-representation. Once the Fifteenth Amendment became law, he was able to focus more fully on and, thus, to understand better the "Woman Question." He now unambiguously attacked the notion that woman was indirectly represented in government, as in society, through her male relations. "The vice of this relation," he now exclaimed, was that "it gives influence and excludes responsibility." He also elaborated upon the importance of responsibility as well as duty. "Divest woman of power [in this case, political power]," he warned, "and you divest her of a sense of responsibility and duty—two of the essential attributes of all useful exertion and existence."

Douglass, along with other nineteenth-century American feminists, black and white, men and women, waged a courageous struggle to reform the status of American women. The staunch opposition they met among most women and men failed to discourage them. In fact, the orthodox male supremacist counterattack forced them to examine and to argue their cause that much more rigorously and righteously. For feminists of Douglass's stripe, sexual equality, like racial equality, was indispensable to the millennium. Notwithstanding the limitations of nineteenth-century feminism generally and Douglass's feminism specifically, notably the failure to comprehend and to attack the conflict between woman's familial (and social) roles and her liberation, the struggle of these feminist pioneers to break out of the prison of male supremacy was remarkably advanced for the times.

The uneasy alliance between the struggles for woman's emancipation and blacks' emancipation, moreover, bore witness to the difficulty of trying to reform racism and sexism either separately or together. That Douglass and his feminist cohorts even attempted to do so attests to their path-breaking social reform vision and their undeniable historical importance. The greatness of their achievement, therefore, was not just what they actually accomplished, but even more important, their vanguard—albeit imperfect—commitment to egalitarianism in a profoundly sexist and racist society. In 1899 at a Douglass memorial meeting in St. Paul of the A. L. E. League of Minnesota, a Negro civil rights organization, Mrs. Rosa H. Hazel, a Negro spokeswoman, reflected upon the "Standard By Which Douglass's Greatness Shall Be Determined." She observed that "it may be that future biographers may think that the greatness of Douglass lay not alone in a life-long consecration for the elevation of his race, but in the breadth of view of this man of the people, who reached out not only for the good of the Negro race, but had the wisdom to foresee the larger good to be accomplished in that kind of justice which ignores both race and sex, giving to all equal opportunities, obligations and incentives in this country."

James M. McPherson

THE CIVIL RIGHTS ACT OF 1875

The Civil Rights Act of 1875 was the last major piece of Reconstruction legislation. Yet the passage of this law barring racial discrimination in public accommodations and jury selection revealed the declining influence of abolitionists and the waning interest of northerners in the "Negro question." As James M. McPherson, Edwards Professor at Princeton University, puts it, the effect of the law was "more symbolic than real." Not only did it lack meaningful enforcement power, but the controversial issue of school segregation was dropped from the final legislation. The Supreme Court in the *Slaughter–House* decision (1873) had already restricted the scope of the Fourteenth Amendment, as it would that of the Fifteenth in the *Reese* case (1876). And in the *Civil Rights* cases (1883) the high tribunal nullified the 1875 law, legitimating an era of Jim Crow segregation that would last until the Civil Rights and Voting Rights acts of 1964 and 1965.

On a brisk spring day in 1870, abolitionists convened in New York City to celebrate the ratification of the Fifteenth Amendment and to dissolve their antislavery societies. "Capstone and

From McPherson, James M. *The Abolitionist Legacy: From Reconstruction to the NAACP.* Copyright 1975 by Princeton University Press. Reprinted by permission.

completion of our movement," the Fifteenth Amendment climaxed 40 years of agitation for the freedom and equal rights of black people. During the last 10 years of this period, change had come with revolutionary swiftness. Four million slaves had been emancipated by force of arms, their freedom and civil equality had been written into the Constitution, half a million had already achieved literacy, and hundreds of their leaders had won election to office in states where they had recently been slaves. Although the veteran crusaders who gathered in April 1870 had hoped all this would one day come to pass, most of them had not expected to see it in their lifetimes. Little wonder that they praised God for His marvelous providence and dismantled their societies in a mood of triumph.

Yet while congratulating themselves on a job well done, the old campaigners warned each other that eternal vigilance would remain the price of the black man's liberty. "While this generation lasts it is probable the negro will need the special sympathy of his friends," said Wendell Phillips. "Our work is not done; we probably never shall live to see it done." The day after the dissolution of the American Anti-Slavery Society, many of its members reconstituted themselves as the "National Reform League" to work against "social persecution of men on account of their color."

Abolition of this "social persecution" was for abolitionists a vital unfinished task of Reconstruction in 1870. Many of them campaigned for civil rights legislation as the best way to accomplish the task. The National Reform League helped to push a public accommodations law through the New York legislature in 1873, and lobbied also for a federal statute. The Civil Rights Act passed by Congress in 1875 climaxed these efforts. But while this law seemed to complete the revolution of racial equality, the victory was more symbolic than real. Running counter to the general retreat from Reconstruction, the Civil Rights Act was passed mainly as a gesture to the departed spirit of Charles Sumner. Stripped of moral authority by the lukewarm commitment of its Republican sponsors, the law had little apparent impact on racial practices. Even its symbolic legal value came to an end in 1883 when the Supreme Court ruled it unconstitutional. Nevertheless the story of the abolitionists' role in events leading to its passage is the best starting point for understanding the part they played in the complex racial developments of the 1870s.

Although discrimination in housing, jobs, hotels, restaurants, and places of amusement long persisted in the North, Jim Crow on trains, steamboats, and streetcars had become rare by 1870. At the same time the visibility of segregation was growing in the South. Several cases were publicized in the antislavery press. In 1869 Lieutenant-Governor Oscar J. Dunn of Louisiana was denied admission to a first-class railroad car in his own state. In 1871 the captain of a Potomac river steamboat refused to allow Frederick Douglass into the boat's dining room. Gilbert Haven, the Massachusetts abolitionist who went south as bishop of the northern-based Methodist Episcopal Church, reported from Georgia that the second-class cars in which black passengers had to ride were "hideous pens."

Abolitionists in the South worked to break down this color line. Haven made a habit of riding in the "Negro car" when traveling with black clergymen. After the Mississippi legislature passed an antidiscrimination law in 1873, Haven visited Vicksburg, where he took two black pastors to breakfast at the city's best hotel. The waiter tried to serve them at a corner table behind a screen, but Haven walked over to a central table and said "we'll take our breakfast here." The owner refused; Haven threatened to sue. The owner gave in and the three men enjoyed a good breakfast at the table of their choice. Two abolitionist carpetbaggers in South Carolina, Gilbert Pillsbury and Reuben Tomlinson, helped persuade the commander of the federal occupying forces to abolish Charleston's streetcar segregation in 1867. The next year one of the first measures enacted by the new Republican legislature, which contained several former abolitionists, was a civil rights law forbidding discrimination in public facilities. This law was never fully enforced, but South Carolina blacks reportedly suffered less segregation than those of other southern states during Reconstruction. In Nashville, Fisk University's abolitionist president, Erastus M. Cravath, reacted swiftly when a ticket agent refused to sell him a dozen Pullman berths for the Fisk Jubilee Singers. Cravath telegraphed George Pullman himself, who wired a rebuke to the agent ordering him to sell Cravath the tickets. For the next quarter-century Pullman cars were officially nonsegregated.

Most abolitionists considered public school segregation one of the worst forms of discrimination. In a democratic society, wrote one, "the majority have no right to exclude the children of the minority from the schools, even though they open others 'as good' for their use. Such a separation in childhood would breed two races of citizens, hostile in their interests." By 1874 all of the New England states plus Michigan, Iowa, Minnesota, and Kansas had prohibited *de jure* segregation in public schools. Abolitionists were active in the antisegregation movements in these and other northern states. Freedmen's schools in the South established by abolitionist missionary societies were open to both races. In the early 1870s two Methodist abolitionists sat on the New Orleans school board, which presided over the desegregation of about one-third of that city's public schools and the assignment of black teachers to some of the mixed schools. When Henry J. Fox, a northern Methodist clergyman and abolitionist, was elected president of the University of South Carolina in 1873, he ordered the admission of a black applicant. Three southern white faculty members promptly resigned. "We are victors—and are going on to greater conquests," wrote Fox, who appointed sympathetic professors to the vacancies. In 1874 a black man joined the faculty. Large number of Negroes entered the university, most white students left, and by 1875 nine-tenths of the students were black. One of the new students had been a slave who remembered "standing in the door of one of the [university] buildings and crying because I could not go to school. Now thank God there has been a great change, the mountains have been brought low and the valleys are exalted."

Except in Louisiana and at the University of South Carolina, no public schools in the South were integrated during Reconstruction. In the North the schools in the states where most of the black population lived were segregated. And many other forms of discrimination persisted in both North and South. The failure of local and state efforts to banish these evils caused many abolitionists to call for national legislation. "Why sit supinely and let these insolent [hotel] proprietors virtually trample upon the great Constitutional guarantees?" asked one. "The hour for fawning, begging, and cringing has gone by. . . . It is necessary and proper that the *law* be appealed to."

Senator Charles Sumner led the drive for a national civil rights law. On May 13, 1870, he introduced a bill to forbid discrimination by railroads, steamboats, public conveyances, hotels, restaurants, licensed theaters, public schools, juries, and incorporated church or cemetery associations. Offenders would be tried by federal courts and punished with fines or imprisonment. When this bill became bottled up in the Senate Judiciary Committee, Sumner pushed for passage of an act to desegregate public schools in the District of Columbia as a pilot project for national legislation. Opponents maintained that integration would drive away white students and destroy public education in the District. Several abolitionists branded this argument specious. William Lloyd Garrison cited the success of desegregation in Boston and other northern cities despite the dire predictions of skeptics; after an initial shakedown period, he said, it would work as well in Washington. Even if white parents did threaten to take their children out of school, "surely it is not for Congress to grant them any indulgence." Arthur Edwards, young editor of the *Northwestern Christian Advocate* who had grown up as an abolitionist in the 1850s, thought that whites "afflicted with colorphobia" must "originate for themselves at their own expense select schools; the public schools must be for the public."

Though the Senate also buried the District of Columbia bill, Sumner made a determined bid for passage of his national civil rights act at the next session of Congress. Abolitionist journalists tried to stir up support for the measure. Editor George William Curtis of *Harper's Weekly* insisted that its passage was required to "remove the last lingering taint of slavery." Theodore Tilton proclaimed that "it is not enough to provide separate accommodations for colored citizens, even if in all respects as good as those of other persons; equality is not found in equivalent, but only in equality." Blacks and abolitionists in both North and South circulated petitions in behalf of the bill; scores of such petitions bearing thousands of signatures soon found their way to congressional desks. The Republicans' landslide victory in the 1872 election gave the party a two-thirds majority in both houses of Congress. Though President Ulysses S. Grant opposed efforts to legislate "social equality," he did recommend "civil rights" legislation in 1873. Whatever this ambiguous endorsement may have meant, most Republicans by this time favored some kind of civil rights law.

But two serious obstacles soon materialized, one legal and the other educational. In the *Slaughter–House* decision (April 1873) the Supreme Court ruled that the Fourteenth Amendment applied only to the privileges and immunities of national citizenship, leaving protection of state citizenship to the states themselves. Though the Court did not clearly define the respective spheres of state and national citizenship, opponents of civil rights legislation cited *Slaughter–House* when arguing against Sumner's bill as an unconstitutional extension of federal power into the realm of states' rights.

The ruling also raised the doubts of a few abolitionists. Although Henry C. Bowen of the *Independent* had been a strong supporter of civil rights legislation, he now stated that "an interpretation of the Fourteenth Amendment which . . . makes *all* the rights of citizenship subject to the legislative will of Congress" was never intended by the framers. When other abolitionists accused Bowen of backsliding, he replied that he did not abate a jot of his opposition to caste. "All such discriminations are oppressive, cruel, and unjust. We denounce them." But "we would not have Congress attempt to do even a good thing beyond the reach of its constitutional powers." Bowen tried to prove his sincerity by urging the states to pass civil rights laws, but a number of Negroes criticized him for deserting the cause. The black abolitionist George T. Downing told him that "the very nice concern you manifest for state rights might receive more consideration did it not oppose efforts in behalf of *personal rights.*"

The second obstacle to Sumner's bill was a growing conviction, shared by some abolitionists, that any attempt to force school desegregation on the South would destroy public education there. As an "abstract question" integrated schools were desirable, wrote an abolitionist carpetbagger in Virginia, but as a "practical question" nothing was "more certain than the utter ruin of our free schools if mixed schools are attempted in Virginia." Even though opposition to integration was based on "unreasonable prejudice," added the *Independent,* we "have lived long enough to know that this prejudice, so far as it exists, is not to be corrected by the legislative coercion of a civil rights bill. It is far better to have both [races] educated, even in 'separate' schools, than not to have them educated at all."

Although Bowen's belief that coercion could not abolish

racism was spreading among former abolitionists, most of them still believed that race prejudice "will perish when the law refuses to sanction the distinction to which it leads." The phalanx of old crusaders remained fairly solid on the civil rights issue. . . .

The bill's most influential supporter outside Congress was George William Curtis, editor of *Harper's Weekly* whose circulation of 150,000 made it the largest weekly in the country. An antislavery man from his youth, Curtis became even more closely identified with the movement in 1856 when he married Anna Shaw, daughter of the prominent abolitionist Francis G. Shaw. On the question whether law could curb prejudice, Curtis took an aggressive stand in 1874. By penalizing its consequences, he said, law would "clear the way for its disappearance." When "hotels and restaurants may turn respectable guests away because they are of the colored race, and theatres and cars, all doing business by legal licence, may refuse them entrance for the same reason, it is plain that the law fosters the prejudice." But when "the law enables the colored guest to call the offending host to account . . . the prejudice will begin to wane." As for the argument that school desegregation would cripple public education in the South and was therefore a "false friendship" for the Negro, Curtis thought it "much wiser to take the risk of closing some of the schools now than of nourishing a prejudice of this kind indefinitely."

Abolitionists mounted a journalistic barrage in 1874 to reinforce and amplify these propositions. Bishop Gilbert Haven insisted that "there is no cure for this evil except by law. . . . Moral suasion never killed so much as a mosquito sin." William W. Patton, a long-time abolitionist and future president of Howard University, considered it "to little purpose that we give the freedman other rights and privileges, if we are powerless to protect" his right to "go from place to place, to eat and drink and sleep, to be sheltered from the storm, to enjoy as do others the ordinary comforts of life." After a visit to Georgia a Methodist abolitionist declared that "there is nothing [the South] so much needs as good laws thoroughly enforced." Of course southern whites say "they don't want to be compelled to concede social equality to 'niggers,' they don't want this, and that and the other. Well, suppose they don't; what then? Are they to dictate and domineer as in the past? . . . We have had enough of that."

Conceding that the "school argument is the only one used by the opponents of the bill which deserves the slightest respect," abolitionists realized that to answer it they would have to do more than point to the integration of a few black children in the Boston schools. Fortunately, more relevant examples existed. The experience of New Orleans, said one abolitionist, "strongly disputes" the assumption that desegregation would destroy public education in the South. And faculty members at abolitionist-founded Berea College, where 167 black and 117 white students attended classes together peacefully from the elementary to the college grades, insisted that what had been done there "can be done again elsewhere . . . If Christian men and women will stand for the right."

Despite these efforts to mobilize support, Sumner's bill languished in Congress. On March 11, 1874, the senator died. On his deathbed he said to a close friend: "My bill, the civil-rights bill,—don't let it fail!" Two months later the Senate finally passed the measure (minus the provision on church associations). Several senators voted aye as a memorial gesture to their departed colleague; the House, perhaps less affected by Sumner's passing, adjourned without action.

The 1874 congressional elections muddied the crosscurrents of civil rights pressures. The campaign produced fierce outbreaks of violence against black voters in several southern states. Commenting on this, the *Boston Commonwealth,* edited by political abolitionist Charles Wesley Slack, stated that "there has been too much shilly-shallying about the civil rights bill. It is seen everywhere that no Southern hate has been placated by deferring action on that bill. The Republicans had better stake the enhanced devotion of the blacks by passing that bill than longer hope to conciliate a set of worthless Southerners by refraining from so doing." But the Democrats made large gains in both North and South in November, winning control of the next House of Representatives. President Grant was reported to believe that popular hostility to the civil rights bill was partly responsible for Republican defeat (this may have been true in several districts) and it was rumored that he would veto the bill if it reached his desk.

Since the outlook for civil rights legislation seemed bleak when Congress convened in December 1874, the bill's managers decided to amputate the school clause to save the rest of the measure. In response to radical protests against this surgery, some Republican congressmen suggested the addition of a provision requiring that any school district maintaining separate schools must insure their equality in every respect. But Curtis considered such a proposal "puerile." Anyone with "common sense knows that in a community where color prejudice is so strong as to abandon the whole school system rather than to provide for schools in common, schools of equal excellence are simply impossible." Wendell Phillips agreed that separate schools even if equal in theory were seldom so in fact. "Herd together the children of the poor, no matter whether the colored poor or those of any other race—whose parents have not the education to see defects, or the influence to secure attention to their complaint," and the schools would deteriorate. "The negro child loses if you shut him up in separate schools, no matter how accomplished his teacher or how perfect the apparatus." And Congressman James Monroe, a veteran abolitionist from Oberlin, opposed the separate but equal amendment as "a dangerous precedent. . . . If we once establish a discrimination of this kind we know not where it will end."

Despite abolitionist opposition, the House cut the school and cemetery provisions from Sumner's bill and then passed the emasculated civil rights act on February 4, 1875. The Senate concurred, and the measure became law when Grant signed it on March 1. Few observers seemed to take the Civil Rights Act seriously. The *Washington National Republican* described it as a "piece of legislative sentimentalism"; the *Nation* thought it "amusing . . . tea-table nonsense." Several officials in the Justice Department considered the law unconstitutional. And not only were many of the 162 Republican congressmen who voted for it in the House lukewarm if not skeptical, but 90 of them were lame ducks, having been retired by the voters at the previous election. Under such circumstances, prospects for enforcement were dubious.

Abolitionists were far from jubilant over what they considered a hollow victory. Though the bill was "good as far as it goes," said one, the deletion of the school clause "simply postpones the question to the future." Curtis believed that "to say that half a loaf is better than no bread" was "absurd" because "the bill recognizes and indirectly authorizes the very prejudice against which it is supposed to be directed," while John D. Baldwin of the *Massachusetts Spy* considered its passage almost "a cause for regret [rather] than congratulation."

But the Civil Rights Act may have had some initial impact in the South. Although abolitionist Anna Dickinson reported during a southern trip in the spring of 1875 that she found a tacit agreement among blacks to avoid trouble by refraining from testing the law, Gilbert Haven maintained that Negroes could now get into first-class cars on some railroads. When Thomas Wentworth Higginson traveled through the south Atlantic states in 1878, viewing matters with "the eyes of a tolerably suspicious abolitionist," he professed to find little overt discrimination. "I rode with colored people in first-class cars throughout Virginia and South Carolina," he said, "and in street cars in Richmond and Charleston." He added, almost as an afterthought, that "in Georgia, I was told, the colored people were not allowed in the first-class cars; but they had always a decent second-class car."

Many Negroes in Georgia, however, did not consider the second-class accommodations "decent." "The fact is," reported a black clergyman whose duties made it necessary for him to travel widely, "pushing the colored people off to themselves is the practice of all the South. . . . In Atlanta everything is separate. You go to the depot, and you find three sets of rooms—*to wit,* 'Ladies' Rooms,' 'Gentlemen's Rooms' and 'Freedmen's Rooms'! You enter the cars, and the same heathen rule bears sway, only to be broken when white men wish to smoke, and then they come into the 'Freedmen's Car.'"

One can find scores of such complaints in newspapers of the period. One can also find reports of nonsegregated public carriers similar to Higginson's. This seemingly contradictory evidence only confirms C. Vann Woodward's thesis that, before the onset of legalized segregation in the 1890s, uncertainty and fluidity characterized racial patterns in the South. It does appear that in the first months after passage of the Civil Rights Act some public facilities obeyed it, but as it became clear that the Justice Department intended to do little to enforce the law, practices reverted to local custom, which varied widely.

After several cases had been appealed through lower courts,

the Supreme Court in 1883 ruled the Civil Rights Act unconstitutional on the ground that the Fourteenth Amendment gave Congress no power to legislate against discrimination by *individuals* (as opposed to states). The *Nation* noted that the public's general indifference to the decision showed "how completely the extravagant expectations as well as the fierce passions of the war have died out." Nevertheless several abolitionists denounced this "new Dred Scott decision." George B. Cheever, an old abolition warhorse whose rehetoric was still untamed at the age of 76, said that "a resurrected band of Ku-Klux savages could hardly have done worse" than the Court whose decision consigned the freedmen "back to the reign of contempt, injury, and ignomy." But some abolitionists who had advocated the Civil Rights Act a decade earlier viewed the Court's ruling with resigned acquiescence. The law had long been a dead letter, they said, so the Negro had lost only an empty symbol. William W. Patton thought that the Court's decision "leaves colored people as to legal protection just where it leaves white people." Most civil rights, said Patton, "including that of life itself," fell within the province of state law, and he urged blacks to keep up "a steady agitation" for the passage of state civil rights laws. He also suggested a new federal statute based on the interstate commerce clause of the Constitution to guarantee equal treatment in interstate travel.

Although several northern states did pass civil rights laws in the 1880s, they were weakly enforced. Abolitionist journalists continued to publicize Jim Crow incidents in both North and South, but never again did their militancy on this issue reach the level of 1874–1875. Experience seemed to confirm that laws alone could not change racial mores. And the question of segregation per se tended to lose significance as the whole edifice of Reconstruction began to collapse in the 1870s. Republican victory in the 1872 presidential election temporarily shored up the edifice, but the issues of the election alarmed many of those abolitionists who had gathered only two years earlier to celebrate the "consummation of the anti-slavery struggle."

SUGGESTIONS FOR FURTHER READING

Journals and Surveys

The literature on abolitionism is extensive. Historical journals that often publish essays on abolitionism include *The Journal of the Early Republic, Civil War History, The Journal of Southern History,* and *Slavery and Abolition: A Journal of Comparative Studies.* Along with *The Journal of American History,* these quarterlies have regular bibliographies in which current studies on abolitionism can be identified.

Books that place abolitionism in the broad context of history are C. Duncan Rice, *The Rise and Fall of Black Slavery* (New York, 1975); David Brion Davis, *The Problem of Slavery in Western Culture* (Ithaca, N.Y., 1966); Davis, *Slavery and Human Progress* (New York, 1984); and Robert W. Fogel, *Without Consent of Contract: The Rise and Fall of American Slavery* (New York, 1989). Racial perspectives in America are discussed over the long view in Winthrop Jordan, *White Over Black: American Attitudes Toward the Negro, 1550–1812* (Chapel Hill, N.C., 1968) and George

Frederickson, *The Black Image in the White Mind: The Debate on Afro-American Character and Destiny*, 1817–1914 (New York, 1971).

The standard survey on American abolitionism is James B. Stewart, *Holy Warriors: The Abolitionists and American Slavery* (New York, 1976). More interpretative works are Ronald G. Walters, *The Antislavery Appeal: American Abolitionism after 1830* (Baltimore, 1976); Peter Walker, *Moral Choices: Memory, Desire and Imagination in Nineteenth-Century American Abolition* (Baton Rouge, 1978); and Lawrence J. Friedman, *Gregarious Saints: Self and Community in American Abolitionism, 1830–1870* (New York, 1982). Though neoabolitionist and antiGarrisonian, Dwight L. Dumond's *Antislavery: The Crusade for Freedom* (New York, 1961) is filled with facts and illustrations.

A good place to begin with the voluminous writing on the related subject of slavery is with Peter Kolchin, *American Slavery, 1619–1877* (New York, 1993) and Lawrence B. Goodheart, Richard D. Brown, and Stephen G. Rabe, eds., *Slavery in American Society*, 3d ed. (Lexington, Mass., 1993). John Hope Franklin and Alfred A. Moss, Jr., *From Slavery to Freedom: A History of Negro Americans*, 6th ed. (New York, 1987) is the standard text on African-American history. For antebellum reform, see Ronald G. Walters, *American Reformers, 1815–1860* (New York, 1978).

Historiography

Older works, now superceded, are Albert B. Hart, *Slavery and Abolition, 1831–1841* (New York, 1906); Alice D. Adams, *The Neglected Period of Anti-Slavery in America, 1808–1831* (Boston, 1908); and Jesse Macy, *The Anti-Slavery Crusade* (New Haven, Conn., 1919). Modern abolitionist studies began with Gilbert H. Barnes, *The Anti-Slavery Impulse, 1831–1860* (New York, 1933). Barnes placed antebellum abolitionism in the context of the religious revivals and social reforms of the era, but his work, like Dwight Dumond's, draws too simple a distinction in favor of Theodore Weld and the Lane seminarians and against William Lloyd Garrison and New England abolitionists. In contrast, another early survey, Louis Filler's *The Crusade Against Slavery, 1830–1860* (N.Y., 1960), is more even-handed.

David Donald's argument in "Toward a Reconsideration of

Abolitionists" in *Lincoln Reconsidered* (New York, 1956) is that abolitionist leaders were a displaced social elite. The status theory is effectively challenged by Robert A. Skotheim, "A Note on Historical Method: David Donald's 'Toward a Reconsideration of Abolitionists,'" *Journal of Southern History*, 25 (1959), 356–365 and Gerald Sorin, *New York Abolitionists: A Case Study of Political Radicalism* (Westport, Conn., 1971).

Stanley Elkins's "Slavery and the Intellectual" in *Slavery: A Problem in American Institutional and Intellectual Life* (Chicago, 1959) disparaged abolitionists as moralists without institutional responsibility. In reaction to Elkins and other critics of abolitionists, Martin Duberman in "Abolitionists and Psychology," *Journal of Negro History*, 47 (1962), 183–191 and in the influential volume *Antislavery Vanguard: New Essays on the Abolitionist* (Princeton, 1965) argued that abolitionists were not neurotic malcontents but courageous radicals confronting actual social ills. For a qualified appreciation of Elkins' thesis, see Bertram Wyatt-Brown, "Stanley Elkins' Antislavery Interpretation: A Re-examination," *American Quarterly*, 25 (1973), 154–176. And a relevant theoretical examination of social change is Aileen S. Kraditor, "American Radical Historians on Their Heritage," *Past and Present*, 56 (1972), 136–152.

In addition, Aileen S. Kraditor revised the interpretation of the abolitionist schism of 1837–1840 in *Means and Ends in American Abolitionism: Garrison and His Critics on Strategy and Tactics* (New York, 1969). Contrary to the prevailing wisdom, she found that the anti-Garrisonians were intolerant and inflexible. Bertram Wyatt-Brown's "William Lloyd Garrison and Antislavery Unity: A Reappraisal," *Civil War History*, 13 (1967), 5–24, and James B. Steward in "The Aims and Impact of Garrisonian Abolitionism, 1840–1860," *Civil War History*, 15 (1969), 197–209 and "Peaceful Hopes and Violent Experiences: The Evolution of Reforming and Radical Abolitionism, 1831–1837," *Civil War History*, 17 (1971), 293–309 further clarified the Garrisonian position. In addition, the intellectual assumptions of Garrisonians are given sophisticated treatment in Lewis Perry, *Radical Abolitionism: Anarchy and the Government of God in Antislavery Thought* (Ithaca N.Y., 1973).

By the early 1970s the abolitionists, including Garrison, had been rehabilitated as serious social reformers whatever their flaws.

The issue had become, as Lewis Perry announced in "Psychology and the Abolitionists: Reflections on Martin Duberman and the Neoabolitionists of the 1960s," *Reviews in American History,* 2 (1974), 309–322, not to praise or to damn the abolitionists but to understand their lives and times, which is currently the dominant mode of historiography.

The following works are important evaluations of abolitionist studies: Merton L. Dillon, "The Failure of the American Abolitionists," *Journal of Southern History,* 25 (1959), 159–177; Dillon, "The Abolitionists: A Decade of Historiography, 1959–1969," *Journal of Southern History,* 35 (1969), 506–522; Richard O. Curry, ed., *The Abolitionists* (Hinsdale, Ill., 1973); Lewis Perry and Michael Fellman, eds., *Antislavery Reconsidered: New Perspectives on the Abolitionists* (Baton Rouge, 1979); Lawrence J. Friedman, "Historical Topics Sometimes Run Dry: The State of Abolitionist Studies," *The Historian,* 43 (1981), 177–194; Richard O. Curry and Lawrence B. Goodheart, " 'Knives in the Heads': Passionate Self-Analysis and the Search for Identity in Recent Abolitionist Historiography," *Canadian Journal of American Studies,* 14 (1983), 401–414; and Betty L. Fladeland, "Revisionists vs. Abolitionists: The Historiographical Cold War of the 1930s and 1940s," *Journal of the Early Republic,* 6 (1986), 1–21.

Primary Sources

A guide to printed, original sources is Dwight L. Dumond, ed., *A Bibliography of Antislavery in America* (Ann Arbor, 1961). Contemporary works by abolitionists are Richard O. Curry and Joanna D. Cowden, eds., *Slavery in America: Theodore Weld's American Slavery As It Is* (Itasca, Ill., 1972); William Lloyd Garrison, *Thoughts on African Colonization* (Boston, 1832); Oliver Johnson, *William Lloyd Garrison and His Times* (Boston, 1879); Samuel J. May, *Some Recollections of Our Anti-Slavery Conflict* (Boston, 1868); Parker Pillsbury, *Acts of the Anti-Slavery Apostles* (Concord, N.H., 1883); and Henry B. Stanton, *Random Recollections* (Johnstown, N.Y., 1885); Lewis Tappan, *The Life of Arthur Tappan* (New York, 1870); and Elizur Wright, *Myron Holley and What He Did for Liberty and True Religion* (Boston, 1882).

For collections of letters and documents, see Wendell Lloyd Garrison and Francis P. Garrison, *William Lloyd Garrison, 1805–1879,* 4 vols. (New York, 1885–1889); Walter M. Merrill and Louis Ruchames, eds., *The Letters of William Lloyd Garrison, 1805–1879,* 6 vols. (Cambridge, Mass., 1971–1981); Gilbert H. Barnes and Dwight L. Dumond, eds., *The Letters of Theodore Dwight Weld, Angelina Grimké Weld and Sarah Grimké, 1822–1844,* 2 vols., (New York, 1934); Dumond, ed., *The Letters of James Gillespie Birney,* 1831–1857, 2 vols. (New York, 1938); John W. Blassingame, et al., eds., *The Frederick Douglass Papers,* 5 vols. (New Haven, 1979–1992); Philip S. Foner, *The Life and Writings of Frederick Douglass,* 4 vols. (New York, 1950–1955); Milton Meltzer and Patricia G. Holland, eds., *Lydia Maria Child: Selected Letters, 1817–1880* (Amherst, Mass., 1982); and C. Peter Ripley, et al., eds., *The Black Abolitionist Papers,* 5 vols. (Chapel Hill, N.C., 1985–1992).

Useful guides to newspapers are John W. Blassingame and Mae G. Henderson, eds., *Antislavery Newspapers and Periodicals,* 5 vols. (Boston, 1984); Donald Jacobs, ed., *Antebellum Black Newspapers* (Westport, Conn., 1976); and Truman Nelson, *Documents of Upheaval: Selections from The Liberator* (New York, 1966). Howard H. Bell has edited the *Minutes of the Proceedings of the National Negro Conventions, 1830–1864* (New York, 1969). Anthologies of original sources include Louis Ruchames, ed., *The Abolitionists* (New York, 1964); William H. Pease and Jane H. Pease, eds., *The Antislavery Argument* (Indianapolis, 1965); and John L. Thomas, ed., *Slavery Attacked* (Englewood Cliffs, N.J., 1965); and Herbert Aptheker, ed., *A Documentary History of The Negro People in the United States* (New York, 1969).

Revolutionary Era and Early Republic

For the Quakers, the first whites to question slavery, see Thomas Drake, *Quakers and Slavery in America* (New Haven, Conn., 1950) and Jean R. Soderlund, *Quakers and Slavery: A Divided Spirit* (Princeton, N.J., 1985). David Brion Davis's *The Problem of Slavery in the Age of Revolution, 1770–1823* (Ithaca, N.Y. 1975) is a magisterial treatment of the period.

On race and revolution, consult Benjamin Quarles, *The Negro in the American Revolution* (Chapel Hill, N.C. 1961); Duncan J.

McLeod, *Slavery, Race and the American Revolution* (Cambridge, Mass., 1974); Ira Berlin, "The Revolution in Black Life," in Alfred E. Young, ed., *The American Revolution: Exploration in the History of American Radicalism* (DeKalb, Ill., 1976), 347–382; Ira Berlin and Ronald Hoffman, eds., *Slavery and Freedom in the Age of the American Revolution* (Charlottesville, Va., 1983); Gary B. Nash, *Race and Revolution* (Madison, Wis., 1990); and Sylvia R. Frey, *Water From the Rock: Black Resistance in a Revolutionary Age* (Princeton, N.J., 1991). Howard A. Ohline, "Republicanism and Slavery: Origins of the Three-Fifths Clause in the U.S. Constitution," *William and Mary Quarterly* 28 (1971), 563–584 and Paul Finkelman, "Slavery and the Constitutional Convention: Making a Covenant with Death," in Rechard Beeman, Stephen Botein, and Edward C. Carter II, eds., *Beyond Confederation: Origins of the Constitution and American National Identity* (Chapel Hill, N.C., 1987) are important on the Constitution.

The standard work on northern abolitionism in the early republic is Arthur Zilversmit, *The First Emancipation* (Chicago, 1967). Case studies are Gary B. Nash *Forging Freedom: The Formation of Philadelphia's Black Community, 1720–1820* (Cambridge, Mass., 1988); Gary B. Nash and Jean R. Soderlund, *Freedom by Degrees: Emancipation in Pennsylvania and Its Aftermath* (New York, 1991); and Shane White, *Somewhat More Independent: The End of Slavery in New York City, 1770–1810* (Athens, Ga, 1991). P. J. Staudenraus, *The African Colonization Movement* (New York, 1961) remains the best book on this subject.

Religion

The subject of antebellum reform is put into a broad perspective of the Second Great Awakening in John L. Thomas, "Romantic Reform in America, 1815–1865, *American Quarterly,* 17 (1965), 656–681. Studies that stress the relationship between evangelicalism and abolitionism are Gilbert H. Barnes, *The Anti-Slavery Impulse, 1830–1844* (New York, 1933); Whitney R. Cross, *The Burned-Over District: The Social and Intellectual History of Enthusiastic Religion in Western New York, 1800–1850* (Ithaca, N.Y., 1950); Anne C. Loveland, "Evangelicalism and 'Immediate Emancipation' in American Antislavery Thought," *Journal of Southern History,* 32 (1962), 172–188; and Bertram Wyatt–Brown,

"Prelude to Abolitionism: Sabbatarian Politics and the Rise of the Second Party System." *Journal of American History*, 58 (1971), 316–341. See also John R. Bodo, *The Protestant Clergy and Public Issues, 1812–1848* (Princeton, N.J., 1954); Charles C. Cole, Jr., *The Social Ideas of Northern Evangelists, 1826–1860* (New York, 1954); Timothy L. Smith, *Revivalism and Social Reform in Mid-Nineteenth Century America* (New York, 1957); William G. McLoughlin, *Modern Revivalism: Charles Grandison Finney to Billy Graham* (New York, 1959); Charles I. Foster, *An Errand of Mercy: The Evangelical United Front, 1790–1837* (Chapel Hill, N.C., 1960); Clifford S. Griffin, *Their Brothers' Keeper: Moral Stewardship in the United States, 1800–1865* (New Brunswick, N.J., 1960); and Victor B. Howard, *Conscience and Slavery: The Evangelistic Calvinistic Domestic Missions, 1837–1861* (Kent, Ohio, 1990).

The social origins of revival religion are explored in Paul E. Johnson, *A Shopkeeper's Millennium: Society and Revival in Rochester, New York, 1815–1837* (New York, 1978). The connection between abolitionism and religion is addressed in Christine Bolt and Seymour Drescher, eds., *Anti-Slavery, Religion and Reform.; Essays in Memory of Roger Anstey* (Folkestone, Eng., 1980) and John R. McKivigan, *The War Against Proslavery Religion: Abolitionism and Northern Churches, 1830–1865* (Ithaca, N.Y., 1984).

Abolitionists and Antiabolitionists

Identifying the abolitionists is the concern of Betty Fladeland, "Who Were the Abolitionists?" *Journal of Negro History*, 43, (1964), 99–115; Bertram Wyatt-Brown, "New Leftists and Abolitionists: A Comparison of American Radical Styles," *Wisconsin Magazine of History*, 13 (1970), 256–268; Lawrence B. Goodheart, "Abolitionists as Academics: The Controversy at Western Reserve College, 1832–1833," *History of Education Quarterly*, 22 (1982), 421–433; and Bertram Wyatt–Brown, "Conscience and Career: Young Abolitionists and Missionaries Compared," in *Yankee Saints and Southern Sinners* (Baton Rouge, 1985), 43–75. John B. Jentz, "The Antislavery Constitutency in Jacksonian New York City," *Civil War History*, 27 (1981), 101–122 and Edward Magdol, *The Antislavery Rank and File: A Social Profile of the Abolitionists' Constituency* (Westport, Conn., 1986) seek to find out who supported the abolitionists.

The phenomenon of northern antiabolitionism is discussed in Linda K. Kerber, "Abolitionists and Amalgamators: The New York City Race Riots of 1834," *New York History,* 58 (1967), 28–40; Lorman Ratner, *Powder Keg: Northern Opposition to the Antislavery Movement, 1831–1840* (New York, 1968); and Leonard L. Richards, *"Gentlemen of Property and Standing": Anti-Abolition Mobs in Jacksonian America* (New York, 1970).

Biography

Collective studies include Jane H. Pease and William H. Pease, *Bound with Them in Chains: A Biographical History of the Antislavery Movement* (Westport, Conn., 1972); Dorothy Sterling, ed., *We Are Your Sisters: Black Women in the Nineteenth Century* (New York, 1984); R. J. M. Blackett, *Beating Against the Barriers: Biographical Essays in Nineteenth Century Afro-American History* (Baton Rouge, 1986); and Leon Litwack and August Meier, eds., *Black Leaders of the Nineteenth Century* (Urbana, Ill., 1988).

For ease of reference the following biographies of abolitionists are arranged by race and gender; the authors are listed alphabetically.

Black Men   David W. Blight, *Frederick Douglass' Civil War: Keeping Faith in Jubilee* (Baton Rouge, 1989); George V. R. Carol, *Segregated Sabbaths: Richard Allen and The Rise of Independent Black Churches, 1760–1845* (New York, 1973); Thomas D. Lamont, *Rise to Be a People: A Biography of Paul Cuffee* (Urbana, Ill., 1986); Waldo E. Martin, *The Mind of Frederick Douglass,* (Chapel Hill, N.C., 1984); William S. McFeely, *Frederick Douglass* (New York, 1991); and Joel Schor, *Henry Highland Garnet: A Voice of Black Radicalism in the Nineteenth Century* (Westport, Conn., 1977).

White Men   Robert H. Abzug, *Passionate Liberator: Theodore Dwight Weld and the Dilemma of Reform* (New York, 1980); Richard H. Abbot, *Cobbler in Congress: The Life of Henry Wilson, 1812–1875* (Lexington, Ky., 1971); Robert C. Albrecht, *Theodore Parker* (New York, 1971); Irving H. Bartlett, *Wendell Phillips, Brahmin Radical* (Boston, 1961); Frederick J. Blue, *Salmon P. Chase: A Life in Politics* (Kent, Ohio, 1987); Fawn Brodie, *Thaddeus Stevens, Scourge of the South* (New York, 1959); Hugh Davis, *Joshua Leavitt: Evangelical Abolitionist* (Baton Rouge,

1990); Merton L. Dillon, *Benjamin Lundy and The Struggle for Negro Freedom* (Urbana, Ill., 1966); Dillon, *Elijah P. Lovejoy, Abolitionist Editor* (Urbana, Ill., 1961); David Donald, *Charles Sumner and The Coming of the Civil War* (New York, 1960); Donald, *Charles Sumner and The Rights of Man* (New York, 1970); Martin Duberman, *Charles Francis Adams, 1807–1886* (Boston, 1961); Tilden G. Edelstein, *Strange Enthusiasm: A Life of Thomas Wentworth Higginson* (New Haven, Conn., 1968); Betty Fladeland, *James Gillespie Birney: Slaveholder to Abolitionist* (Ithaca, N.Y., 1955); Frank O. Gatell, *John Gorham Palfrey and The New England Conscience* (Cambridge, Mass., 1963); Lawrence B. Goodheart, *Abolitionist, Actuary, Atheist: Elizur Wright and the Reform Impulse* (Kent, Ohio, 1990); Stanley Harrold, *Gamaliel Bailey and Antislavery Union* (Kent, Ohio, 1986); Charles A. Jarvis, "Admission to Abolition: The Case of John Greenleaf Whittier," *Journal of the Early Republic*, 4 (1984), 161–176; Edward Magdol, *Owen Lovejoy, Abolitionist in Congress* (New Brunswick, N.J., 1967); Walter M. Merrill, *Against Wind and Tide: A Biography of William Lloyd Garrison* (Cambridge, Mass., 1965); Russell B. Nye, *William Lloyd Garrison and The Humanitarian Reformers* (Boston, 1955); Stephen Oates, *To Purge This Land with Blood: A Biography of John Brown* (Amherst, Mass., 1984); Lewis Perry, *Childhood, Marriage and Reform: Henry Clarke Wright, 1797–1870* (Chicago, 1980); Harold Schwartz, *Samuel Gridley Howe, Social Reformer* (Cambridge, Mass., 1956); Milton C. Sernett, *Abolition's Axe: Beriah Green, Oneida Institute and The Black Freedom Struggle* (Syracuse, 1986); Richard H. Sewell, *John P. Hale and The Politics of Abolition* (Cambridge, Mass., 1965); James B. Stewart, *Joshua R. Giddings and The Tactics of Radical Politics* (Cleveland, 1970); Stewart, *Wendell Phillips, Liberty's Hero* (Baton Rouge, 1986); Stewart, *William Lloyd Garrison and The Challenge of Emancipation* (Arlington Heights, Mass., 1992); Benjamin P. Thomas, *Theodore Weld, Crusader for Freedom* (New Brunswick, N.J., 1950); John L. Thomas, *The Liberator: William Lloyd Garrison, A Biography* (Boston, 1963); Bertram Wyatt-Brown, *Lewis Tappan and The Evangelical War Against Slavery* (Cleveland, 1969); and Donald Yacovone, *Samuel J. May and The Dilemmas of the Liberal Persuasion, 1797–1871* (Philadelphia, 1991).

White Women   Catherine Birney, *The Grimké Sisters: Sarah and Angelina Grimké, The First Woman Advocates of Abolition and Woman's Rights* (Boston, 1885); Ira V. Brown, *Mary Grew: Abolitionist and Feminist, 1813–1896* (Selinsgrove, Penn., 1991); Deborah P. Clifford, *Crusader for Freedom: A Life of Lydia Maria Child* (Boston, 1992); Gerda Lerner, *The Grimké Sisters from South Carolina: Pioneers for Woman's Rights and Abolition* (New York, 1967); Katharine D. Lumpkin, *The Emancipation of Angelina Grimké* (Chapel Hill, N.C., 1974); Milton Meltzer, *Tongue of Flame: The Life of Lydia Maria Child* (New York, 1965); and Dorothy Sterling, *Ahead of Her Time: Abby Kelley and The Politics of Antislavery* (New York, 1991).

African Americans

Two older works still provide the most comprehensive overview of African-American abolitionists; they are Benjamin Quarles, *Black Abolitionists* (New York, 1969) and William H. Pease and Jane H. Pease, *They Who Would Be Free: Blacks' Search for Freedom, 1830–1861* (New York, 1974). Shirley J. Yee, *Black Women Abolitionists: A Study in Activism, 1828–1860* (Knoxville, Tenn., 1992) and Nell Irwin Painter, "Sojourner Truth in Life and Memory: Writing the Biography of an American Exotic," *Gender and History*, 2 (1990), 3–16 examine a largely neglected topic. Important primary sources are Charles M. Wiltse, ed., *David Walker's Appeal* (New York, 1965) and Brenda Stevenson, ed., *The Journals of Charlotte Forten* (New York, 1988), the latter are the records of a free black woman. For white racism among abolitionists, consult William H. Pease and Jane H. Pease, "Antislavery Ambivalence: Immediatism, Expediency, Race," *American Quarterly*, 17 (1965), 682–695 and their "Boston Garrisonians and The Problem of Frederick Douglass," *Canadian Journal of History* 2 (1967), 29–48.

For the struggle and condition of free blacks, see Leon Litwack, "Abolitionist Dilemma: The Anti-Slavery Movement and The Northern Negro," *New England Quarterly*, 34 (1961), 50–73; Litwack, *North of Slavery: The Negro in the Free States, 1790–1860* (Chicago, 1961); Ira Berlin, *Slaves Without Masters* (New York, 1974); James O. Horton and Lois E. Horton, *Black Bostonians: Family Life and Community Struggle in the Antebellum North* (New York, 1979); Leonard P. Curry, *The Free Black in Urban*

America, 1800–1850: The Shadow of a Dream (Chicago, 1981); William D. Piersen, *Black Yankees: The Development of an Afro-American Subculture in Eighteenth-Century New England* (Amherst, Mass., 1988); Julie Winch, *Philadelphia's Black Elite: Activism, Accommodation, and The Struggle for Autonomy, 1787–1840* (Philadelphia, 1988); David E. Swift, *Black Prophets of Justice: Activist Clergy Before the Civil War* (Baton Rouge, 1989); James O. Horton, *Free People of Color: Inside the African-American Community* (Washington, D.C., 1993); and Donald M. Jacobs, ed., *Courage and Conscience: Black and White Abolitionists in Boston* (Bloomington, Ind., 1993).

Abolitionists made effective use of slave autobiographies and narratives. Interpretative guides are Frances S. Foster, *The Development of Ante-Bellum Slave Narratives* (Westport, Conn., 1976); Charles T. Davis and Henry Lewis Gates, Jr., eds., *The Slave's Narrative* (New York, 1984); and William L. Andrews, *To Tell a Free Story: The First Century of Afro-American Autobiography, 1760–1865* (Urbana, Ill., 1986). Frederick Douglass' *A Narrative of the Life of Frederick Douglass* (Boston, 1845) is available in several reprints. See also Arna Bontemps, *Five Slave Narratives: A Compendium* (New York, 1960) and Solomon Northup, *Twelve Years a Slave* (Baton Rouge, 1968; originally 1853). A history written by a fugitive slave, William Wells Brown, *The Black Man, His Antecedents, His Genius, and His Achievement* (New York, 1863) is important. Oxford University Press has reprinted a series on the experiences of black women. See Harriet Jacobs, *Incidents in the Life of a Slave Girl* (New York, 1988; originally 1861); *Collected Black Women's Narratives* (New York, 1988); and *The Narrative of Sojourner Truth* (New York, 1991; originally 1850).

For the literature on slave resistance, two broad, comparative interpretations are Eugene D. Genovese, *From Rebellion to Revolution: Afro-American Slave Revolts in the Making of the Modern World* (Baton Rouge, 1979) and Michael Mullin, *Africa in America: Slave Acculturation and Resistance in the American South and British Caribbean, 1736–1831* (Champaign, Ill., 1992). An important specialized study is Douglas R. Egerton, *Gabriel's Rebellion: The Virginia Slave Conspiracies of 1800 and 1802* (Chapel Hill, N.C., 1992). An extended bibliography on the subject is in Lawrence B. Goodheart, Richard D. Brown, and Stephen G. Rabe, eds., *Slavery in American Society* (Lexington, Mass., 1993).

On the issues of fugitive slaves, see Larry Gara, *The Liberty Line: The Legend of the Underground Railroad* (Lexington, Ky., 1961); Stanley W. Campbell, *The Slave Catchers: Enforcement of the Fugitive Slave Law, 1850–1860* (Chapel Hill, N.C., 1970); Jonathan Katz, *Resistance at Christiana: The Fugitive Slave Rebellion, Christiana, Pennsylvania, September 11, 1851* (New York, 1974); Thomas O. Morris, *Free Men All: The Personal Liberty Laws of the North, 1780–1861* (Baltimore, 1974); William H. Pease and Jane H. Pease, *The Fugitive Slave Law and Anthony Burns* (Philadelphia, 1975); Nat Brandt, *The Town That Started the Civil War* (Syracuse, N.Y., 1990), which is set in Oberlin, Ohio; and Thomas B. Slaughter, *Bloody Dawn: The Christiana Riot and Racial Violence in the Antebellum North* (New York, 1991). Howard Jones, *Mutiny on the Amistad: The Saga of a Slave Revolt and Its Impact on American Abolition, Law and Diplomacy* (New York, 1987) describes an event in which abolitionists played a major role.

Women

An important primary source is Milton Meltzer and Patricia G. Holland, eds., *Lydia Maria Child, Selected Letters, 1817–1880* (Amherst, Mass., 1982). The issue of race and gender is discussed in these major studies of women abolitionists; see Alma Lutz, *Crusade for Freedom: Women of the Antislavery Movement* (Boston, 1968); Ellen Carol DuBois, *Feminism and Suffrage: The Emergence of an Independent Women's Movement in America, 1848–1869* (Ithaca, N.Y., 1978); Blanche G. Hersch, *The Slavery of Sex: Feminist-Abolitionists in America* (Urbana, Ill., 1978); Jean F. Yellin, *Women and Sisters: The Antislavery Feminists in American Culture* (New Haven, Conn., 1989); and Wendy H. Venet, *Neither Ballots nor Bullets: Women Abolitionists and the Civil War* (Charlottesville, Va., 1992).

Economics and Class

Two early studies still worth consulting are Joseph Rayback, "The American Workingman and the Anti-Slavery Crusade," *Journal of Economic History,* 3 (1943), 152–163 and Bernard Mandel, *Labor—Free and Slave: Workingmen and the Anti-Slavery Movement* (New York, 1955). Important recent studies are Eric Foner, "Abolitionism and The Labor Movement in Ante-Bellum America," in *Politics and Ideology in the Age of the Civil War* (New

York, 1980), 57–76; Louis Gerteis, *Morality and Utility in Anti-slavery Reform* (Chapel Hill, N.C., 1987); Richard H. Abbott, *Cotton and Conscience: Boston Businessmen and Antislavery Reform, 1854–1868* (Amherst, Mass., 1991); and Jonathan A. Glickstein, *Concepts of Free Labor in Antebellum America* (New Haven, Conn., 1991).

South and West

Overviews of antislavery sentiment in the South are Carl Degler, *The Other South: Southern Dissenters in the Nineteenth Century* (New York, 1971) and Merton L. Dillon, *Slavery Attacked: Southern Slaves and Their Allies, 1619–1865* (Baton Rouge, 1990). Specialized studies include Gordon E. Finnie, "The Antislavery Movement in the Upper South before 1840," *Journal of Southern History*, 35 (1969), 319–342; Joseph C. Robert, *The Road from Monticello: A Study of the Virginia Slavery Debate of 1832* (New York, 1970); James B. Stewart, "Evangelicalism and The Radical Strain in Southern Antislavery Thought During the 1820s," *Journal of Southern History*, 39 (1973), 379–396; and Lawrence B. Goodheart, "Tennessee's Antislavery Movement Reconsidered: The Example of Elihu Embree," *Tennessee Historical Quarterly*, 41 (1982), 224–238.

On the West, see Eugene H. Berwanger, *The Frontier Against Slavery* (Urbana, Ill., 1967) and V. Jacques Voegeli, *Free But Not Equal: The Midwest and The Negro during the Civil War* (Chicago, 1967).

Politics

The most systematic study of antislavery politics is Richard H. Sewell, *Ballots for Freedom: Antislavery Politics in the United States, 1837–1860* (New York, 1976). A significant collection of essays is Alan M. Kraut, ed., *Crusaders and Compromisers: Essays on the Relationship of the Antislavery Struggle to the Antebellum Party System* (Westport, Conn., 1983). For the Liberty and Free Soil parties, see Vernon L. Volpe, *Forlorn Hope of Freedom: The Liberty Party in the Old Northwest, 1838–1848* (Kent, Ohio, 1990); Frederick J. Blue, *The Free Soilers: Third Party Politics, 1848–1854* (Urbana, Ill., 1973); John Mayfield, *Rehearsal for Republicanism: Free Soil and The Politics of Antislavery* (Port Washington, N.Y., 1980). William E. Gienapp's *The Origins of the Republican Party,*

1852–1856 (New York, 1987) is the definitive treatment on the subject, but also see Eric Foner, *Free Soil, Free Labor, Free Men: The Ideology of the Republican Party before the Civil War* (New York, 1970). The concept of the Slave Power is the subject of Larry Gara, "Slavery and The Slave Power: A Crucial Distinction," *Civil War History*, 15 (1969), 5–18 and David Brion Davis, *The Slave Power Conspiracy and The Paranoid Style* (Baton Rouge, 1969).

Legal

Specific studies of abolitionism and the law are Russel B. Nye, *Fettered Freedom: Civil Liberties and The Slavery Controversy, 1830–1860* (East Lansing, Mich., 1949); Robert M. Cover, *Justice Accused: Antislavery and the Judicial Process* (New Haven, Conn., 1975); Paul Finkelman, *An Imperfect Union: Slavery, Federalism and Comity* (Chapel Hill, N.C., 1981). and William M. Wiecek, *The Sources of Antislavery Constitutionalism in America* (Ithaca, N.Y., 1977).

Violence

The growing acceptance of violent means by most abolitionists by 1860 has been the subject of a number of works. See Carleton Mabee, *Black Freedom: The Nonviolent Abolitionists from 1830 through the Civil War* (New York, 1970) for an overview. Other pertinent works are John Demos, "The Anti-Slavery Movement and The Problem of Violent Means," *New England Quarterly*, 37 (1964), 501–526; Robert B. Abzug, "The Influence of Garrisonian Abolitionist Fears of Slave Violence on the Antislavery Argument, 1829–1840," *Journal of Negro History*, 55 (1970), 15–28; Jane H. Pease and William H. Pease, "Confrontation and Abolition in the 1850s," *Journal of American History*, 58 (1972), 923–937; and Richard O. Curry, "Ambivalence, Ambiguity, and Contradiction: Garrisonian Abolitionists and Nonviolence," *The Journal of Libertarian Studies*, 6 (1982), 217–226.

On John Brown, see C. Vann Woodward, "John Brown's Private War," in Daniel Aaron, ed., *America in Crisis* (New York, 1952), 110–130; Stephen B. Oates, *To Purge This Land with Blood: A Biography of John Brown* (New York, 1970); Bertram Wyatt-Brown, "John Brown, Weathermen, and the Psychology of Antinomian Violence," *Soundings*, 58 (1975), 417–440; and Robert E. McGlone, "Rescripting a Troubled Past: John Brown's

Family and the Harpers Ferry Conspiracy," *Journal of American History,* 75 (1989), 1179–1200; and Seymour Drescher, "Servile Insurrection and John Brown's Body in Europe," *Journal of American History,* 80 (1993), 499–524.

Civil War and Reconstruction

The literature on this period is vast, but a good introduction is James M. McPherson, *The Struggle for Equality: Abolitionists and the Negro in the Civil War and Reconstruction* (Princeton, N.J., 1964). The emergence of emancipation is discussed in Louis S. Gerteis, *From Contraband to Freedman: Federal Policy Toward Southern Blacks, 1861–1865* (Westport, Conn., 1973); LaWanda Cox, *Lincoln and Black Freedom: A Study in Presidential Leadership* (Columbia, S.C., 1981); and Ira Berlin, et al., *Slaves No More: Three Essays on Emancipation and the Civil War* (New York, 1992).

A classic on black soldiers is Thomas Wentworth Higginson, *Army Life in a Black Regiment* (New York, 1869). Another recommended primary source is Edwin S. Redkey, ed., *A Grand Army of Black Men: Letters from African-American Soldiers in the Union Army, 1861–1865* (New York, 1992). Authoritative secondary sources on black soldiers are Dudley T. Cornish, *The Sable Arm: Negro Troops in the Union Army, 1861–1865* (New York, 1956) and Joseph T. Glatthaar, *Forged in Battle: The Civil War Alliance of Black Soldiers and White Officers* (New York, 1990).

Magisterial books on Reconstruction are Leon Litwack, *Been in the Storm So Long: The Aftermath of Slavery* (New York, 1979) and Eric Foner, *Reconstruction: America's Unfinished Revolution, 1863–1877* (New York, 1988). Willie Lee Rose, *Rehearsal for Reconstruction: The Port Royal Experiment* (New York, 1964) deals with the early stages of abolitionist involvement in emancipation, while James M. McPherson, *The Abolitionist Legacy: From Reconstruction to the NAACP* (Princeton, N.J., 1975) traces the abolitionist legacy into the twentieth century. An important historiographic essay is Richard O. Curry, "Abolitionists and Reconstruction: A Critical Appraisal," *Journal Southern History,* 34 (1968), 527–545. Specialized studies are Patrick Riddleberger, "The Radicals' Abandonment of the Negro During Reconstruction," *Journal of Negro History,* 45 (1960), 88–102; James M. McPherson, "Abolitionists and the Civil Rights Act of 1875," *Journal of American History,* 62 (1965), 493–510; and

McPherson, "Grant or Greeley? The Abolitionist Dilemma in the Election of 1872," *American Historical Review,* 71 (1965), 43–61.

Comparative and International

British abolitionism had an important influence on its American counterpart. A collection of nearly 500 letters mostly to and by Garrison is found in Clare Taylor, ed., *British and American Abolitionists: An Episode in Transatlantic Understanding* (Edinburgh, Scotland, 1974). Major overviews are Christine Bolt, *The Anti-Slavery Movement and Reconstruction: A Study in Anglo-American Cooperation, 1833–1877* (London, 1969) and Betty Fladeland, *Men and Brothers: Anglo-American Antislavery Cooperation* (Urbana, Ill., 1972). On black abolitionists in England, see R. J. M. Blackett, *Building an Antislavery Wall: Black Americans in the Atlantic Abolitionist Movement, 1830–1860* (Baton Rouge, 1983). See also David Brion Davis, "The Emergence of Immediatism in British and American Antislavery Thought," *Mississippi Valley Historical Review* 49 (1962), 209–230 and Anthony J. Barker, *Captain Charles Stuart: Anglo-American Abolitionist* (Baton Rouge, 1986).

Surveys of British abolitionism are Frank Klingberg, *The Anti-Slavery Movement in England* (New Haven, Conn., 1926); Reginald Coupland, *The British Anti-Slavery Movement* (London, 1933); Howard Temperley, *British Antislavery, 1833–1870* (London, 1972); and David Turley, *The Culture of English Antislavery, 1780–1860* (London, 1991). For abolitionism elsewhere, see C. Duncan Rice, *The Scots Abolitionist, 1833–1861* (Baton Rouge, 1981); Lawrence C. Jennings, *French Reaction to British Slave Emancipation* (Baton Rouge, 1988); and Allen P. Stouffer, *The Light of Nature and the Law of God: Antislavery in Ontario, 1833–1877* (Baton Rouge, 1992).

The abolition of the Atlantic slave trade has received much attention. A classic work is Thomas Clarkson, *The History of the Rise, Progress and Accomplishment of the Abolition of the African Slave Trade by the British Parliament,* 2 vols. (London, 1808). See also Christopher Lloyd, *The Navy and the Slave Trade: The Suppression of the African Slave in the Nineteenth Century* (London, 1949); Roger T. Anstey, *The Atlantic Slave Trade and British Abolition, 1760–1810* (Atlantic Highlands, N.J., 1975); Roger T. Anstey and P. E. H. Hairs, eds., *Liverpool, The African Slave Trade and Abolition* (Liverpool, 1976); E. Phillip LeVeen, *British Slave*

Trade Suppression Policies, 1821–1865 (New York, 1977); David Eltis and James Walwin, eds., *The Abolition of the Atlantic Slave Trade: Origins and Effects in Europe, Africa and the Americas* (Madison, Wis., 1981); and David Eltis, *Economic Growth and The Ending of the Transatlantic Slave Trade* (New York, 1987).

The modern discussion of the relationship between abolitionism and the maturation of capitalism was initiated by Eric Williams, *Capitalism and Slavery* (Chapel Hill, N.C., 1944). Williams' provocative thesis that the economic decline of West Indian slavery was the cause of abolitionism has been refuted by modern scholars. See particularly Seymour Drescher, *Econocide: British Slavery in the Era of Abolition* (Pittsburgh, 1977) and *Capitalism and Anti-slavery: British Mobilization in Comparative Perspective* (New York, 1987). A related issue is explored in Betty Fladeland, *Aboli-tionists and Working Class Problems in the Age of Industrialization* (Baton Rouge, 1984).

The broad view of abolitionist ideology in the Western world is discussed in Howard Temperley, "Capitalism, Slavery and Ideology," *Past and Present,* 75 (1977), 94–118; Temperley, "The Ideology of Antislavery," in David Eltis and James Walvin, ed., *The Abolition of the Atlantic Slave Trade* (Madison, Wis., 1981), 21–35; and David Brion Davis, "Capitalism, Abolitionism, and Hegemony," in Barbara Solow and Stanley L. Engerman, eds., *British Capitalism and Caribbean Slavery* (New York, 1987), 209–227. Davis' formulation of an abolitionist hegemony is challenged by Thomas H. Haskell, in "Capitalism and The Origins of the Humanitarian Sensibility," Part 1, *American Historical Review,* 90 (1985), 339–361, Part 2, *Ibid.,* 90 (1985), 457–566. For the rebuttal, see Davis, "Reflections on Abolitionism and Ideological Hegemony," *American Historical Review,* 92 (1987), 797–812; John Ashword, "The Relationship between Capitalism and Humanitarianism," *Ibid.,* 813–828; and Haskell's final comment, *Ibid.,* 829–878.

An introduction to current research on postemancipation societies in the New World are provided by David Richardson, ed., *Abolition and Its Aftermath: The Historical Context, 1790–1916* (London, 1985) and Frank McGlynn and Seymour Drescher, *The Meaning of Freedom: Economics, Politics, and Culture after Slavery* (Pittsburgh, 1992).